THE WARREN BUFFET WAY

Complete Biography • Success Secrets • Money Making Skills

THE WARREN BUFFET WAY

Complete Biography • Success Secrets • Money Making Skills

DINKAR KUMAR
N. CHOKKAN
PRADEEP THAKUR

Published by
PRABHAT PRAKASHAN PVT. LTD.
4/19 Asaf Ali Road,
New Delhi-110002 (INDIA)
e-mail: prabhatbooks@gmail.com

ISBN 978-93-5562-692-9

THE WARREN BUFFETT WAY: COMPLETE BIOGRAPHY, SUCCESS SECRETS & MONEY MAKING SKILLS
by Dinkar Kumar, N. Chokkan & Pradeep Thakur

Edition
2025

Price
₹ 650 (Rupees Six Hundred Fifty Only)

Printed at
Sita Fine Arts, Delhi

Author's Note

The world hardly knows him by Warren Buffett than, 'the magician of the share market', 'Omaha's Saint', 'the Emperor of Berkshire, 'the biggest player of Wall Street' and 'the Oracle of Omaha'. A person with normal stature and jolly nature, nobody can guess that he is the world's third richest and Americas' second richest person. In the issue of April 2007 of *Forbes* magazine, he got the third place in the list of the world's billionaires, after Bill Gates of America and Carlos Slim Helu of Mexico. He created history in the field of Philanthropy by donating 37 billion dollars (83 per cent of his total wealth) to the Bill and Melinda Gates Foundation (31 billion). Not only this, he donated 6 billion for other four charitable trusts for the welfare of world's need.

The story of young Warren Buffett's struggle is like a case study for the students studying management world-wide. The story of Warren Buffett, who sold chewing gums, soda, coke and newspaper to school children in America is narrated often to inculcate the value of self-dependence.

To understand Warren Buffett's personality or to form an opinion about him is as complex as understanding the share market. On one hand, he keeps track of stock and shares in the Wall Street, on the other hand he does not hesitate to donate most of his wealth in charity.

This book tries to explain this complexity by looking into different aspects of his life which are filled with qualities like struggle, restraint, frugality, philanthropy and foresight.

– Dinkar Kumar

❑

Author's Note

Contents

Author's Note 5

COMPLETE BIOGRAPHY **13**

- ❖ A Brief Biography: Warren Buffett 15
- ❖ Earning and Spending Skills 32
- ❖ Story of the World's Most Successful Investor 34
- ❖ Wife, Children and Profession 42
- ❖ Childhood 44
- ❖ From Golf Course to Graduate School 51
- ❖ Intelligent Investor 57
- ❖ Life Partner 60
- ❖ Wealth Creation 72
- ❖ Warren Buffett's Principles of Investment 91
- ❖ Women in Warren's Life 93
- ❖ A Turning Point 95
- ❖ Warren and Madam B 114
- ❖ Most Prosperous Period of His Life 118
- ❖ Charlie Munger and Warren Buffett 137
- ❖ Warren's Ten Formulas to Earn Money 139

- ❖ Warren Buffett's Seven Formulas to Success 141
- ❖ Warren's Interest in India 143

References 145

SUCCESS SECRETS **147**

Author's Note 149

1. Innovators, Imitators and Idiots 151
2. Tools and their Value 153
3. Read and Analyze the Raw Data 155
4. Dealing with Gaps 157
5. Are you the Smartest Person in Every Room? 159
6. A Great Deal, Rejected 161
7. Knowable and Urgent 163
8. Is Time a Friend or an Enemy? 165
9. Income and Consumptions 167
10. What does a Leader Really do? 169
11. Best Salespeople 171
12. The "Easy" Way to Make Mistakes 173
13. Being a Complete Leader 175
14. Margin of Safety 177
15. Be Your Own Compliance Officer 179
16. Tails and Legs 181
17. Circle of Competence 183
18. Views of Others 185
19. A Car you can't Replace 187

20. The Perfect Choice 189

21. Dealing with Bad Decisions 191

22. Possibilities: Good and Bad 193

23. Best Person for the Job 195

24. The Selection Criteria 197

25. Making People Listen to You 199

26. Don't Teach a Fish How to Swim 201

27. Watch the Puck 203

28. Clear Boundaries 205

29. Don't Keep Scores 207

30. Standard of Living 209

31. Working with Smart Customers 211

32. Products that Travel Well 213

33. The Path to Expertise 215

34. Learning from Friends 217

35. Prescriptive Approach vs. Descriptive Approach 219

36. When it is Raining Gold... 221

37. What Makes a Product Great? 223

38. Every Employee Contributes to the Success (or Failure) 225

39. Addressing Self-Doubt 227

40. Meeting Obligations 229

41. Short Read, Long Read 231

42. Necessary Prudence 233

43. A Successful Day 235

44. The Win-Win Deal 237

45. Value of Hard Work 239

46. The Right Seed 241

47. Talk and Action 243

48. The Orangutan Effect 245

49. Good Decisions and Bad Decisions 247

50. The "Because" Test 249

51. Average Office, Amazing Portfolio! 251

52. Lunch with Warren 253

53. Difficult Problems don't Need Difficult Solutions 255

54. The Need for Immediate Help 257

55. Earning and Spending 259

56. Facing Pain 261

57. Success, Guaranteed! 263

58. Heroes won't Let you Down 265

59. Use the Available Interstate 267

60. Focus on Positivity 269

61. The Pricing Power 271

62. The Game of Liked and Disliked Qualities 273

63. Compounding Value of Learning 275

64. Win Some, Lose Some, then Win Some More 277

65. My Luxury 279

66. The Unsalaried Employee 281

67. I Don't Know! 283

68. The Right Story 285

69. Financial Support from Customers 287

70. Great Author, But… 289

71. Doing after Understanding 291

72. Fair or Wonderful? 293

73. Same Question, Fifth Time! 295

74. Compatible Partners 297

75. Environment Makes Us 299

76. Be Kind, Oh, Stranger 301

77. The Cream-Skimming Approach 303

78. The Other Guy is Doing It 305

79. Super Skill that Increases your Value by at Least 50% 307

80. Finding Our Strength(s) 309

81. The Brain Work 311

82. The Narrow Vision 313

83. An Unusual Race 315

84. The Ideal Job 317

85. The Real Boss 319

86. The 'No Games' Approach to Negotiation 321

87. Cross-learning 323

88. Good Information and Quick Information 325

89. When your Hypothesis is Wrong… 327

90. Looking for 1-foot Bars 329

91. Loving What We Do 331

92. The Power of Habits 333

93. Finding a Good Partner 335

94. Only Twenty Punches 337

95. The Light Calendar 339

96. Intentional Confusion 341

97. Sitting on the Sidelines 343

98. Feeling Good About You! 345

99. The Confidence 347

100. Important Things 349

MONEY MAKING SKILLS **351**

Author's Note 353

1. Picking the Right Business 357

2. Economic Test of a Business 387

3. Picking the Right Manager 409

4. Motivation of Workforce 435

5. Risks, Challenges and Opportunities 451

Complete
Biography

A Brief Biography: Warren Buffett

The Evolution of Warren Buffett

1936 - Age 6

Buffett started selling Juicy Fruit chewing-gum packs. When asked for 1 piece, he would not sell as he thought he may be left with 4 pieces he could not sell. He made 2 cents profit per pack.

Buffett would also purchase Coca-Cola six packs for 25 cents from his grandfather's grocery store–Buffett and Son. He would sell each Coke for 5 cents. Profit of 5 cents per pack.

1941 - Age 11

At 11 years old, Buffett bought his first stock – 6 shares of Cities Service (now known as CITGO – an Oil company) at $38 per share. He bought 3 for himself and 3 for his sister Doris.

That is all the money he had at that time. Practised little to no diversification at a young age, which he continued to do throughout his investment career. The stock price fell to $27 but soon went to $40. He sold the stock at $40, but the stock shot up to $202 in the next few years.

He later cited this experience as an early lesson in patience in investing.

1943 - Age 13

Buffett files his first tax return and deducts his bike as a work expense for $35.

1945 - Age 15

Buffett makes $175 a month selling *Washington Post* newspapers and saves $1200 to buy 40-acre farmland in Omaha, Nebraska.

1947 - Age 17

He went to Woodrow Wilson High School, Washington D.C. Buffett joins his friend Donald Danley to start a company called Wilson Coin Operated Machines. The business buys a pinball machine at a cost of $25 and places it in a nearby barber shop. Wilson Coin makes $50 per week for Buffett and Donald.

Buffett does tax returns for himself and Wilson Coin. In the next few months, they own three machines and a year later sells it for $1200.

1949 - Age 19

At the age of 19, when Warren was studying at Pennsylvania University's Wharton School, he joined the Alpha Sigma Phi fraternity. His father and uncle were also in the fraternity.

1950 - Age 20

B.Sc. degree from Nebraska University. Warren applied for admission in Harvard Business School but his application was rejected as he was under age. Then he sought admission in Columbia Business School, because he knew that security analysts like Benjamin Graham and David Dodd were teaching there.

1951 - Age 21

M.S. Degree in Economics from Columbia University. Twenty One year old Warren came to know that Benjamin Graham was the Chairman of G.I.E.C.O. Insurance Company in Washington. On one Saturday he boarded a train and reached Washington. He kept knocking at the headquarter door till he was allowed to enter. There he met the Vice-Chairman of the company Lotimer Davidson, who was not only extremely impressed by him, but they also became good friends. He discussed about the insurance business for 4 hours. Later

Davidson recalled that within 15 minutes dialogue with Warren made him understood that he was an, 'extraordinary person.'

1952 - Age 22

Twenty two year old Warren married Susan Thompson.

1953 - Age 23

Twenty three year old Warren became father. His daughter was named Susan Alice Buffett.

1954 - Age 24

Benjamin Graham offered him a job in his partnership company on an annual salary of $ 12,000. He worked there with Walter Schloss.

1956 - Age 26

Warren's second child, a son Howard Graham Buffett was born. Graham decides to retire and fold his business. Buffett's savings have grown from $9,800 to $140,000.

Buffett returned to Omaha and on May 1, created Buffett Associates Ltd. Seven family members and friends invest a total of $105k. Buffett invested only $100k.

1957 - Age 27

Buffett created more partnerships and was managing a total of 5 partnerships, all from his home.

1958 - Age 28

After 3 years, Buffett doubled the partner's money.

1959 - Age 29

Buffett was introduced to Charlie Munger by his friend Edwin Davis at a dinner. Charlie Munger later became the Vice Chairman of Berkshire Hathaway.

1961 - Age 31

Buffett is running seven partnerships by 1961; Buffett Associates, Buffett Fund, Dacee, Emdee, Glenoff, Mo-Buff, and Underwood.

The partnerships are worth a few million and Buffett made his first million-dollar investment in Dempster - a windmill manufacturing company.

Sanborn Map Company accounted for 35% of the partnerships' assets. He explained to the partners that in 1958, Sanborn was selling at $45 per share when the value of its investment portfolio itself was at $65 per share which meant that it was undervalued by $20 per share with a map business coming in for nothing.

Buffett reveals that he earned a spot on the board of Sanborn.

1962 - Age 32

Buffett goes to New York to meet his old acquaintances to include more partners and raise capital. He collects a few hundreds of thousand dollars. Buffett Partnership is worth $7.2 million. Buffett then merges all partnerships into one and renames it as Buffett Partnerships Ltd.

Munger introduces Buffett to Harry Bottle, CEO of Dempster Mill, who cut costs, laid off workers, and turned around Dempster to generate cash. At this time, Buffett notices Berkshire Hathaway selling for $8 a share and starts buying aggressively.

1963 - Age 33

Buffett sells Dempster for a $2.3 million gain, three times the invested amount.

Buffett aggressively purchases Berkshire paying $14.86 per share while the company had working capital of $19 per share. This did not include the value of fixed assets. Buffett Partnership becomes the single largest shareholder of Berkshire Hathaway.

1964 - Age 34

American Express is victim to the salad oil scandal and shares fall to $35. Buffett saw the value and bought 5% of the company.

1965 - Age 35

Buffett invests $4 million in Walt Disney after a meeting with Walt Disney himself, which is almost 5% of the company. Buffett takes full control of Berkshire Hathaway and names Ken Chace to be the CEO.

1966 - Age 36

Buffett closes the partnership to new money. Buffett writes in his letter that "unless it appears that circumstances have changed (under some conditions, added capital would improve results) or unless new partners can bring some asset to the partnership other than simply capital, I intend to admit no additional partners to BPL."

Buffett invests in Hochschild Kohn's which was a department store in Baltimore.

Buffett's personal investment in the partnership is now approximately $6.8 million.

1967 - Age 37

Buffett Partnership now owns 59.5% of Berkshire Hathaway. Berkshire Hathaway pays a 10 percent dividend. This is the first and only dividend it has paid ever.

The Partnership is worth $65 million. Buffett's personal investment is $10 million. Buffett tells his partners that in the current-raging bull market, he is unable to find good investments.

He also briefly considered leaving investing to pursue other interests.

American Express hits $180, making a $20 million profit on a $13 million investment.

Berkshire Hathaway acquires National Indemnity Insurance for $8.6 million.

Berkshire acquires National Fire and Marine Insurance Company.

1968 - Age 38

Partnership is worth $104 million.

1969 - Age 39

Berkshire acquires the *Sun* Newspapers (Publishing), Rockford Bank (Banking), Illinois National Bank (Banking) and Blacker Printing Company (Publishing).

Buffett decides to close the partnership and liquidate the assets to the partners.

From 1957-1969, Buffett Partnership returns were 29.5%.

Warren has three recommendations to partners.

1970 - Age 40

The Buffett Partnership is completely dissolved and divested of its assets.

1972 - Age 42

Through the Blue Chips Stamps Company, Berkshire buys See's Candies (Chocolates) and Wesco Financial Corp. (Financial Services).

1973 - Age 43

Berkshire starts buying stocks in the Washington Post company (Publishing). Buffett becomes close friends with Katharine Graham who controlled the company and its flagship newspaper and becomes a member of the Board of Directors.

1974 - Age 44

Due to falling stock prices, the value of Berkshire Hathaway portfolio begins to fall. Warren's personal network falls by more than 50%.

1975 - Age 45

Buffett merges Berkshire and Diversified – the firm controlled by Munger.

Munger gets 2% stock of Berkshire and becomes its Vice Chairman.

1976 - Age 46

Berkshire invests $4 million in GEICO (Insurance) when its stock price was just above $2. Buffett continually invests in GEICO until 1996, when Berkshire acquires the company.

Berkshire's subsidiary, National Fire and Marine Insurance Company, acquires Cypress Property and Casulty Insurance Company.

1977 - Age 47

Berkshire invests in the *Buffalo Evening News* (Publishing) for $32.5 million. He also invests in Interpublic (Advertising) and Ogilvy & Mather (Advertising), Kaiser Industries (Metals and Mining), and Knight-Rider (Publishing).

1978 - Age 48

Berkshire invests in SAFECO (Insurance), ABC Broadcasting (TV Network).

1979 - Age 49

Berkshire is trading at $290 per share.

Warren's personal net worth is now approximately $100 million and receives a $50k annual salary.

Berkshire starts to buy shares in General Foods (Foods), Handy & Harman (Metals and Mining), Affiliated Publications (Publishing), Media General (Publishing), FW Woolworth (Retail), Amerada Hess (Oil), Precision Steel Warehouse (Materials and Construction).

1980 - Age 50

Berkshire buys stock in RJ Reynolds (Tobacco), ALCOA (Metals and Mining), Pinkerton (Professional Services), Cleveland-Cliffs Iron (Metals and Mining), National Detroit (Banking), Times Mirror (Publishing), National Student Marketing (Financial Services).

Berkshire Hathaway Performance from 1970 to 1980.

1981 - Age 51

Berkshire buys Arcata (Forest products/Paper), and GATX (machinery).

1982 - Age 52

Buffalo Evening News is the only local newspaper of Buffalo and its name is changed to Buffalo News.

The newspaper earns $19 million in its first year without competition. By the late eighties, the Buffalo News starts earning $40 million a year.

Berkshire invests in Time (Publishing), Crum & Forster (Insurance).

1983 - Age 53

Berkshire merges with Blue Chip Stamps which was a majority-owned subsidiary of Berkshire.

Berkshire Hathaway purchases Nebraska Furniture Mart (Furniture) for $60 million.

Berkshire portfolio is worth $1.3 billion.

Begins with a stock price of $775 and ends the year at $1310.

Warren's personal net worth has ballooned to $620 million and he makes the Forbes millionaire list for the first time.

1984 - Age 54

Berkshire buys $139 million of Washington Public Power Supply System Bonds, invests in Exxon (Oil) and Northwest Industries (Diversified).

1985 - Age 55

Buffett shuts down Berkshire Hathaway's textile business.

He helps in the merging of ABC TV Network and Capital Cities (Communications). Buffett is forced to leave the board of Washington Post, as the legislation prohibited him from sitting on the boards of both Capital Cities and Washington Post.

Berkshire purchases Scott and Fetzer who boast products like Kirby vacuums and World Book Encyclopedia. Also buys Fecheimer Brothers (Uniform Company) and Beatrice (Food).

1986 - Age 56

Berkshire acquires Fechheimer Brothers Company and invests in Lear Seagler (Aerospace).

Berkshire's stock price soars above the $3,000 mark.

1987 - Age 57

The stock market crashes in October and Berkshire loses 25% of its value.

The stock prices go from $4,200 to $3,100 and Buffett's wealth falls by $320 million.

Berkshire buys 12% of Salomon Brothers (Investment Bank).

1988 - Age 58

Buffett starts buying Coca-Cola (Beverages) and eventually gains a 7% stake in the company for $1.2 billion.

Berkshire buys Freddie Mac (Financial Services).

1989 - Age 59

Berkshire acquires Borsheim's (Jewelry) from the Friedman Family. Berkshire's stock price rises from $4,800 to $8,000 per share.

Berkshire buys Gillette (Toiletries) and Buffett's personal fortune rises to $3.8 billion.

1990 - Age 60

Berkshire buys 10% of Wells Fargo (Banking).

1991 - Age 61

Berkshire acquires H.H. Brown (Footwear) and starts buying M&T Bank (Banking).

Buffett serves as the CEO of Solomon Brothers following the firm's treasury bond-trading scandal. Berkshire invests in Guinness (Beverages).

1992 - Age 62

Berkshire acquires Central States Indemnity Company (Insurance) of Omaha and Buffett continues to serve as interim Chairman at Solomon Brothers.

Berkshire becomes the largest shareholder of General Dynamics (Aerospace).

Berkshire's stock shoots past the $10,000 mark.

1993 - Age 63

Berkshire acquires Dextor (Footwear) which turns out to be a bad investment.

1994 - Age 64

The Warren Buffett Way by Robert G. Hagstrom Jr. is published and becomes a bestseller.

Berkshire invests in McDonald's (Restaurants), Gannett (Publishing) and PNC Bank (Banking).

1995 - Age 65

Berkshire acquires Helzberg's Diamond Shops (Jewelry) and R.C. Willey (Home Furnishings).

Berkshire Hathaway's annual meeting is so well attended that it is held in Omaha's Holiday Convention Center for the first time. Berkshire stock crosses $25,000 per share.

1996 - Age 66

Berkshire acquires the remaining stake in GEICO to become 100% owned subsidiary.

Berkshire acquires Flight Safety International (provider of professional aviation training).

Wesco Financial, a subsidiary of Berkshire, acquires Kansas Bankers Surety Co. (Insurance).

1997 - Age 67

Berkshire acquires Star Furniture (Furniture) and International Dairy Queen (Fast Food restaurants), and also invests in Travelers (Insurance).

Buffett invested 2% of his investment portfolio in silver.

Buffett makes a huge investment in US Airways (Airlines) which turns out to be a bad investment decision.

1998 - Age 68

Berkshire acquires General Re (Re-insurance) and Executive Jet, later renamed as NetJets (Private Aviation).

1999 - Age 69

Berkshire acquires Jordan's Furniture Company, a Massachusetts-based furniture powerhouse. Also buys parts of Mid-American Energy Holdings Company, a utility company.

2000 - Age 70

Berkshire Gains 1580% vs. Dow Jones 280%

Buffett is still going strong.

Berkshire acquires a long list of companies.

Ben Bridge (Jewelry)

CORT, the leading national provider of rental furniture, accessories and related services in the growing "rent-to-rent" furniture rental industry.

Justin Industries including Acme Building Brands.

Shaw Industries, the world's largest manufacturer of tufted broadloom carpets.

Benjamin Moore, a leading manufacturer and retailer of premium paints, stains and industrial coatings that was founded in 1883.

Buffett is named the top money manager of the 20th century in a survey by the Carson Group, ahead of Peter Lynch and John Templeton.

2001 - Age 71

The acquisitions and purchases continue to increase.

Berkshire acquires Johns Manville Corp (building products), MiTek, and a provider of steel connector products, design engineering software and ancillary services for the global building components market.

Berkshire goes on to acquire XTRA Corporation (transport containers), H&R Block (Financial Services) and Moody's Corporation (Financial Services).

Insurance claims from the 9/11 terrorist attack total $2.28 billion.

Buffett apologises to his shareholders for failing to foresee the risk and properly price insurance coverage.

2002 - Age 72

Warren entered into 11 billion dollars worth of forward contracts to sell American Dollars against other currencies. (After 4 years he earned a profit of more than 2 billion dollars on these contracts).

Berkshire acquires Larson-Juhl, a custom picture-frame-maker, Fruit of the Loom (textile), Albecca (picture framing), Garan (apparel), CTB (farming equipment) and The Pampered Chef (kitchenware).

Berkshire and other investment groups buy $500 million in bonds issued by Level 3 Communications, the former Omaha fiber network company.

Buffett enters a deal where $11 billion worth of forward contracts is delivered in US dollars against other currencies. By April 2006, his total gain on these contracts is over $2 billion.

2003 - Age 73

Berkshire acquires McLane (wholesale distributor), Clayton Homes (housing) and Burlington Industries, one of the world's most diversified marketers and manufacturers of soft goods for apparel and interior furnishings.

2004 - Age 74

Warren's wife Susie passes away. Bill Gates is elected as a director for Berkshire Hathaway.

2005 - Age 75

Berkshire acquires Medical Protective Company (Medical malpractice carrier) and Forest River (leisure vehicles).

Despite insurance business losses of about $2.5 billion caused by Hurricane Katrina, Berkshire records a gain of $5.6 billion.

Berkshire's subsidiary, Shaw Industries, buys stock in Honeywell International. Berkshire joins the fun by buying Procter and Gamble (Consumer Goods) and Anheuser-Busch (Food and Beverage).

Berkshire stock crosses $90,000 per share.

2006 - Age 76

Buffett announces in June that he will give away more than 80%, or about $37 billion of his $44 billion fortune to five foundations in annual gifts of stock, starting July 2006. The largest contribution will go to the Bill and Melinda Gates Foundation.

Berkshire stock crosses $100,000 per share.

The list of acquisitions and stock purchases continues:

- Business Wire (media distributor)
- Russell Corporation (athletic apparel)
- 80% of the Iscar Metalworking Companies (IMC) in a transaction that valued IMC at US$5 billion.
- Applied Underwriters (insurance)
- TTI Inc (electronic components distributor)
- Southern Energy Homes (utility)
- Brooke Sports (athletic apparel)

2007 - Age 77

In a letter to shareholders, Buffett announces that he is looking for a young successor or perhaps successors to run Berkshire.

Buffett had previously selected Lou Simpson, who manages the investment via GEICO, to fill that role. However, Simpson is only six years younger than Buffett.

The companies bought that year include:

- ❖ Boat America Corporation, which owns Seaworthy Insurance Company and controls the Boat Owners Association of the United States.
- ❖ Leading jewelry manufacturers Bel-Oro International and Aurafin LLC, which merges into Richline Group.
- ❖ 60% of Marmon Holdings (holding company that owns companies producing electrical components).
- ❖ SE Homes (home construction).
- ❖ BoatUS (Boat America Corporation is the main supplier of towing, insurance and other services to the nonprofit boater's association).

2008 - Age 78

'Forbes' magazine names him the richest man in the world. Before this, Bill Gates held this distinction for the last 13 years.

Berkshire buys out Marmon Holdings and Coachmen Industries becomes a part of Forest River (leisure vehicles).

Berkshire buys $4.4b in bonds from Mars Inc (food and beverage). Makes $680 m in profit off the investment.

2009 - Age 79

Berkshire's subsidiary, Shaw Industries, acquires Sportexe (a leading synthetic turf company).

Berkshire acquires Cavalier Homes (home-building company).

A $5 billion 'paper' loss on investments and derivatives triggers a first-quarter loss for Berkshire. It is the biggest loss since the 9/11 terrorist attack. But earnings rebound later in the year.

2010 - Age 80

Berkshire buys out railroad company Burlington Northern for $44 billion. As a result of the acquisition, Berkshire enters the S&P 500, replacing Burlington Northern Santa Fe.

Berkshire subsidiary, McLane Company, acquires Kahn Ventures.

Berkshire invests in Munich Re (Insurance).

2011 - Age 81

Berkshire acquires Lubrizol (Speciality Chemicals).

2012 - Age 82

Berkshire acquires Omaha World-Herald (Publishing) and invests in IBM (Technology).

2013 - Age 83

Berkshire acquires a 50% stake in H.J. Heinz Company (Food and Beverage).

Berkshire is worth $176,140 as on October 22.

2014 - Age 84

In May, Buffett's company, Berkshire Hathaway, completed its acquisition of the Nevada utility NV Energy for $5.6 billion. In November, it was announced that Berkshire Hathaway had invested $3 billion in the initial public offering of Chinese tech giant Alibaba.

2015 - Age 85

In March, Buffett wrote his annual letter to shareholders, in which he announced that he had been diagnosed with early-stage prostate cancer. He said the diagnosis was not life-threatening and would continue to work as usual. In September, Berkshire Hathaway agreed to acquire Precision Castparts, a maker of aerospace and industrial components, for $32 billion.

2016 - Age 86

In his annual letter to shareholders, Buffett criticized hedge funds and their high fees, saying that they often underperformed the market. In December, he joined the board of directors of the Canadian oil company Suncor Energy.

2017 - Age 87

In January, Buffett wrote in his annual letter to shareholders that he had sold off a large portion of his holdings in IBM and invested more heavily in Apple. In June, Berkshire Hathaway invested $377 million in Store Capital, a real estate investment trust.

2018 - Age 88

In January, Buffett announced that Berkshire Hathaway had received a $29 billion boost from the recent corporate tax cut passed by the US government. In February, he released his annual letter to shareholders, in which he praised Apple and its CEO, Tim Cook. In May, he revealed that Berkshire Hathaway had purchased more than 75 million shares of Apple.

2019 - Age 89

In February, Buffett's annual letter to shareholders warned of the risks of investing in bonds, saying that they were a "terrible" investment choice in the current economic climate. In August, he announced that Berkshire Hathaway had acquired a 10% stake in the Indian digital payments company Paytm.

2020 - Age 90

In April, Buffett announced that Berkshire Hathaway had sold off all its airline stocks, citing the uncertainty caused by the COVID-19 pandemic. In July, he revealed that the company had acquired more than $2 billion worth of Bank of America stock. In November, he disclosed that Berkshire Hathaway had invested in four pharmaceutical companies working on COVID-19 treatments.

2021 - Age 91

In January, Buffett's annual letter to shareholders acknowledged that the COVID-19 pandemic had caused significant economic upheaval, but expressed confidence in the long-term prospects of the US economy. In February, it was announced that Berkshire Hathaway had invested more than $8 billion in Verizon. In May, Buffett announced that he would be stepping down as the trustee of the Bill and Melinda Gates Foundation, a role he had held for more than a decade.

2022 - Age 92

Due to market volatility, Warren Buffett's Berkshire Hathaway (BRK.A, BRK.B) reported a net loss of $22.8 billion in 2022. However, Berkshire's "operating income," excluding certain capital gains and losses, rose to a record $30.8 billion. In his much-awaited shareholder letter, Buffett reiterated his faith in the American economy and aimed for overpriced share buybacks.

The story is not over yet.

❑

Earning and Spending Skills

American Warren Buffett's name does not need any introduction. There is no business magazine, newspaper or TV channel in the world which does not cover or discusses him. After Bill Gates and Carlos Slim, he is the third richest person in the world. There are several reasons why he is counted in the world's richest's list. Here, we are not discussing him for being rich rather we are here to highlight the fact of his lifestyle, which he embraced in spite of possessing huge amount of wealth.

In our country, every now and then, we witness the arrogant display of pomp and show of the novo rich. But Warren is totally unlike the other rich persons of the world in all respects. Warren, who has a sharp eye over his business, possesses several qualities which distinguish him from the others.

There is no account of the wealth which he possesses, but in America he is the second richest person after Bill Gates. According to *'Forbes'* Magazine, he is worth 65.1 billion dollars (4297 billion Indian rupees). He created history by donating 83 per cent of his wealth in charity. Warren still lives in the house which he purchased in 1953.

Now let us also find out how he earned the immense wealth and what he does with it.

Warren was born in Nebraska, Omaha on 30th August, 1930. His father was a stock broker. At the age of eleven Warren joined his father's stock broking business and also sold newspapers to earn his pocket money. At the age of thirteen, he filed his first income tax return. He regretted the fact that he started his money earning career pretty late. At the age of fifteen, Warren along with his school classmate set up a pinball machine in a barber's shop by investing 25 dollars. He made good money and bought a 40 acre farm.

He then used his business acumen and started investing in the share market and made lots of money.

At the age of twenty after being unable to get admission in America's reputed Harvard Business School, Warren sought admission in the Columbia Business School. There he learned the tricks of investing in the share market from economic Gurus like Benjamin Graham and David Dodd.

Warren has been known as the Oracle of Omaha or 'Omaha's Saint.' Warren is the single largest investor in several large American companies, of which Coca Cola, Gillette etc. That is to say that irrespective of whosoever might be the promoter or may be running these companies, the real owner is Warren.

Warren's simple lifestyle contrasts with his immense wealth. Warren still lives in the house which he bought fifty eight years earlier. He drives his own car. He neither employs a driver or a security guard. He never travels in a private plane. His company Berkshire Hathway owns 63 companies. He only writes one letter every year to all his CEOs in which he give details of the plans for a complete year.

He never conduct meetings with his Officers or his business associates. He has specified two rules for all his Officers – one, never allow your shareholders wealth to erode in any manner and second, never forget rule one. He never attends parties of important and influential people.

His message to the youth of the new generation:

"Stay away from the mentality of using the credit card compulsorily and invest on yourself. Wealth has not created mankind but mankind has created wealth. Live your life in the simplest manner possible."

❑

Story of the World's Most Successful Investor

The nineteenth century was coming to an end. With the rise of Europe, America was emerging as a super power. After the social and industrial upheaval, the lives of people were gradually becoming normal. The conditions in Nebraska District situated on the banks of Missouri river in America were more or less similar. Due to the efforts of its hard working farmers Omaha, a big city of the famous Nebraska was getting back on its feet. But for the Buffett family, living there, the days of struggle were far from over.

In the year 1869 Warren's grandfather opened a small grocery store to earn his living. Grandfather Buffett's business acumen coupled with his good behaviour resulted in the grocery store doing well in a very short time. Gradually the store became his hallmark. His family of two sons started growing.

Warren's father Howard Homan was studying in Nebraska University. Here he met Leila Stahl. While working together for the universities newspaper 'Daily Nebraska', their closeness led to marriage. On 30th August, 1930 in Omaha, a son was born in their house. He was their second child after their daughter Doris and was named Warren Edward Buffett. Warren meant, 'keeper' and he justified his name in the future.

Even though they continued to struggle, the Buffett family was always on the lookout for new rightful business opportunities. Warren's father Howard's interest was less in his father's store and more in the stock market and politics. Seeing his family's hardship, nobody could understand as to when Warren learnt the alphabet of self-sufficiency. To improve the financial condition of his family little Warren also started earning. Little Warren unlike other children of his age, who would be playing and having fun after school, would be involved in earning quarters, dimes and nickels.

Profit from Selling Chewing Gum and Some Innocent Questions

His father's business was still shaky and his grandfather was somehow managing the family through his grocery store. Warren would observe all this, think about it and ask his grandfather as to why their condition was like that? Why are we struggling so much? Can't we become rich quickly? His grandfather would evade his queries and assign him odd jobs. Reminiscing about his childhood on CNBC TV Warren said, "I must have been 7-8 years old, my grandfather would sell chewing gum to me from the store; I would go door-to-door, sell it and earn a few nickels profit. He would sell 6 bottles of coke to me for a quarter and I would sell them and earn a nickel profit. Doing such small odd jobs and earning a small profit became my favourite past time. I was always on the lookout for doing something new and earning a little more profit."

In addition to selling chewing gum, soda and coke, Warren started making schemes along with his schoolmates to earn profit. He worked out a mathematical formula and named it 'Stable Boy Selection', to find out the probable winner in horse racing. He would sell tips to find out the winning horse for a few dollars outside the race course. But before he could earn much, he had to stop it, as he did not have a license for this job. After all why was a 4 feet tall, 10 year old boy so serious about earning money, when he could have enjoyed a carefree life!

But Warren was not at all interested in having fun, all he wanted to do was to earn profit, his habit had turned into an obsession. But the good thing was that whatever he did, he did it honestly and seriously. Cheating did not suit him. When he could not think of doing anything new, he would go and help his grandfather at the store. He would also learn the tricks of the trade.

At 13, A Stock Market Player

During 1941, when the world was embroiled in the Second World War, Warren was also preparing for his own war. He started getting involved in his father's stock broking business. Even though his father could not spare any time to explain the intricacies of the stock market, Warren started understanding the rise and fall of the stock markets on his own. He was able to understand that 'bull' and 'bear' were not animals but were terminology used to describe a rising and falling market, respectively.

Eventually at the age of eleven, he made his first investment in the stock market. He bought 3 shares of Cities Service Preferred at 38 dollars per share. He bought 2 shares in his name and 1 share in his sister Doris's name. But his luck did not favour him, the market entered a bear phase and the shares of Cities Service dropped to 27 dollars a share. But Warren was not discouraged and he held on to the shares till they rose to 40 dollars a share and then he sold them. He regretted for his decision later as the shares of Cities Service rose to 200 dollars a share. This event taught him his first and basic rule that one must exercise control; investment in the shares should be for long durations. This rule helped him to become the most successful investor in the world. At this tender age, Warren who had a completely different identity when compared to his classmates. He had clearly realised two things about himself–one, that he can be successful and second, he can earn money from the work in which he had interest. He was saving money and building his courage to implement both these self-realisations. The only thing that was diminishing was his fear and hesitation.

He was able to strike a balance between studying his school books and using his business acumen. To protect himself and to do something different, he was encouraged by his father to file his income tax return. At that time, Warren was only 13 yrs old. He claimed rebate on expense on his cycle as 'being an expense for conducting his business, when he filled in the details of income and expense for income tax return.

New Location, New Business, Studies and Family

In 1942, the Buffett family moved from Omaha to Washington D.C. so that his father could fulfil his political ambitions. The struggle to re-establish in a new place started all over again. On arriving in Washington, his father became involved in his work, Warren also increased his activities. He became a paper delivery boy. He distributed papers in the streets of Washington and its posh colonies, in morning and evening. He carried two papers with him, 'The Washington Post' and 'The Times Harold', so that if anyone stopped one paper, he could offer the second paper and continue maintaining his clientele. Gradually, he increased the number of papers to five and started selling different magazines also.

He was able to earn about 175 dollars a month, which was equivalent to a grown up man's earning. He was able to save nearly 1200 dollars in a few months. He took a bold step and bought 40 acres of farmland in Thurston County and hired it out to a farmer. It was interesting to note that nobody in the Buffett family could achieve what Warren achieved at the age of 14. Now he was no longer an ordinary boy, he was a land owner.

As Warren was growing older, his understanding was becoming sharper and clearer. Like his classmates, he was not interested in picnics, parties, football, rugby or having girl friends. He distanced himself from all such activities and was busy in creating a new world for himself. At the age of 15, along with one of his classmates, formed a company called, 'Venture Wilson Line Updated Machine Corp', to set up pinball machines. They would place pinball machines in barber's shops and earn up to 50 dollars a week.

It was not as if his family was not aware of his activities. Even though he had got full freedom from his family, yet along with his father, his family desired that he should study properly and do something big. Seeing that his involvement in small and transient jobs was affecting his studies, his father Howard insisted on sending him to University of Pennsylvania's famous, 'Wharton Business School.' Warren was not at all interested in going there. At that time he had 50,000 dollars and he was dreaming to multiply it several times by investing in new businesses. But he had to give up to his father's pressure and he joined Wharton. Though he was not very happy to go to Wharton but anyhow he completed two years of study there and returned home. He completed his last year of study at University of Nebraska in Lincoln. When he reached Nebraska, he returned to his old form. He tied up with the University's paper, 'Lincoln Journal' and took up the responsibility of managing a team of 50 boys for its distribution in six rural districts.

After completing his one year study in Nebraska, he applied for doing post graduation in the reputed Harvard Business School. But the School rejected his application on the grounds that he was underage and will have to wait for two years. However, he was able to get admission in Columbia Business School. Here he completed his M.S. under the guidance of the famous market analyst Benjamin Graham. His association with Graham paved his way to new heights, which he was very anxious to attain.

Association with Graham, Marriage with Susan

The year was 1949 and Warren was 19 years old. While in Columbia for his Master's degree, Warren got an opportunity to read Benjamin Graham's famous book, 'The Intelligent Investor.' After reading the book he realised that he had not made any mistake in joining Columbia Business School. His understanding of proper and steady investment planning matured. In two years, under the guidance of other Investment Guru's (apart from Graham) like Phillip Fisher, David Dodd, Walter, Walter Schloss and Edwin Kahan, Warren himself became a Guru. Benjamin Graham considered Warren as his best student and placed him in the A+ category.

In 1951, Warren completed his Masters Degree in Economics from Columbia and started formulating his future plans. Warren wanted to work in association with Graham, but Graham refused. Warren had now turned into an intelligent and capable young man and he saw no valid reason to stay at Columbia. Planning to use his academic knowledge in his father's brokerage firm, he returned to Washington and started working as an investment salesman. It was not as if he had given up his desire to work with Graham. He still wished for a chance to work with Graham, so he continued to pursue Graham. Finally he received an offer from Graham to work for him at an annual salary of 12,000 dollars. Warren worked with Graham for two years and gained practical and professional knowledge of all the tricks of the trade which he had studied in Columbia.

During this period he met Susan Thompson. She was a singer in a night club. Their meetings turned into love and led to marriage.

In 1954, when Graham decided to retire and close down his business, Warren and Graham separated. Warren returned to Omaha, but this time he had with him Susan and the tricks of the trade taught by Graham. He now had an open field to trade in the stock market and to do whatever he wished.

From Buffett Associates to Berkshire Hathaway

In 1956, Warren formed a partnership firm 'Buffett Associates.' In this firm, apart from Warren, there were 8 other partners, consisting of his family members and friends. Warren invested 105,000 dollars and the other 8 partners totally invested an equal amount, that is, 105,000 dollars. This partnership firm operated very successfully for nearly 13 years and established Warren's identity in Wall Street. The partnership firm's investment grew by 30 per cent annually, whereas the market grew by 7 to 11 per cent annually. The tricks of the trade which he had leant from Graham played an important role in this achievement.

As his investment grew, his courage also reached new heights and he thought of doing something new. In 1962, Warren started buying shares of a struggling textile company called, 'Berkshire Hathaway.' The immediate Vice-President of Hathaway called it Warren's mistake, as during that period, all the textile companies were incurring losses.

However, that did not deter Warren. He increased his holding to 49 per cent at less than 8 dollars a share. He now focused all his attention to turning the biggest deal of his life, so far, to a profitable one.

He also started investing the available funds into acquisitions in public limited companies. Strategically, on the top of his hit list were insurance companies. He got a positive response from the market on account of his good track record. By now, Charlie Munger had become his trusted associate. After Benjamin Graham, Charlie Munger had impressed him the most. Now his investment strategy was armed with the experience of Charlie Munger, in addition to the fundamentals of Graham.

Gradually, Warren effectuated a successful turnaround of the company and brought Berkshire out of loss. It had now become his leading company. To strengthen it further, he merged all his other partnership firms into Berkshire and made his partners shareholders of it. Warren had estimated that the Dow Jones Industrial Index's growth would be about 10 per cent every year. Between the years 1957 and 1969, if someone had invested 10,000 dollars then it would have become 28,570 dollars in 1969, whereas if someone had invested in Buffett's firm then it would have become 150,350 dollars, that too after deducting Warren's share. These figures indicate Warren's business acumen and his involvement.

In the 70's decade, it was being said that if Warren showed interest in any company, then the shares of that company would rise by 10 per cent overnight. In case of some companies, it did actually happen. From 1962 to 1980, the shares of Berkshire rose from 8 dollars to 800 dollars and in 1990 it rose to over 7,000 dollars. He limited his salary to 50,000 dollars annually initially and later raised it 100,000 dollars annually. He maintained a strict control over his expenses. Replying to a colleague he said that whatever he gets by the way of income, he invests a large portion of it in Berkshire and retains the rest for his expenses.

After the turnaround of the business, Warren sold the yarn mill of Berkshire and converted it to a purely holding company, which had investments companies which were growing at a healthy rate. Some of these companies were Washington Post, Coca Cola, Gillette, and

American Express, in which Warren started acquiring core holdings, that too for long periods. He also continued to acquire smaller companies. The share price of Berkshire kept on rising and so did the wealth of Warren. He kept on rising to new heights and entered the league of world's richest persons. His wealth can be a source of envy for a lot of business and other tycoons.

Born in the 20th century, he was known as the, 'Saint of Omaha', whereas in the 21st century he was known as the 'Greatest Philanthropist.' In June 2006, he unexpectedly announced donation of 83 per cent of his wealth to the Bill and Melinda Gates Foundation and surprised the world. The contribution amounted to 37 billion dollars or 2400 billion Rupees, which is the largest donation given by anyone in the world. There was a time when he was mocked as the C.E.O., who did not own a private plane. He then bought a private jet for 100 million dollars and silenced all the mockery cast on his extreme austerity.

His decision therefore, to donate a major portion of his vast wealth for philanthropy was indeed a great surprise for the world.

❑

Wife, Children and Profession

While he was reaching new heights in his profession, he was not happy at home. There was no happiness in his married life and there were signs of cracks. The Warren family consisting of his wife and 3 children were unsatisfied, as he was unable to fulfil his responsibilities towards them. The children were growing up but Warren was not devoting enough time to them. He was completely engrossed in his business. Consequently in 1977 his wife Susan left him and started living in San Francisco. But they stayed in contact.

A waitress named Astrid Menks used to like Warren. After Susan left, she tried to fill the vacuum in Warren's life. The interesting fact is that Astrid was introduced to Warren by Susan herself. In spite of the separation Warren and Susan remained in close contact. They would talk over the phone almost daily, would spend the holidays together and along with the children celebrate Christmas together at their beach house in California. Susan was not disturbed by Astrid's presence. Till Susan died in 2004 due to heart attack, all the three had cordial relations. Two years later on his 75th birthday, Warren formally married Astrid. The arrangements for their marriage were done by his daughter.

Warren's children did not join his business. They chose radically different professions. It could also be on account of Warren's decision to donate his entire wealth for charity. His one son is a photographer and the other son a music composer. His daughter is married; in addition to looking after her family, she is managing Susan Thompson Buffett Foundation and doing charitable work. At the age of 83 Warren and his holding company Berkshire are healthy and active in the world of investing.

While investing money or spending money, Warren is extremely disciplined. In spite of the fact he is a major and an experienced investor in the share market, he does not look for small or quick gains. He had not sold even a single share of his holding in Berkshire. He has been giving his children 10,000 dollars only once in a year on Christmas and that too for claiming rebate on tax. Whenever he helps his children, he does so with proper documentation. Once when his daughter asked him for 20 dollars for parking fee, he paid her by cheque.

Warren prefers to stay in his house in Dundee-Happy Hollow, Omaha which he bought in 1958, 57 years back for 31,500 dollars. In spite of being such a well-known celebrity, he is a very simple person and the people of Omaha do not crowd him. He does not like having bodyguards around him.

❑

Childhood

In 1942 Warren's father was elected as the Representative to the U.S. House of Representatives from Omaha in Nebraska, for the first time. When the Buffett family moved to Fredericksburg, Virginia (about 50 miles from Washington D.C.), in January, then Warren was allowed to stay in Omaha along with his grandfather and Aunt to complete his 8th class studies. Thereafter, he completed his 9th class studies from Alice Deal Middle School in Washington. By now, he had become used to Washington's ambience. During this period he had established his newspaper business by distributing 'Washington Post' and other papers and magazines. As far as his studies were concerned he was an average student.

In June, 1943 the 13 year old Warren along with two friends, ran away from his home in Fredericksburg, Virginia and reached a place called Hershey in Pennsylvania. There they wanted to work as Caddy's in the golf course. They spent the night in a hotel in Hershey. Next day some policemen made enquiries from them and after being satisfied by their replies, left. After this, the boys also decided to return home.

His father, therefore, placed a conditional challenge before him – either get better marks or shut down the newspaper business.

Warren loved making money, so he concentrated not only on his studies over the next several months and improved his performance; he also expanded his newspaper business. He started delivering 5 newspapers and magazines. Any customer who did not want the 'Washington Post', he would offer 'Times Harold' to them. By 1945, he was earning 175 dollars a month. This amount was equivalent to many grown-ups monthly salary.

In the same year when he went to Omaha during summer with his family, merely at the age of 14 he decided to buy 40 acres of farmland in Nebraska. From the newspaper business earnings he bought the land for 1200 dollars and rented it out to a farmer. It was beginning of the career of the world's most successful investor.

Warren Edward Buffett was born on 30th August, 1930 in Omaha. From his father's side, his ancestors were Huguenots from France, who had moved to America in 1600. For the next 250 years they did farming in Huntington in Long Island. One of them Sidney Homan Buffett decided to move to the west to start a new life. This was in the year 1867, when the civil war had ended and America was expanding towards the West. Sydney reached the main town Omaha. He saw wooden houses by the side of Missouri river and flat land beyond. He started working as a stage coach driver and later opened S.H. Buffett grocery store.

Only three months earlier the country's east and west regions had been connected by train. There was two way movement of people between the east and west parts of the country. In 1970, people had started arriving and settling in Omaha. Houses with steel structures were also being built and even an Opera House had been built. Consequently, Omaha town was growing and so was the business of S.H. Buffett grocery store. The store was supplying provisions of all kinds from flour to salt in hotels, restaurants and homes.

In the year 1900, the population of Omaha had grown to 1,40,000. Sydney Buffett expanded his store. He also got married; he had two sons, who started helping him in his business. In 1915, one of his sons Ernest opened another store named 'Buffett and Sons' in the newly developing western part of the town. The affluent people of Omaha were developing this part of the town.

Ernest got married and had a son, who was named Howard. It was expected that after Howard grew up, he will manage the family business, but he had no interest in business. He did not want to manage the grocery store. As a student at Nebraska University in Lincoln his inclination for journalism was growing and he became the editor of 'Daily Nebraska.' There he met a simple girl named Leila Stahl, whose father was publisher for a weekly paper in the suburbs of Nebraska. The 16 year old Leila had completed her high school and was looking for a job in a newspaper, so that she could meet her college expenses. She had gained good experience in journalism. When she was in 5th class, she had started helping her father in his weekly paper's work. She herself would compose the matter and even operate the linotype machine. She could conduct interviews and even write the articles nicely. Every Thursday she would operate the printing machine and print the paper.

Howard employed her and also fell in love with her. They got married on 26th December, 1925. By then Howard had completed his college studies. Even though he had wanted to work as a journalist, but when a friend of his father proposed him a job in an insurance company, he accepted it. After this job, Howard got a job in Union Street Bank, where he was assigned the responsibility for selling shares.

In 1928 Leila gave birth to a daughter, who was named Doris. Two years later on 30th August, 1930 Warren was born. That day it rained and the rain cooled the 89 degrees Fahrenheit heat.

Within a year, two weeks before Warren's first birthday the bank where his father used to work closed down. In 1924, when recession set in, countless American companies became bankrupt. Consequently, Howard Buffett also lost his job and exhausted all his savings.

Howard was a determined, hard working person who was dedicated towards his goal. He started a new business with a colleague. He started trading in investment securities, Municipal Corporation and public utilities stock and bonds. He earned commission on their sales. The commission was not much and it was uncertain. Howard and his colleague were also inexperienced in the securities trading. Moreover, when the population of Nebraska was finding it difficult to meet two ends, they could not think of investing. The poor farmers were constrained to eat in charitable messes.

Leila was fulfilling her responsibilities as a housewife with due care, keeping in mind his husband's limited income. Several times she would feed her husband and children and go to bed without eating. However, gradually their financial condition started improving. When Warren was three years old his younger sister Roberta was born. When Warren was six years old his father bought a large mansion on 53rd street in North Omaha and the entire family moved there.

Bottle Caps and Golf Balls

When Warren started going to school, his parents realised that he was born with a fascination for numbers and capabilities to earn money. At the age of five, he set up a kiosk in front of his house and started selling Chicklet bubble gum to the passersby. At the age of six when he went for holidays with his family by a lake side in Iowa, he found out that he could buy a pack of six cokes for a quarter. He sold a single bottle of coke at a time for a nickel to the visiting tourists, thus he earned a profit of 5 cents after selling six bottles of coke. After he returned to Omaha, during his summer holidays, he started earning money by buying soft drinks from his grandfather's store and selling them in the neighbourhood.

When Warren was nine years old, his mother saw that he was collecting bottle caps from a vending machine located in a gas agency near his friend Bob Russell's house. He and Bob counted the brand-wise soft drinks bottle caps to know which soft drink brand was selling the most. At the same time, they started collecting the usable golf balls from Omaha Country Club. They would sell such balls. Warren's mother saw different brand golf ball stored in separate baskets, in his bedroom. Each basket was labelled with the brand name of the golf ball and its price. Warren starting selling the golf balls through his friends and started earning commission on it.

When he was not busy on the golf course he would go to the Ak-Sar-Ben racetrack. He would collect any useful thing he found thrown near the betting window and the grand stand. He would earn some profit from such collection also.

As a child Warren's favourite game was to study the symbols of corporate stocks and bonds. These symbols were marked on the ticker tape, which his father used to bring home from his brokerage office. Warren had memorized hundreds of symbols. Warren would also study in-depth the stock and bond certificates available in large numbers in his father's office. Warren was a welcome visitor in the office of a neighbourhood brokerage firm 'Harris Upham', because he would note down the current stock prices on their blackboard accurately.

Thereafter he started making chart of the movement of different share prices at his home only. When he was 11 years old, he decided to buy 3 shares of, 'Cites Service Preferred', at 38 dollars per share, in his and his sister Doris's name. The share quickly dropped to 27 dollars a share and then gradually rose to 40 dollars a share. Warren immediately sold the shares. After deducting the commission on the trade his father gave him, he earned his first profit of 5 dollars in the share market. He sold the shares at a small profit but regretted his decision when the share rose to 200 dollars. He learnt his lesson of patience in investing.

Warren and his friend Bob Russell would spend hours playing mental games. For instance, they would keep record of how many times some words appeared in a newspaper. They would learn details about different towns, thereafter Bob would name the town and Warren would immediately tell the total population of the town and so on. Bob would ask him questions on the history of baseball and Warren would start narrating the players betting averages and other team details. On Sundays in the Church, his mother would watch him preparing the age records of the people who had written the prayers.

Warren would enjoy spending time in Bob's house. Whereas Warren's house was located in a quite locality, Bob's house was located in a crowded locality. There was constant traffic jams in that area. Once Warren said to Mrs. Russell, "This area is so much crowded, it is a matter of shame that you are not making any money here in spite of so much traffic of people".

Warren and Bob started learning mathematical formulas. Pretty soon they developed a mathematical technique, which could help in betting on the race course. After testing their technique at the Ak-Sar-

Ben racetrack, they were convinced that they could make money at the betting window. For the next race they brought out a hand written horseracing tip sheet called, 'Stable Boy Selection'. While they were selling the tip sheet, they were told by the Officers that a license was required for selling it. But as they were under age, they could not get the license. So they had to stop it.

In Washington D.C.

In 1942, there was a major turn in Warren's life. On 7th December, 1941, the Japanese bombed Pearl Harbour, which sucked America into World War II. The Democratic President Franklin Delano Roosevelt was so popular that in 1940, he was elected President for the third time in a row. The Republican's of Omaha were on the lookout of a candidate who could defeat the Democratic candidate for the Representative election. They selected Omaha's businessman Howard Buffett, who was well-known for being critical of Roosevelt's current policies.

Many persons including his father wanted that Howard should win the Representative elections. Howard won the election. Twelve year old Warren had to pack his bags and baggage, bid his friends goodbye with whom he had spent joyous days. He had to move to Washington D.C. with his family. Washington D.C. being the capital city had become overcrowded on account of the war. So the Warren family had to rent a house in the suburbs in Fredericksburg, Virginia.

Now his father, with whom Warren had a closer attachment as compared to his mother, was staying in a hotel room in Washington D.C. He would visit his family only at the weekends. Warren was desperately missing Omaha and he expressed his inner turmoil in a letter, which he wrote to his grandfather Ernest. His grandfather wrote back that he could stay with him and his Aunt Alice in Omaha, till he completed his 8th class studies. Warren's parents agreed to send him to Omaha.

Warren returned to Omaha and was pleased to meet his friends. During the next four months, while studying to complete his 8th class, he would roam around the western areas of Omaha on a motorbike. After returning from school and on holidays his grandfather would ask him to work in his store 'Buffett and Sons.' He soon learnt to successfully manage the business. He would arrange the stock on the shelves, clean the fruit and vegetable baskets and even pick up the heavy items. He did not very much like these types of jobs and could not tolerate the smell of the groceries. Yet he liked arranging the stock on racks placed against the wall and handing over the items asked by the customers. He learnt a basic lesson that for a business to be successful, one must always remain busy. He had observed that all the workers in the store were constantly busy day or night.

On his way to school, frequently Warren would have lunch at his father's business partner Carl Falk's house. There one day he told Mrs. Falk that he wanted to become a millionaire before he turned 30 years old.

Mrs. Falk asked him, "Warren why do you want to earn so much money?"

The 13 years old guest Warren answered, "It is not as if I only want to earn money, I enjoy earning money and its growth pleases me."

❑

From Golf Course to Graduate School

In September 1943, after bidding goodbye to his dear grandfather and Aunt Alice, Warren returned to Washington. There he joined Alice Dale Junior High School for his 9th class studies. His parents had moved to a house on 49th Street in Washington. The house was located in the north-west district of the city, next to Massachusetts Avenue.

Warren, who was always eager to earn money, started distributing the 'Washington Post', newspaper door-to-door. He used to get up early and complete the distribution of the newspaper before it was time to go to school. Yet he was not at all happy to stay in Washington. He was younger than his classmates. While studying in Omaha, he had moved one class higher. He had very few friends in Washington. His school principal had warned his mother about his shabby dressing habits and asked her that she should send him to school properly dressed. By June Warren had turned to be a young man who could defy conventional set up and rules.

This was the time when Warren had run away to Hershey along with his two friends. He was sure that they will get caddy's job in the golf course there. However, after they were questioned by the policeman the next morning, Warren decided to return home. When he returned home his father clearly told him, 'Either secure good marks or stop selling the newspaper.' This had the desired effect on Warren who did not want to stop the newspaper business.

By winter, his teachers also felt that Warren was concentrating on his studies and there was improvement in the marks secured by him. On the other hand, the circulation Manager of 'Washington Post', had also tied up with the fourteen year old Warren to sell more copies of the newspaper. By now Warren was selling approximately 500 copies in five localities. He had to put in a lot of effort to distribute the newspaper in apartment blocks. He would take the lift up to the 4th floor in an 8 floor building, leave half of the newspapers there, take the balance newspapers up to the 8th floor and deliver the newspaper to each apartment using the staircase.

'Times Harold', newspaper was a competitor of 'Washington Post.' Warren took up the distribution of this newspaper also. When a customer discontinued 'Washington Post' then Warren would persuade him to subscribe to 'Harold Times.' In addition he was supplying magazines also. By the summer of 1944, he was earning approximately 175 dollars a month through the newspaper and magazine business.

In November 1944, Warren's father was elected to the House of Representatives for the second time. At that time Warren was studying for his 10th class in Washington's Woodrow Wilson High School. He was making new friends and was playing golf for his school team. He and his friends would collect the thrown golf balls. They would clean and sell them. One friend of Warren, Donald Denali used to play the piano. He also enjoyed playing number game like Warren. They would play the number games for hours, without using any paper or pencil. They would question each other and solve them orally, even the two digit multiplications.

Pin Ball Machines and Tennis Shoes

Donald had expertise in repairing broken machines. In the spring of 1946, while studying for his senior grade, Donald bought an old pin ball machine for 25 dollars. He repaired it and made it operational. Warren and Donald operated it repeatedly but it broke down every time. However, Donald was able to repair it every time. When Warren saw that Donald was able to repair the machine every time with ease, he suggested that they hire it out to the barbers shop in the neighbourhood.

The barber agreed to keep the machine in the shop provided it earned him a decent income. On the first day there was an earning of 14 dollars. Within a month Warren and Donald hired out seven machines in such shops and started earning 50 dollars a week. They named their company, 'Wilson Coin Operated Machine Company.' They had named their company prompted by the name of their school. Warren had bought the used machines between 25 to 75 dollars. On the other hand, Donald would service the complaints. He would reach the shop on his motorbike. They would introduce themselves as employees of a large business corporation.

Several years later Warren had told that, "The owners of the barber shops would demand for new machines and we would assure them that we shall inform the higher officials about it. We would pretend that we were salaried employees and our job was to provide the machines and manage the cash".

Many years later Warren's high school classmates still remembered a particular thing about him, "We often joked that Warren would only wear tennis shoes, howsoever, cold it might be."

Another friend said, "We would frequently make fun of him about it. He would wear the same shoes round the year. Even when there was knee deep snow he would not feel any difficulty in moving around wearing his tennis shoes."

At home, 16 year old Warren was fond of his father, who in November 1946 successively for the third time won the Representative election from Nebraska. Warren was aware that his father had a conservative attitude. When he was appointed for the first time as Representative, then the Representative's had decided to enhance their salary from 10,000 dollars to 12,500 dollars. His father had protested against the enhancement stating that the people had appointed him as their Representative on a salary of 10,000 dollars, so he will not accept the higher pay.

It was almost time for Warren to enter college. His father suggested that he should seek admission in Pennsylvania University's Horton School of Finance and Commerce. Warren said, "There was no need for him to study any further. He had already earned more than 5,000 dollars by selling 600,000 copies of newspapers. He was earning a regular income from the pin ball machines and the 40 acres land purchased in Nebraska. He had already read more than 100 books on business topics. What new things could any school teach him about business?"

His father reminded him that he was not even 17 years old. Warren hesitantly agreed to seek admission in Horton School.

In the June of 1947 Warren completed his high schooling from Woodrow Wilson High School and secured 16th position out of 347 students. In the Wilson year book, below his photograph was the caption– 'Likes mathematics, a future stock broker.'

When his friend Donald Denali's girl friend asked him if he was going to settle in Washington, then Warren replied, "No, I will settle in Omaha."

Rolls Royce Ride

After taking admission in Horton, Warren soon realised that what he had thought was right and told his father so. No Professor knew more than what he had already learned. During holidays when he returned to Omaha, his father's business partner's wife Mary Falk asked him whether he was concentrating on his studies or not?

He replied, "All I have to do is to open my books and empty a large bottle of coke on the eve of the examination. I shall secure 100 per cent marks."

After spending a year in Horton, when he returned to Washington during summer holidays, he had already made up his mind to discontinue his studies. His father, however, convinced him to continue with his studies for the second year also. During this period he would ride in his friend Donald's Roll Royce car all through Washington. Donald had purchased this 1928 model car from a scrap dealer. He had repaired the car and painted it deep blue colour. Just for fun sake,

Donald would don a chauffer's uniform, whereas Warren and Donald's girl friend would dress as a rich couple and occupy the back seat. They would then drive through Washington's affluent areas. Donald would stop the car anywhere in-between, open the hood of the car and pretend to examine it. After some time when a crowd of curious onlookers gathered, Warren would get down from the car and point his cane towards any part of the engine. Donald would then pretend to repair that part, after which all of them would carry on with their drive.

In Horton, Warren used to stay at a friend's house, where he would be engrossed in very challenging games of bridge. He would freely chat with his friends. One of his friend told, "He was a very funny boy. He was very clever. Whenever he was with us, he would make us laugh."

Weekend beer parties were held at his friend's place. Many of Warren's classmates had become his pals just to drink free beer. Warren himself used to drink only Pepsi-cola. In the party, Warren's ideas on politics and economics used to impress everyone. They had realised that Warren's knowledge was much more extensive than their own knowledge. Compared to his Professors dull lectures, Warren could talk in a more interesting way. One of his classmates told, "Warren had realised that there was nothing new which he could learn at Horton. I think, he was right."

In November 1948, Howard Buffett lost the Representative election and returned to Omaha with his wife and daughters. In June 1949, Warren completed his second year term at Horton and took admission in Nebraska University in Lincoln for his further studies. He never looked back but later he told, "I always had the feeling that I was not learning much."

50 Hawkers and 2,640 Golf Balls

After studying for 2 years at Horton, Warren decided to complete his Bachelor's degree in 3 years instead of 4 years. In the winter of 1949, Warren started studying five syllabuses of economics and business, whereas the scheduled starting time was 1950. During this time he also took up a job in the newspaper, 'Lincoln Journal.' He became the supervisor of 50 hawkers in the 6 rural districts of Nebraska. He used to get 75 cents per hour. In the afternoons, he would tour his area in a car and reappoint new hawkers.

In the winter of 1950, Warren decided to restart his golf balls business. He appointed Jerry, a classmate from Horton as his sales agent in Philadelphia and started supplying him used golf balls. By July, he sold 2640 balls and earned 1,200 dollars. After the summer holidays he returned home and started studying three syllabuses in the Omaha precinct of Nebraska University for his degree. By then he had earned 9,800 dollars from the newspaper job and sale of golf balls.

Thereafter Warren applied for admission in Harvard Business School. Nineteen year old Warren was called to Chicago for the interview. The interview lasted for 10 minutes only. Later Warren told, "The snoot nosed interviewers at Harvard thought that I was under aged and so they asked me to wait for one or two years."

But Warren could not wait. He applied for admission in New York's Columbia University Graduate School of Business. One of the Professor of Columbia University, Professor Benjamin Graham had written the book 'Intelligent Investor', which Warren had read and liked it very much. Professor Benjamin could never have known that very soon he would become lifelong guide of a 19 year old inquisitive youth.

❑

Intelligent Investor

The title of Benjamin Graham's book, 'Intelligent Investor', aptly describes as to what Warren had wanted to become in life. Warren used to constantly ponder about Investors. People used to buy shares of proprietary companies and hoped that they would make some profit. Warren liked Graham's fundamental advice that an intelligent investor should not blindly follow the other Wall Street investors. Instead Graham had advised in his book that the investor should invest in companies which were trading below their intrinsic value.

According to Graham, it was not easy to identify such companies. It required a lot of patience. It was necessary to study every aspect of the working of the company- its assets, its earnings and its future plans. After conducting such an analysis the investor could determine the true price of the share of the company, in other words the price, which had no relation to the price being quoted in the share market.

Graham believed the prices in the market were like a popularity contest. The prices reflected the sentiments of the investors towards that company. The movement of share prices in the share market was often based on rumours and false propaganda and they may have no relationship with the facts. One could not decide the correct price of the share of any company on the basis of prices quoted in the market.

Graham had concluded that the intelligent investor should buy the shares of any company when they are trading below their intrinsic value. Thereafter, the investor should patiently wait for the share price to rise. It is definite that the share price would rise sooner or later.

After reading the book Warren discovered the mantra of investing. He was impressed by the basic rules described by Graham. While buying shares from his father's brokerage or while studying in Horton from a brokerage in Philadelphia, Warren followed these basic rules. He saw that the people who bought shares on rumours or on guess work had to face the uncertainties of the share market. He firmly believed that by buying share on guess work could never earn any profit for the investor. He believed that this practice was totally wrong.

In September, 1950 Warren was one of twenty students who were studying in Graham's class. He was quite impressed by Graham's style of teaching. Graham never used to accept or reject instantly the reply of any student, to the queried question. Instead he would ask, "On what basis have you arrived at this conclusion?"

Graham would teach his students how to study and analyse the annual report of a company; how to determine the true value of its share based on its financial statement. He would present two balance sheets of two purportedly different companies to the students for comparison. Later, he would dramatically disclose that the balance sheets were of the same airplanes manufacturing company- Boeing; but of different periods. He was in fact training the students of the manner in which the companies preferred to disclose their information for record. The students can determine the true value of its shares based on the information provided on record only.

Warren was imbibing the knowledge into his blood streams. He had answer to all the questions. Later, one of his classmates told, "He would frequently raise his hand to reply and he would participate in the discussions enthusiastically. He possessed amazing zeal. As compared to others, he would always speak without any hesitation."

He was greatly impressed by his Professor's intelligence and friendly nature; so he wanted to compile all the available information on him. During his second semester at Columbia, he came to know that Graham was the Head of the Government Employees Insurance Company G.E.I.C.O. Its headquarter was in Washington D.C.

In November 1950, his father Howard Buffett again won the Representative election, after remaining out of the House of Representatives for two years. In 1951, Warren joined his family in Washington for a week's holiday. He arrived at Washington railway station on a Saturday morning and the same day he went to the headquarter of G.E.I.C.O. located on K Street. There he met a guard and told him that he wanted to meet an Officer of the Company. He was introduced to the Deputy Finance Officer Lorimer A. Davidson. An unknown young man posed numerous questions to Davidson.

Later Davidson told, "After talking to him for 15 minutes, I realised that the stranger was not an ordinary person. He was asking intelligent questions based on the facts. What is G.E.I.C.O.? How did it conduct his business, what are its objectives, what are its growth prospects? He was asking questions which could have only been raised by an experienced investor. He wanted to gain all the information which I had."

Both talked for about 4 hours. Warren came to know that two persons from Texas, Leo Goodwin, Sr. and Lillian Goodwin had founded G.E.I.C.O., who planned to sell insurance policies directly to Government Employees. Government Employees claims were much less than any other group of persons. Direct sales also meant that there was no need to pay any commission to agents.

❑

Life Partner

The young Warren used to stay away from girls. Even though he desired that he had a girl friend, but his attitude would become a hindrance. Later he said, "In the presence of girls, no one was as shy as I was. Maybe I was hesitant in continuing a conversation." Except for talking about shares and politics, he had little else to talk about. He felt nervous in asking a girl out for a date. In school or college, he could not mix freely with girls. His limited interactions with girls were not very pleasant.

While going out to witness a baseball game with a girl named Jackie Gideon, his car crashed against a cow. While he had gone out with another girl, he got hit by a golf ball. While he had gone out with a girl named Ann Beck, he kept sitting in front of her but could not utter a single word, as if he was a mute. He could not decide if she would like to hear him speak about Ben Graham. A girl named Bunny Merlin tried to befriend Warren for many days but nothing came out of it.

Finally in the summer of 1950 before he left for California his sister Berty introduced him to her roommate Susan Thompson. She came from the North-Western part of the country and was a cute girl with a round chin. She had impressed Berty at once, who was one and half years younger than her. Berty was an expert in understanding people. When Warren met Susan, he was enamoured by her; but somehow he doubted her appearance.

"I can most certainly say that in the beginning she was acting. I was impressed by her and was trying to attract her; but I also wanted to know her real self. I could not believe that there could be any girl like that in reality."

In fact Susan was not attracted towards Warren, as she was in love with someone else.

After leaving Columbia Warren read in the Earl Wilson's gossip column in, 'New York Post', that the year 1949 'Miss Nebraska' Vanita Brown was staying in Webster Women's Residence. She was participating in a T.V. show with singer and idol of the youngsters Eddy Fisher.

Vanita was studying in Nebraska University, when Warren was also studying there. Even though, till now he had not specifically noticed her and since the glamorous Miss Nebraska was staying in New York, he called her at the Webster residence. Gradually Warren had been overcoming his shyness.

Vanita decided to meet him and try her luck. They had met once in the past. Warren knew that she had been brought up in totally different circumstances. She had grown up in the neighbourhood of the southern Omaha's storages, where after returning from school she used to skin chickens in Omaha Cold Storage. Her shapely body and intoxicating face attracted lots of people. She got her first job in Paramount Theatre. Then she participated in the local beauty contests.

"I think her real talent lied in charming the judges." Warren said.

After winning the 'Miss Nebraska' title, Vanita participated in the beauty contest in Washington D.C. Thereafter she came to New York and tried to establish herself in the show business there.

Even though she knew that Warren was not a boy who would take a girl to a stark club or to cope cabana for a show; yet she welcomed the boy from her home town warmly. Pretty soon they were seen roaming about on the streets of New York. Both of them started visiting the Marble Collegiate Church to listen to the lectures of Norman Vincent Peel on personality development. Peel had written several books on personality development and was a powerful orator.

Warren used to take Vanita by the side of Hudson River for cheese sandwiches. Even though Vanita did not like cheese sandwiches but she wanted to retain her relationship with Warren. Warren found her entertaining and witty. While talking to Vanita he felt the same pleasure as if he was playing oral ping-pong. Vanita's beauty had its own charm. In spite of Vanita's company Warren could not fully develop the art of mixing freely in society. As time passed, he became increasingly concerned about this shortcoming in his personality. He saw an advertisement offering a course on the Dale Carnegie style of speaking. Warren had lot of faith in Dale Carnegie who had mastered the techniques of 'How to win friends and influence people.' He reached the institute in New York to join the course with a 100 dollar cheque in his pocket.

"I went to join the Dale Carnegie public speaking course because I was facing difficulty in mixing socially. I gave the cheque, but then I stopped its payment because I changed my mind."

During winter, Warren kept on writing letters to Susan Thompson. But there was no improvement in their relationship. She neither prompted him to write nor told him to stop writing. Warren thought that if he met Susan's parents it might help him to get closer to her. Warren went with Susan's parents to see a football match in West Side and then went out for dinner with them. But during dinner Susan left them to meet a friend.

After spending his holidays, Warren returned to New York. He felt a little handicapped there, but did not give up hope. In the meanwhile he kept meeting Vanita.

Later Warren said, "Of all the people I met, Vanita was the most imaginative girl."

In fact becoming intimate with Vanita was like giving invitation to uncertainty and insecurity. She had threatened Warren several times that she will go to Washington and when Howard Buffett was addressing the House of Representatives; she will kneel down on her knees in front of him and scream, 'Warren is the father of the child in my womb.' Warren was apprehensive of her carrying out the threat. Once she created such an ugly scene in the cinema hall that Warren had to drag her out of the cinema hall and left without her.

Vanita was beautiful and bewitching. But she was hot-headed and dangerous. Warren had realised that getting closer to her could be perilous. But Warren felt an exhilarating pleasure in retaining her friendship. It was like taming a tigress.

"Vanita could take care of herself. She could do so quite easily. The question was whether she wanted to do it or not? She was not a nuisance for others unless she so desired."

Once Warren arranged a dinner party in New York Athletic Club, in the honour of a distinguished Lawyer and Navy's Secretary Frank Mathews and also invited Vanita. He thought that the presence of the beautiful Miss Nebraska will add glamour to the party. Mathew himself was a resident of Nebraska. The other invitees were also well-known personalities of the society. Warren wanted to impress the guests. However, while cocktails were being served Vanita embarrassed Warren. When Warren introduced her as a friend, she contradicted him and said that she was his wife. She said, "I don't know why he is feeling embarrassed in telling the truth? Whenever he takes me out he says that I am his friend; whereas the fact is that we are married."

Eventually Warren understood that Vanita could take care of herself, but, "In reality she could always create difficulties for me and she always enjoyed acting in a whimsical manner," Warren told later. She would often behave whimsically. She had a superiority complex and had no inkling as how she would behave at any particular moment.

Whenever Warren visited his home in Nebraska, he would meet Susan Thompson. Even these meetings were brief. He thought that she was cultured, imposing and compassionate. Warren later told, "As compared to me, she was much more mature."

His attraction for Susan was getting stronger, so he started looking for ways to distance himself from Vanita. Warren later told, "Even though I knew that I was not her first love, but I was convinced that it was not going to affect our relations."

Susan's family and Buffett family knew each other quite well. In fact it was Susan's father, William Thompson who had managed Howard Buffett's election campaign for the fourth term, which Howard lost. In spite of the acquaintance, there were a lot of dissimilarities between the two families. Susan's mother Dorothy Thompson was a sweet natured, courteous, generous and erudite woman, who always fulfilled her obligations towards her family consciously. She would ensure that dinner was served on the dinning table exactly at 6 O'clock in the evening. She fully assisted her husband Dr. William Thompson, so that he could manage his busy schedule smoothly. William Thompson always formally dressed in a suit and would move around as if everyone was praising him.

He was the Dean of the Arts and Science College of Omaha University. He also taught psychology and as the Assistant Athletic Director was responsible for the athletic activities of the University also. As a former football player and sports lover he used to be involved in all the activities enthusiastically. Warren told later, "His role made him so famous in the town that all the policemen recognized him, which was a boon for him as he was a rather careless driver." He had also designed IQ and psychology tests for the students. He was especially interested in conducting examinations for the town's school children. He did not like spending even a single holiday at home, away from his hectic schedule. On Sundays, he would give sermons in the Church, in an earnest but soft voice. His two daughters gave him company by singing hymns. In the remaining time he would discuss his political beliefs in different groups of people. His political beliefs were more or less similar to the political beliefs of Howard Buffett.

Whenever William Thompson would ask for anything, it was meant to be taken as an order. He used to talk about the pride of women, but he himself disregarded it. He used to study in-depth the psychology of mankind, but he was unable to properly understand their sentiments. He wanted to see the people whom he liked, to remain close to him. He used to be disturbed if he did not see them around. He felt that his dear ones might get into unexpected troubles. He used to adore people who followed his advice as directed.

Thompson's elder daughter, Dotty was temperamentally averse to following his orders. According to the family members, in Dotty's initial years when her father had become extremely annoyed with her, he used to lock her in the cupboard.

His second daughter Susan was born seven years after Dotty's birth. Mother Dorothy was shaken by the father's behaviour towards her elder daughter Dotty, so she told her husband, "The elder daughter is yours, I will bring up the younger daughter as I choose.

Susie was a sickly child from birth. She was troubled by her allergy and ear infection. In the first eighteen months her ear had to be cleaned a dozen times. She was fever prone. In the second grade of kindergarten, she was confined to her home for four to five months due to her sickness. Later, she told that she used to watch her friends playing from the window and feel annoyed with herself.

Her parents used to pay special attention towards her on account of her sickness. Warren had said "Susie could do no wrong, whereas faults were found in everything Dotty did. Nobody treated her properly."

Even after Susie recovered and there was no need for her to be confined, she showed no interest in going out to play. Instead she took special interest in making new friends because she was completely isolated from everyone, on account of her sickness.

Later Susie reminisced, "After you suffer pain, relief from it provides an amazing feeling of freedom. The feeling is just fantastic. Relief from pain heals your heart. I understood this at my tender age itself. This realization changes your outlook towards life and it becomes simplistic. Then while developing new acquaintances all that comes to your mind is how good the people are."

Susie was growing up. Her round chin was very attractive. Her babyish voice used to impulsively draw attention towards her. In her teens, she took admission in Omaha's Central High School. Students from different sections of the society used to study together in this school, which was a very unusual thing for the forties. Even though she used to mix with the elite group, yet all her classmates remembered her as popular and simple student. The kind of intensity she used to display and used to open her heart innocently easily impressed people. She was more interested in oration and performing arts instead of being immersed in studies. In debating competitions, she would present her views confidently and sincerely. People noticed that her ideology was mostly opposite to her father's ideology. In the school plays, she used to act forcefully and in musical shows she would sing melodiously. Many of her musical shows became memorable events for the audience. The magnetism of her personality had impressed everyone in the school and her classmates elected her, 'Senior Class President.'

Susie's first boyfriend was a pleasant boy named John Gilmore whom she liked very much. While studying at Central High School even though John was one feet taller than Susie, she used to dominate her.

During that period she made a new friend, an intelligent boy whom she had met in a debating competition. Milton Brown was a student of Thomas Jefferson High School in Council Slough, Iowa. He had an enticing smile. He was a tall, dark haired pleasant boy. They would meet frequently. Susie's close friends were aware of her friendship with Milton. Her friendship with Gilmore was also intact and she would attend parties and school functions with him.

Susie's father did not like Milton Brown, who was the son of an illiterate Russian-Jew immigrant labourer and used to work on the Labour Union Pacific Railway Track. Susie took him to her home three or four times. Her father was rude to Brown and used to lecture him on FDR and Truman. Her father was against her daughter's friendship with a Jew boy and never bothered to hide his negative feelings towards him. Susie's father also used to believe in Omaha's conventional family traditions like the Buffett family. He was not prepared to deviate from this traditional thinking. But Susie was trying to cross over the traditional social boundaries. Yet in high school, she was popular for following traditions.

Facing such dilemmas, for her college studies Susie took admission in North Western University in Winston, Illinois. Milton was also studying there. There they both felt the sense of having freedom. Susie shared her room with Berty Buffett. While studying for Journalism, Susie planned her schedule so that she had time to meet Milton every day.

Milton was doing odd jobs to fund his studies. Susie and Milton would meet in the library. Students of her community were not happy to see her getting close to a Jew boy. They were particularly annoyed when she took him along for a dance performance. Even though she was hurt by this treatment, she did not stop seeing Milton. They both started learning 'Baudh Dharma', to attain mental peace.

During this time unaware of all these happenings, Warren went to Winston to see a football match and in the winter holidays went to Omaha to meet Susie. By then he had made up his mind to express his affection to her. She had all the qualities which Warren wanted to see in a woman. But it was Milton Brown on whom she wanted to shower her affection.

In 1951, Milton was elected 'Class President' and Berty Buffett elected 'Vice-President'. Susie would weep while reading letters from home which directed her to terminate her relationship with Milton. Berty could only watch her shedding tears emotionally as Susie never shared her feelings with her. It seemed as if she wanted to keep others out of the emotional trauma which she was undergoing. Just before the session ended, Susie's father directed her over phone to return home. When she reached Omaha her father told her that she could not see Milton under any circumstances and she could also not go back to North Western University. Susie's world came crashing down and she started weeping bitterly. But her father did not relent.

At that time, Warren had also returned to Omaha after completing his graduation from Columbia. Warren's parents were living in Washington at that time and Warren was to stay in his parental home. He also had to serve time with the National Guards for some time during the summer holidays. Even though he was not fully fit to join the National Guards but it was a better option than fighting war in Korea. Every year he had also to attend the training camp in La Crosse Wisconsin for a few weeks. Even after attending such training camps he had not matured.

"In the National Guards the other boys would eye me suspiciously because my Dad was a Congressman. They thought that I was a strange animal. But this belief was short-lived. The organization was established on core democratic values. What I mean is that it does not matter what you are outside. Here to develop team spirit you must even be prepared for reading comics. I was reading comics within the hour of reaching there. When the others were doing the same, how could I be different? Four words were added to my vocabulary, which I am sure you can easily guess."

"I learnt that when you are in the company of people who are better than you then you also develop. Whereas when you are in the company of people who are inferior to you then it quickly leads to your downfall."

After returning from the training camp, based on his experience Warren said, "I use to hesitate while speaking to a group. You will not believe the state of my mind I used to be when it was my turn to address the group. I was so scared that I could not even utter a single word. I wished that I should somehow disappear. In fact, I had designed my life-style so that I need not speak in front of others. When I returned to Omaha after completing my graduation, I saw an advertisement. I knew that at some point of time, I will have to speak in front of others. I was terribly scared of this thought, so to overcome this fright, I enrolled for the art of speaking course.

This however, was not the single objective which he had in mind. He understood that to win over Susan Thompson's affection, it was necessary for him to be able to talk to her freely and leave a lasting impression. Earlier on several occasions, he had stammered while talking to her. He was prepared to do anything to improve his shortcoming and also knew that this year's summer holidays were his last chance to do so.

Dale Carnegie's public speaking classes were held in Hotel Rome, which was the favourite spot of the shepherds.

"I took the fees for the course with me, which I paid to the Instructor were Poly Kennan and told him to keep it before I changed my mind. There twenty-five to thirty students. We were all perturbed. We could not even pronounce our names. We all stood there but were unable to talk to each other. I was, however, impressed by Poly Kennan's ability to remember names of all the students and the ease with which he called our names. He was a good teacher and he used to teach us the tricks to sharpen our memory; but I was unable to learn them. We were given copies of keynote speeches, election speeches, Lt. Governor's speech etc. to memorise and it was expected that we will be able to narrate the speeches. This would motivate us to overcome our hesitation. Why is it that you do not hesitate to talk freely to a single person, but are unable to utter even a single in front of a group? He used to teach us psychological tricks to overcome our fear. We had to practice some of these tricks. We were helping each other to overcome our hesitation. It had helped me quite a bit by the time I completed the course."

However, Warren did not use this ability on Susie. He understood that Susie was influenced by her father, so he was thinking of ways to impress him, when he was alone. William Thompson liked to play the mandolin in his garden during summer. Warren would sing sitting in front of him. Susie would then quietly leave to meet Milton.

Warren liked to spend time with William Thompson. In his company, he was reminded of his father, who blamed the Democrats for all the wrongs. Like Warren's father, William was also interested in discussing sporting activities, in addition to politics. He had no son and he considered Warren to be the perfect future son-in-law. Warren was hot-blooded, was a Protestant, was a Republican and most importantly Warren was not Milton Brown.

But William's acceptance was not enough to bring him closer to Susie. In spite of lot of efforts, Warren could not win over Susie's affection. She might have overlooked his loose socks and cheap dress, but his other qualities did not impress her as well. He was a Congressman's son, who had a special status in the society. He was a graduate with handsome savings and was progressing rapidly. He would always talk about shares. It was a topic in which Susie had no interest. During his outings with Susan, he would narrate memorized jokes, quiz riddles and ask her questions to test mental ability. Since William liked Warren, she saw her father's personality's reflection in him. William had almost forced Susie to be with Warren. Warren later told, "It was one against two."

Milton liked Susie and he needed him also but since he was a Jew, he had to face injustice. He was a handsome youth, but Susie's father disliked him.

That year during summer, Milton Brown was working for Council Sloughs. He received information from North Western University regarding hike of fees; he realized that he will not go to Evanston for further studies. So he handed over a letter to Berty Buffett, in which he had written that he was going to take admission in Iowa University. That year Susie was taking admission in Omaha University. By then both of them realized that their paths were separated on account of Susie's father's interference. Susie spent the summer holidays weeping.

On the other hand, in spite of her initial dislike for Warren, Susie could not spend time with him without knowing everything about him. She soon realized that her initial impression about Warren was not right. Warren was not what she had thought– Warren was not a pampered young man, full of self-confidence.

"I was confused." Warren told later. He needed support. "I could not understand my state of mind. I was not able to mix socially. In addition till now I had not experienced a fast paced life." Susie's friends were also feeling that the overtly confident Warren was inertly restlessness. Gradually, Susie also started understanding that he was lonely. Even though he would talk fascinating things about shares, but in fact he was in search of love, as he was lonely. He was like a child in search of a safe place. Later Warren said, "I was confused. The wonderful thing was that Susie had perceived the state of my mind."

Warren was not bothered how others dressed. He was not even attracted by the attire of women. But now since he was deeply in love with Susie, he particularly started noticing her dresses. He remembered going out with Susie in a blue dress. Also when she was dressed in a black and white dress, he had called it a 'newspaper dress'. They were dancing on the dance floor of Peony Park Pavilion. Warren had not learnt dancing, so he was somehow trying to match the steps. He was blushing like a child on the dance floor. Later he said, "I was ready to do whatever she asked me to do. I wanted to feel the warmth of her arms around my back."

On the Labour Day, Warren took her to the fair. Both reached there like lovers.

Susie took admission in the University to study journalism. She joined the debating team. She also became a member of a psychological institution.

In October of 1951, Warren wrote in a letter to his Aunt Dorothy Stahl– "I am having a good time with a girlfriend. I have become pretty close to a local girl. After I receive the go ahead from Uncle Fred and you, I will take the next step. This girl has one shortcoming, she does not understand anything about shares, otherwise she is superb."

Warren was making progress. He had prepared well. Instead of proposing he was gradually getting intimate with her. Susie understood that he had decided about her, even though she could not figure how it happened.

Full of enthusiasm, he rejoined the Dale Carnegie course. Warren said, "They used to reward a pencil if you were able to complete a difficult assignment. In the same week, I won a pencil and proposed to Susie."

After this, Susie wrote a detailed and sorrowful letter to Milton Brown. He was stunned. He knew that Susie used to meet Warren, but he never took their friendship seriously.

Warren went to meet Susie's father to seek his blessings. He was confident that Susie's father would grant the blessing easily. But William Thompson took a lot of time before giving his approval. He started discussing the political situation in the country and cursing the Government's policies. He painted a bleak picture of the country's economy and expressed concern that Warren's plans to trade in the stock market could fail. However, he considered him to be a smart boy and capable of facing any eventuality with courage. So even if such an eventuality occurred and her daughter faced hardship, then he would not blame him.

Warren had by now become used to hearing such talk from his father and Susie's father. So he was not disturbed. He kept listening patiently and waited for him to say 'Yes'. Finally after three hours William Thompson gave him permission to marry his daughter.

In April of the same year, Warren and Susie were married.

❑

Wealth Creation

'Wealth creation is the outcome of a man's thinking capability.'

—Ayn Rand

If you had invested 10,000 dollars in 1956, the year in which Warren Buffett had started investing then today, you would have been worth 350 million dollars.

Warren's success is significant in many ways, because he did not create wealth by patenting a product, or by setting up an industry, or by setting up a retail operation nor by starting his own business. The assets which he used can be easily applied in this capitalist world by everyone– following the principles of extraordinary discipline and investment based on value.

Warren has earned 100 billion dollars till now and is still creating wealth. He believes that there is no magic spell for making profit by investing in others business and anyone can create wealth by doing so. For this one must follow the same rules and principles, which Warren has followed in his life. Anyone can earn money like this and save it for his next generation.

Warren's success story seems unreal and one cannot easily believe it. How a person without the support of his family's wealth, without assuming any responsibility in his family's business, without any recommendation or approach from the higher ups, without working for a fat salary can generate so much wealth and also give most of it towards philanthropy.

It is easy to become rich: by being born in a rich family, by marrying a wealthy a woman or by winning lottery. But becoming rightfully rich is the one tested by Warren- managing your own business and managing it by spending less than your earnings. Like Warren did, you can also convert your dreams of becoming rich into reality by investing in part of others business through the share market. By learning the tricks of investing and management, you can even take controlling stake in that company.

Warren's billions made him the richest man in the world. But he also generated lots of wealth for his partners and shareholders. He generated two dollars for them, for every dollar he generated for himself, his family's four foundations.

By investing over long periods of time, the manner in which he created wealth for himself and others is not really surprising. He strictly followed his principles and became wealthy. Even though, it took him several decades to do so.

First in the middle of sixties, Warren along with his partners started buying shares of a textile mill named Berkshire Hathaway. By 1965, he bought most of its shares for 20 million dollars and took management control of the mill. In 1967, the turnover of the mill was 39 million dollars. In the next four decades by investing his capital he generated 100 billion dollars, he only had to borrow a minor amount.

Extraordinary Capability for Creation of Wealth

In all probability the American writer, poet and philosopher Ralph Waldo Emerson has rightly said that–

"Man is born to become rich and attain prosperity by a mix of his qualities, ideas and nature. Wealth is a product of your mind. To play this game you must learn to be polite, intelligent, swift-footed and patient."

Warren was not born rich but from the very beginning, he had the extraordinary capability to create wealth. All through his life the huge wealth which he created and donated for the welfare of mankind is a result of application of his mental capabilities. He is a polite, intelligent, decisive and a patient person. This amazing story is of a person who started with his hard earned capital and became the richest man in the world in the capitalist system by incessantly using his capabilities appropriately. The wealth which he created is more than the GDP of Iraq, Ethiopia, Costa Rica, Cuba, North Korea and Yemen put together.

Warren was born on 30th August, 1930 in Omaha, a city in Nebraska. Howard Buffett was his father and Leela Stahl Buffett his mother. Jokingly he said that, "He was conceived in his mother's womb in 1929, when the stock market had crashed; because his share broker father had no other work. At that time the senseless behaviour of the investors, is fully registered in my DNA."

Warren often says that being born a white man and an American is his good fortune. He was born in a democratic and capitalist society, where there were immense opportunities for personal growth. If he was born a hundred years earlier or born in a third world country or he had to any other job than investing, then it would not have been possible for him to attain such prosperity. More than 30 books have been written on him, on account of his extraordinary success. From the very beginning he had an uncommon capability to value companies. In addition the time period, in which he was born, was favourable for the economy to expand and capitalism was at its peak. It is equally fortunate that he was born in America where only 2 per cent of the world's population lives; yet has 50 per cent of the world's wealth and has the biggest companies, which has the political and constitutional set up which treats all the professions including investment capabilities equally and had recorded a seven-fold increase in the standard of living in a century.

Warren's friends and Microsoft's creator teased him saying that had he been born a few centuries earlier and did not possess hearing and running capabilities then he would have been gobbled by a wild animal. Or had he been born a woman at a time, when there were a lot of restrictions on women then he would have become a housewife, teacher, secretary or nurse instead of becoming an investor.

Warren's father used to run a stock broking company in Omaha and later became a Congressman from Nebraska. This background also helped to groom Warren's fate. Even though his father did not bestow any money to him because he knew that Warren did not need any ancestral property. His father bestowed him with interest for shares, self-confidence to be independent, high moral standards and developed his political outlook. With the help of all these qualities Warren always succeeded. His father also gave him freedom to form his own opinions. That is why Warren supported his father's opposition party. Both were restless, but Warren's father had a serious disposition whereas Warren was jovial.

20 Per cent Profit at the Age of Six

Warren's grandfather used to run a grocery store, 'Buffett and Son', in Omaha. Being business-minded was in Warren's blood and at the age of six he proved it. He bought pack of 6 cokes for 25 cents from his grandfather's store and sold them separately for a nickel each and earned 20 per cent profit. Thus Warren laid the foundation of being industrious in his future life. At a time when the other children roamed around on the streets in summer evenings, at that time this six year old industrious child was selling coke bottles from door-to-door and learning the art of making money.

From the early years, Warren was interested in arithmetic, numbers, money and coins. His sister told that in his childhood, Warren used to move around with a metal money changer belt. Warren never required a calculator or a computer to solve mathematical problems. From childhood to the present-day, Warren has been continuously involved in making and growing money.

At the age of 8, Warren started reading books on making money and business. '1000 ways to earn 1000 dollars', was his favourite book in the beginning. He read the book several times. By the time he was 10 years old, the billionaire of the future, had read dozens of books on investment, finance, stock market in Omaha's local library. Warren had a sharp memory and he was very good at articulating what he had learnt. He was a wizard with numbers. That is why during his school days, he was promoted by two classes.

His first experience of the stock market was noting down the prices of shares on a blackboard in his father's stock broking office. That is how the prices of shares were displayed before the advent of the electronic display ticker tape and it was called 'marking the board'.

It was while noting down the prices of shares on the blackboard, in June 1942 at the age of eleven, Warren bought his first lot of shares. He bought 6 shares of a company called 'Cities Service Preferred'. He had bought 3 shares in his name and 3 shares in the name of his elder sister Doris. Each share had cost him 38 dollars. So it can be assumed that his personal capital was a little more than 100 dollars at that time. The price of the shares dropped to 27 dollars rapidly, but after some time it increased to 40 dollars. At that time he sold his shares. But from this experience he learnt an important lifelong lesson. Soon after he sold the shares, its price rose to 200 dollars. Possibly at that time he did not realize the error of selling too soon, based on the market price, rather than at its intrinsic value; in his future life he adopted the solid fundamentals of investing.

At the age of 13, displaying exceptional curiosity for learning, Warren had made up his mind to become an investor in the stock market. As a matter of fact he had told a friend of his family that he would become a millionaire by the age of 30. He had also told his father's business partner's wife Mary Falk, while having soup, that if did not become a millionaire, then he would jump from the tallest structure of Omaha.

First Business at the Age of 14

When his father was elected Congressman then Warren had to move to Washington from Omaha to be with his family. There he started studying in high school. He was not very happy to be in the country's capital and he missed Omaha, his birth town. Warren displayed his love and attachment for his birth place all through his life.

At the age of 14 Warren was industrious and ambitious. He started delivering 500 copies of 'Washington Post' newspaper in five localities. He started earning 175 dollars a month.

Like selling coke during his childhood proved to be useful later in life, distributing newspapers also proved to be extremely useful. Later he became the largest shareholder in the newspaper, which he used to distribute in his teens.

Warren's also used to do business of selling used golf balls. For it he took help of his several neighourhood friends. At the age of 14, he bought 40 acres of farmland in Nebraska for 1200 dollars, which he had saved by delivering newspapers and other activities. He leased out the land to a farmer. This investment was the first sign that he was a determined and self-confident youth, who had become capable of taking firm business decisions, like grown-ups. By investing in the farmland in his early years he expressed his deep-rooted affection for his home state Nebraska. Warren maintained this affection all through his life.

The beauty of this real estate deal was that he did not have to take care of it himself. Even in the later years, Warren did not think that it was necessary for him to visit the head-quarters or the offices of the companies in which he held controlling stakes.

While studying in high school, he bought a used pinball machine for only 25 dollars along with his friend Donald Danly. The original cost of this machine was 300 dollars. He had learnt the art of buying a thing worth one dollar for less than 10 cents in his teens itself. In the later years also he displayed this acumen on several occasions. Both the friend's named the company 'Wilson Coin Operated Machine Company', inspired by their school's name. In front of their customers they posed as if they were the employees of the company and Wilson was the owner. They installed the machine at a barber's saloon.

They earned 5 cents per game and the first week's earning was 4 dollars, which could be called a confidence building return on their investment. When the other barber's asked Warren and Donald to install new machines, they would assure them that they will talk to their owner. They would come back and say that Wilson did not want to buy new machines and only wanted to operate used machines. In this manner they bought 7 used machines and by installing at different barber's shops started earning 50 dollars per week. Next year they sold their business to a War Veteran for 1200 dollars. This experience also helped Warren in the later years. After four decades Warren's company, Berkshire Hathaway became the biggest share-holder, in the world's largest vending machines operator 'Coca Cola'.

Even today on Warren's auto license plate holder, in memory of his teen's business 'Wilson Coin Operated Machine Company' insignia is displayed. It was presented to him by a shareholder.

Warren completed his high school studies at the age of sixteen. At that time he had savings of 6,000 dollars, earned by him. By following the principle of spending less than the earnings, he was living a simple life. By then he had read more than 100 books concerning business. Even today, he is an avid reader and believes in reading a complete book in a day. There was also a time in his life when he read 5 books in a day. He can read 5 times faster than an average reader. He has the same capacity to study the balance sheets of companies; 5 times faster than an average investor. He maintains record of the relevant data also.

The record in his high school year book shows that he was a very good student of mathematics and following the footsteps of his father, he was going to become a stock broker in the future. His father was paying for his college fees and creating an atmosphere for him to save and invest.

College Study: Beginning of Investment On Value-Based Principle

Initially Warren had taken admission in Pennsylvania University but later he moved to Nebraska University and from there obtained his Bachelor of Science degree in Economics in 1950. Warren had a special attachment for Lincoln-based Nebraska University as his parents had fallen in love in its campus. Earlier Warren had read Benjamin Graham's book 'Intelligent Investor' and had been quite impressed by it. Graham later became his Professor, employer and lifelong mentor.

While reading Graham's book Warren discovered the basic principle of investing. The book had highlighted the concept of 'value investing'. It said that the best investment was one which was done by the buyer without being influenced by emotion, fear, rumour or movement of the market but done with due consideration based on value.

Warren had saved 9800 dollars at the age of 19. He applied for admission in Harvard Business School for graduation in Economics but his application was rejected as he was under aged. He was bit disappointed, but another golden opportunity was awaiting him in Columbia. He had heard that Benjamin Graham the author of 'Intelligent Investor', was teaching in Columbia. Warren took admission in Columbia to fulfil his longing to be in the proximity of Graham. David Dodd, who was a famous economist, was also teaching there. Together they had written a 735 pages book on 'Security Analysis'. Warren had been advocating to everyone who wished to operate in the stock market to read this book. The formula to work out the true value of a company had been given in the book.

At the age of 21, in 1951, Warren came to know that Graham was working as the CEO of G.E.I.C.O. Auto Insurance. Warren realized that if a person like Graham was associated with this business, then he could get an excellent opportunity to learn the cues for investing under his guidance. Warren proceeded to Washington D.C. from New York by train on a Saturday. He reached the auto insurance company's headquarters and obtained information regarding the company from an Officer of the company. Evidently the learning of the auto insurance business came in handy in the latter years, when his company bought the full ownership of the auto insurance company.

One of the important principles of Warren's is that all information about the company must be gathered before investing so that its true valuation can be assessed. How does the company make money, what is its stability, what are its shortcomings, what are its growth potential, what is the strength of its competitor's, how effective is its management and how honest it is, etc. complete information on all such parameters must be obtained.

His visit to the headquarters of G.E.I.C.O. helped him to understand several such factors. Based on this information, Warren invested in G.E.I.C.O. shares. Next year he was attracted by a new share, so he sold these shares for 15,259 dollars and invested in a new company's shares.

Warren had learnt so much about G.E.I.C.O. that merely at the age of 21 he wrote a research report titled 'The share which I like most', for a magazine called 'The Commercial and Financial Chronicle'. On the basis of his research he found out that G.E.I.C.O. was earning 5 times profit as compared to its competitors because they were selling directly without the help of agents. He was fully aware of the details of this company. So in 1976, through Berkshire Hathaway, he bought one third of the auto insurance company's shares for 45.7 million dollars. Later he bought more shares and increased the shareholding to 50 per cent. In 1995 he bought rest of the 50 per cent shares for 2.3 billion dollars and gained complete ownership. He thus added another company to his list of companies which were continuously earning profit.

In 1951, Warren got his graduation degree in economics. Warren wanted to work in Wall Street, but his father Howard Buffett and Graham asked him not to do so. These two influential persons in Warren's life had seen the depression and were fully aware of the ups and downs of the share market. Both of them advised the young and ambitious graduate to get a secured job in a reputed company. Both believed that there was a lot of uncertainty in share prices in the share market. Warren did not follow the advice.

Warren proposed Graham that he would work for him as a share researcher and analyst for free but Graham rejected the proposal. Even though Warren was the only student to whom Graham had graded with A+ for share analysis. Warren jokingly said that after receiving the proposal, The Honourable Professor, quickly did cost-benefit analysis and concluded that in spite of the fact that Warren was going to work for free, the trade would not be profitable. However, the real reason was that it was the policy of Graham-Newman partnership to employ Jews only. The Jews were not given jobs on Wall Street and so Graham tried to balance the scales by giving opportunities to Jews. Therefore, Warren returned to Omaha and started getting close to his sister's college classmate Susan Thompson.

Choice of the Right Guides and Good Practices

Warren has been telling students, "If you tell me who is your ideal person, then I will tell you the type of person you are. Initially the pressure of the shackles of habit is slight, but later it becomes so overwhelming that it becomes impossible to release it". In other words, the manner in which your leader explains to you, your habits also define you.

To motivate the students Warren used to say, "Choose such a classmate to whom you would like to give 10 per cent of your income in the future. Then the students did not choose the most bright, best sportsman or the most handsome classmate. They used to choose classmates with good habits, who guided you correctly, who observed values and ideals. There is nothing better than honesty and the whole world trusts such a person."

He used to say– "Whomsoever they considered to be their ideal, observed the good qualities of his character and keep noting them down. Continue this practice. As you continue the practice, it will also start changing your mental visualization. When you make the list of habits which you like then you will also like to develop those habits yourself. You can never build your character by trying only once in your life time; nor can you build it by having prerogative, status or wealth. You can build a strong character by observing minute details of your daily activities."

At an age when most of the youngsters considered sports stars and film actors as their ideals, Warren guided by his inner motivation and wisdom had chosen his father and Graham to be his mentors. Instead of considering the famous basketball player Jo DiMaggio or the sensational singer Elvis Presley as his ideals, Warren had chosen a stock broker-cum-state leader and a Professor-cum-teacher of value-based investment as his ideals. Under their guidance he developed the skills of value investing, decision-making and learnt important principles and policies.

Every person can willfully choose his own guide and habits. Our habits define our character. The good thing is that we can change our habits. It is easy to change our habits when we are young. Possibly for this reason, Warren used to like talking to students and motivating them. Warren became a role model for thousands of investors, businessmen, managers and his competitors by choosing the right mentors, achieving extraordinary success and developing disciplinary habits.

Beginning Career As a Stock Broker

Warren started working as a stock broker in his father's company Buffett-Falk Company. He also joined the evening classes in Omaha University. His subject was, Principles of investing. The other students were double his age. Warren was not focusing only on achieving financial success. In 1952, he married his sister's friend Susan. He moved to a small rented apartment. Its rent was 65 dollars a month. After one year, his first child was born. When he had gone for his honeymoon to California by road, he had carried with him Graham's book 'Security Analysis', to study it again, in the back seat of his car.

While working for his father, Warren was in constant touch with Graham. He kept sending him his research papers on stocks and stock picks, which also included his research on G.E.I.C.O. Auto Insurance. In 1954, Graham invited Warren to work in the Company's headquarters. His starting salary was 12,000 dollars a year. It was slightly less than the 13,800 dollars average salary of the premier baseball league players but much more than the 5,000 dollars salary of a New York school teacher. After two years, Graham decided to retire and he dissolved his partnership.

After working with Graham for two years, Warren was now ready to start his own investment partnership in his home town. Six years back when he had completed his college education his saving was 9,800 dollars, which had now grown to 1,40,000 dollars. He would spend sparingly and continued value-investing. A 26 year old youth taking such wise decisions used to astonish every one.

The Beginning of Investment Partnership

Warren returned to Omaha from New York and started a small Investment Partnership Company. He made only his family members and friends as partners. There were only 7 partners in this business, which he operated from his home, who had invested a total sum of 1,05,000 dollars. Warren had invested only 700 dollars. Without having a formal office or Secretary, without using a calculator, in the next 13 years Warren's company earned 29.50 per cent average profit and did not make loss even in a single year. Warren's eldest child and only daughter Susan says that when she was young she used to think that her father did home alarms business because he used to work from home and used to work as a Security Analyst.

In 1957, when Warren's wife was about to deliver their third child, he bought a 5 bedroom stucco house for 31,500 dollars on Farnam Street in Omaha. He had spent 10 per cent of his total wealth on the purchase. He stays in the same house even today. This investment shows glimpse of the future billionaire's adherence to the fundamental principles of investment. His principle has been to save, invest and spend only 10 per cent of your wealth; whereas most people deposit their entire savings towards down payment for buying a house and for the next 20 years continue to pay the instalments and remain as the banks debtors. Warren had given another message that after buying a house, one must not leave it and definitely not sell it at any price. With his intention to never sell his house, Warren will leave his house and his company Berkshire Hathaway as it is, after him.

Warren has impressed his shareholders with such principles and his life's philosophy. Such shareholders who bought the shares at the issue price of 17 dollars, have continued to be associated with his company for more than 27 years. Warren has been winning the faith of his shareholders by his exceptional policies and have decided on retaining their relationship with his company.

When Warren achieved the target of becoming a millionaire by the age of 30, nobody was surprised. By 1962 Warren's company which at start valued at 10,500 dollars was worth 7.2 million dollars. He opened his office in a tall building on Farnam Street itself, where he works even today with handful of employees. The office is close to his house.

In the beginning of the 60's, while researching, he identified a textile manufacturing company named Berkshire Hathaway based in New Bedford, Massachusetts. Before investing, he would undertake thorough research for selecting the right company. He started buying shares of this company at 7 dollars a share, which was lower than its value of 17 dollars a share. The company had a small debt. For investing in this company, he applied the principle of value-investing. By 1963, Warren's partnership company had become the largest shareholder in Berkshire Hathaway.

Building A Stock Portfolio

In 1965 after meeting Walt Disney personally, Warren started investing in Walt Disney Company. He had taken the decision to invest in this company after a lot of analysis as he had done before investing in G.E.I.C.O. Later, he developed so much expertise that he started investing without meeting the management of the company or without visiting the company and just by studying the balance sheet of the company. Warren bought Disney's 5 per cent shares for 4 million dollars. It was a debt free company. If he had 80 million dollars he would have bought the entire company. Today it would have been worth more than 40 billion dollars.

He sold it for 6 million dollars a year later. If Warren had retained his initial investment today, it would have been worth 7 to 12 billion dollars (including the dividends and spin-offs). It seems amazing that a company which totally valued at 80 million dollars at that time, today in that amount only a roller coaster can be bought for its entertainment park. When warren had invested in the company, Disney had spent 17 million dollars to develop its entertainment park and had produced approximately 200 animated films. So if Warren or anyone else had researched the company, it would not have been difficult to find out that the company's true value was much higher. Today, if Warren were to invest in this company, considering its true value, he would prefer to buyout the company provided he had sufficient funds to do so.

In the same year, in the board meeting, Warren took control of Berkshire Hathaway. He appointed Ken Chase as the CEO to manage the textile business of the company. Later this company became his holding and investment company. This company had a working capital of 19 dollars per share, whereas Warren had bought the shares at the rate of 14.86 dollars per share. This price did not include the fixed assets (building and machinery), of the company. At the age of

36, Warren's personal wealth had become 5 million dollars and few years later it became 10 million dollars. His investment partnership company's wealth had become 65 million dollars. It not less than a miracle that at the age of 38 in 1968 Warren's investment partnership company was earning 40 million dollars every year and it was valued at 104 million dollars.

In 1969, the year after his most successful year, he closed his investment partnership and distributed the several hundred million dollars of portfolio to all the partners. He took this decision after he realized that in the changing circumstances, the opportunities based on value investing had become fewer, whereas the shareholders expectations were skyrocketing. The assets which he distributed to the shareholders also included the shares of Berkshire Hathaway. At that time at the age of 39, his personal share holding was worth 25 million dollars and he owned 50 per cent of Berkshire Hathaway.

At this time, he also started writing an annual letter to his shareholders, which later become a very popular communication. Seeing his exceptional ability for creation of wealth, the people wanted to know what was going on in his mind. Through his annual letter, he used to share information about his company and the share market in a very easy to understand language. Warren always used to consider his shareholders as his partners and maintained communication with them through his annual letter. Through this letter he used to explain the fundamentals of investing and his life's philosophy and has been attracting new investors.

There was another turning point in his life, when in addition to making money through his partnership; he started creating wealth by investing in public limited companies.

In that year, when his textile company earned a profit of 45,000 dollars, his investments in insurance, banking other businesses earned more than 10 times, an amount of 4.7 million dollars. Warren started experimenting with new ways to create wealth. He started using the profits from his insurance and operating company to buy other businesses. Thus he started creating wealth much faster and kept continuously advancing towards the peak of his success.

Warren's investment strategy could be understood thus– Berkshire was investing in businesses, who were earning profit and reinvesting in such companies, who delivered a higher profit. Warren used to exercise his say in the operations of the companies in his portfolio and their management. Warren had invested 400 million dollars in the insurance sector which he used for other sectors and kept on increasing the profits. People started calling Berkshire 'Capital Allocating Machine'.

In 1973, when the share market started showing sign of dipping, Berkshire bought shares of 'Washington Post' and became its largest shareholder. Thirty years earlier, Warren used to sell this newspaper. Even today, Warren holds this investment and earns 9 million dollars in dividends every year. This amount was equivalent to the principal amount which he had invested.

After a year in 1974, when the share market entered the bear phase, on account of the global oil crisis, he lost half of his wealth. Later in 1974, when the markets recovered, Berkshire's share rose to 290 dollars and it was worth 140 million dollars. Even at that time he was drawing an annual salary of only 50,000 dollars. He was against any kind of wasteful expenditure.

In the next 4 years, based on value-investing and with the contribution from his insurance and other companies, Berkshire's corporate stock portfolio had amassed wealth of 1.3 billion dollars. In the beginning of 1983 Berkshire's share was quoting at 775 dollars per share, which increased to 1,300 dollars per share during that year itself. At that time Warren's personal stake was worth 420 million dollars and he was fast approaching towards becoming a billionaire. 'Forbes Magazine' added his name in the world's richest persons' list.

In 1985, Warren closed down Berkshire's textile business on account of global competition due to cheaper labour. At one time it was Berkshire Hathaway's core business which had now become insignificant. After one year Berkshire's shares price increased to over 3000 dollars and Warren became a billionaire.

In 1988, Warren made up his mind to initiate his childhood business from a new perspective. At the age of 58 year, Warren started buying Coca Cola Company's shares like an obsessed man. He bought 8 per cent shares of the company for 1 billion dollars and became the largest shareholder. In 1936, when he was 6 years old he had made 20 per cent profit by selling coke. Since childhood Warren's fascination for soft drinks business persisted. In 1988 Coca Cola Company was buying back its shares and Warren was impressed by its managing capabilities. He was buying shares at the price of 5 dollars a share. Compared to technology business, he understood Coca Cola as product much better and knew very well how profits could be generated from this product. The product had been established in the world's markets. He knew that like his other investments, his investment in Coca Cola would yield profits continuously.

Before investing in the company, he had not contacted anyone in the company to ascertain the facts. He had researched the information available to the general public for this purpose. He did not think that it was wise to approach the management because at that time the company was buying back its own shares and believing this to be an opportune signal for investing. He decided to buy as many shares as possible. He bought 200 million shares of Coke. At first the Coke's management was worried about this unexpected buying but when they came to that Warren had bought the shares, their fears were allayed. They were worried because the competing companies also make such purchases in an effort to vest control of the company. Warren respected Coke's management and did not wish to exercise his control over them. The Management appointed him on their Board of Directors. Warren still has been regularly cooperating with the company and playing an important role in its growth. His elder son Howard Graham Buffett is a Board Member of, 'Coca Cola Enterprises', its bottling unit.

Coca Cola controls 70 per cent share of the world's soft drinks market. It sells 1.8 billion bottles of soft drinks every day. Warren invested in Coke because he knew that it would be a value-based investment and it would generate profits continuously.

From the very beginning Warren became involved with Coca Cola, Washington Post and G.E.I.C.O. When he grew up he continued his attachment with these companies by buying their shares. He became owner of a textile company also. He invested the profit from it in other businesses and kept on earning profit continuously.

By 1988, Warren had acquired ownership in different businesses. He had started acquiring ownership of 4-5 companies every year and had become a worldwide famed billionaire. People started calling him the 'Saint of Omaha'. Worldwide students of management and business have researched his success story. If he starts showing interest in any company, its share price shoots up. Taking advantage of this phenomenon, many companies have floated rumours of Warren's interest in their company, in a bid to raise the prices of their shares.

Warren achieved an annual return of 29.55 per cent for 13 years through Buffett Partnership and an annual return of 22.6 per cent for 38 years through Berkshire Hathaway. He created new records of achieving success in the 5 decades of his glorious investment career.

Warren increased the valuation of Berkshire Hathaway from 40 million dollars to 66 billion dollars. Warren is most certainly the greatest experimenter of economic value in a free capitalistic society. He is an extraordinarily talented and lucky person. He has practiced with a unique fusion of mathematics and business skills. He achieved extraordinary success by inculcating qualities like patience, discipline, self-confidence, decisive ability, wisdom and independent thinking. Other people may also possess such qualities but it is not easy for everyone to apply them. It becomes very difficult to defend such human qualities, particularly in an economic environment of professionalism and consumerism.

Warren reached the pinnacle of success in an era of expanding capalist economy. At the beginning of the century the Dow Jones Industrial Index's, average was 66, which reached 11,000 in 100 years. One can gauge the extent of growth of capital through this index. However, it is possible to succeed in any economic set up by following Warren's principles. J.P.Morgan had said, "In business, important decisions can only be taken based on a high degree of character." Warren is a living example of this saying. Like Warren, anyone can create immense wealth by not compromising with one's principles and following simple rules of investing.

Value-based Investing Versus Investing Based On Mass Frenzy

Some people differentiate between value-investor and growth-investor. Warren believes that both are linked to each other. The objective of investing is to earn profit in the future by deploying the funds today.

Are you owner of a business or just a seller? To decide this, Warren suggests raising questions from the beginning. Do you track the present and the future earnings of a business or do you assess it based on its price? Is your investment decision based on study and research or are you influenced by others opinion? People who invest considering the value are independent thinkers. Such people do not take the decision to invest based on mass frenzy. They form their own independent opinion by conducting their own research and studying incessantly. They may study the activities of others but never copy them. Such people like to choose their own path. They decide to invest only after assessing their expectations, time period and risk taking capacity.

It has been the common belief that one must invest more in shares when they are young and switch to safer investment avenues as they grow old. They must also consider their age, marital status etc. while investing.

In contrast Warren believes that age should not be a criterion. Whether you buy shares or invest in fixed return instruments, its merit and value-based price should be the basis. He also believes that one must not be scared by the uncertainties of investing. Problems arise when the investor does not have the information or does not know what he is doing.

Comparison of the Market Beliefs Versus Warren's Beliefs

Market beliefs	*Warren's beliefs*
(a) Mass	Individual
(b) Emotional	Wisdom
(c) Price-based	Value-based
(d) Manifold	Focused
(e) Spectator	Owner

(f) Not committed	Loyal
(g) Higher cost and taxes	Lower cost and taxes
(h) Sell	Study
(i) Average 6 months investment	Life-long ownership

From the above table it is easy to understand the difference between the markets and Warren's techniques of investment.

□

Warren Buffett's Principles of Investment

In the beginning, Warren learnt the principles of investing, under the guidance of his father and later refined those principles under his mentor Benjamin Graham. Warren's investing principles can be expressed by the following two simple rules–

Rule 1. Never lose money.

Rule 2. Never forget Rule 1.

Warren says that, "An active investor must carry out three jobs everyday– study, research and thinking."

Warren's investments principles can be summarized as follows:

- Know what you have.
- Research before investing.
- Become the owner of the business and not of the share.
- Just do 20 important investments in your life time.
- Resolve to be a long-term investor at the time of buying the share.

All the factors which you will consider before you buy a company must also be considered before you buy its shares.

Initially, Warren used the cigar smoking example to invest, according to which he used to buy old companies. Such companies would be almost at the end of their life cycles. Such companies were left with limited earning opportunities, like the few puff of a cigar. The main example of this is Berkshire Hathaway Textile Mill, which was left with only 20 years or less of operational life.

Thereafter, he moved ahead and started investing in companies which were available at fair price but earned much higher profit. His investment in Gillette Company is an example of this. In 1989 Warren bought shares worth 6 million dollars of this company. Warren's holding company owns 11 per cent of the world's largest razor blade company, valued at 3 billion dollars. He had bought the shares at the price of 6.25 dollars per share which started yielding an annual return of 12 per cent in 14 years. Warren learnt that every night the beard of 2.5 billion people grew. Gillette's has 70 per cent share in the world's razor market.

Warren's advice is to try and buy an uncommon business or share, at the lowest price. He himself has been buying a dollar's worth of property, for only 50 cents.

Warren believes that during one's life time, only 20 important investments must be done. This principle was proposed by his Guru Benjamin Graham. He also believes that it takes 20 years to build one's reputation, but it can be destroyed in a moment. An investor must build his reputation to be successful.

❑

Women in Warren's Life

At the age of 78, for the first time Warren Buffett shared the intimate aspects of his life with a female writer Alice Schroeder in detail. His official biography "The Snowball: Warren Buffett and the Business of Life; based on this interview was published."

It has been revealed in this book that Warren did not always spend a peaceful and balanced life. He faced emotional upheavals also. He was an emotional and love starved husband. At the same time as a father, he did not give sufficient attention to his children. He avoided people who were likely to criticize him.

Warren considered his four time elected Congressman Father to be his ideal; but had a difficult relationship with his mother. His mother who was considered as a model housewife by the outside world, used to scold the little Warren and his elder sister until they were in tears. Warren told that he did not cry when his mother passed away, though he felt sad. In Warren's words "My mother had her merits also, but her shortcomings kept me aloof from her."

The book highlights the women in Warren's life, who tried to fill his loneliness and gave him emotional happiness. Susan, his wife for 25 years was the most important woman. After marriage they stayed in Omaha with their 3 children. Warren was busy in his work round the clock. Susan knew that Warren expected her to love him and did not like to be criticized. In their social life, they both appeared to be a happy couple, where Warren would often embrace her. But in their personal life, Warren who was busy creating wealth did not have time for his wife. Then Susan used to think of the time when his husband will have 8 to 10 million dollars and will be able to spend time with his family. But Susan failed to understand the fact that at the age of 6, the boy who while selling coke to his neighbours had decided on his objective, it was going to continue without any break. Warren was one day going to become the richest man in the world by creating wealth by following his principles and spending it frugally.

When their children grew up and settled, Susan decided to stay separately and moved to San Francisco. They separated in 1977 but never divorced. Warren and Susan lived separately for 27 years, but they used to talk regularly with each other over phone. Warren had realized his mistake and was also quite hurt by Susan's annoyance. He used to aimlessly walk in the house. He was neither conscious of his food or his clothes. At first Susan thought of returning back to him, then she decided against it and instead sent Astrid Menks who used to work as a hostess in a restaurant to look after him.

Later Warren told, "Susan used to take care of me; Astrid also started taking care of me." Susan died of heart attack in 2004. Warren married Astrid on 30th August, 2006, at the age of 76.

There were other women also in Warren's life, but his attention was primarily focused on expanding his business. One of the other women was Sharon Osberg, who was a bridge player. On her say, Warren had agreed to use the computer. Earlier Warren had refused even his friend Bill Gates to use the computer. Similarly, he became friends with Carol Loomis who was a writer of 'Fortune', magazine. She used to edit his annual letter to the shareholders.

There was a lot of talk on his close relations with Katherine Graham who was the publisher of, 'Washington Post'. Warren had met Katherine Graham when he had invested in the shares of, 'Washington Post'. Through her, he had got the opportunity of meeting and developing relations with society's elite. Warren played an important role in explaining the finer points of the business to Katherine.

❑

A Turning Point

As Warren became more and more busy with his business trips to New York, Washington, Buffalo and other places, he was becoming more and more distant from his wife Susie. Both were living separate sort of lives. Susie was seriously considering of taking up singing. Musician Neil Sedaka heard her singing in Omaha and suggested to her that she should start singing as a professional. Warren's investment manager and friend Bill Ruane arranged for Susie's audition in Tramp, Ball Room and other night clubs of Manhattan. Warren's New-York based friends were surprised and realized that Susie could sing quite well. According to the reigning singer Rosen Prent, "If she had been a common singer, nobody would have bothered, but she was the wife of a very wealthy man.

After receiving an invitation to participate in a music program in New York, Susie thought of improving her singing and touring different cities. She also entered into an agreement with the talent agency, 'William Morris.'

In the winter of 1977, when Warren was in the process of buying, 'Buffalo Evening News', a music program was being organized for Susie in Omaha's French Cafe. After the conclusion of the program, a party was held at Warren's house, for the guests. After spending a little time in the party, Warren proceeded to his study and Susie kept entertaining the guests. Warren's youngest son Peter later told, "Dad was reading in the study room and Mummy was looking after the guests."

Both of them had become extremely busy, so much so, that in April, 1977 when they were celebrating their weddings Silver Jubilee Anniversary, cartoonist Stan Lipsay drew a cartoon of both of them floating over their anniversary cake.

Both of them had different interests and after the children grew up, Susie felt very lonely in the house. Their family friend and those times well-known artist Kent Bellows believed that Warren's and Susie's married life was a success and referring to their contrasting nature, said that they were an example of how opposites attract each other. Warren often would hide behind a screen like a snail hides in his shell. Even though he would be physically present but his mind would be elsewhere. He would either be reading a book or lost in his thoughts. Socially, he was completely unlike Susie.

Susie had told Bellows, "To be happy, all that Warren needs is a 60 watt bulb and a book," whereas, Susie liked to do lots of things to be happy. She essentially believed in making others happy. She liked to be emotionally involved with people. It was in her nature to live for others and for ages she had been sacrificing her body and soul for Warren's happiness.

Her daughter says, "Mummy went through lot of hardships to help Dad. She made sure that Dad did not face any difficulties in carrying out his work. Dad was an introvert and was always dedicated towards his work. He has been doing the same type of work."

While her son Peter says, "Mummy underwent a lot of hardships to keep others happy. It was only very late in the evening, when she had some time for herself, she used to listen to music."

In an exclusive interview with, 'Omaha World Herald', on her singing career, Susie had praised Warren for fully helping her in her singing career. The article based on this interview was published two days before their marriage's silver jubilee anniversary. On her relationships, Susie had told that she was madly in love with another boy but heeding to her father's advice, she had chosen Warren as her life partner and found out that he was an extraordinary person. In the interview, she never mentioned whether she fell in love with Warren after her marriage nor did she express her pain which she felt after her separation from Milton Brown. Even 25 years after her marriage, she used to remember Milton Brown and used to wonder about her life, if she been married to Milton Brown instead of Warren. At that time Milton had become a successful grain broker in Des Moines.

At that time both of them were feeling pangs of loneliness. Their daughter was married and was working in a company called Century 21 in Irvin, California. She was also studying in college. Howard had left his college studies from Augustana College in Sioux Falls, South Dakota. He was starting his own business by setting up a company near Omaha. To buy the equipment, he was using his shares in Berkshire Hathaway. Peter had taken admission in Stanford University.

In September 1977, Susie performed in Omaha's famous Music Theatre Orpheum. Artists like L. Johnson and Barbara Stanczak used to perform in this theatre, in the 30s. During the program Susie performed in a confident manner in front of her hometown audience and won their hearts. Ecstatically addressing the audience she said, "It feels as if we are madly in love."

After a few days of this event, 45 year old Susie decided to part ways with her husband Warren. She left Warren's house on Farnam Street in Omaha and moved to San Francisco, where she started living in a rented apartment. She also informed her children about this. While Howard was shocked, Peter was not much surprised. Susie told her children that she was not legally separating from Warren, but she wanted to lead her life as she wished.

Susie's leaving was like a deadly blow for Warren, the suffering of which could not be expressed in words. Warren was shocked and stunned. He could not understand the reason why Susie left him. She was like a shield for him who used to protect him from calamities and difficulties; she used to maintain the right ambience in the house so that he could focus on his work. With her love and affection, she used to generate a feeling of warmth in the house and she used to take care of even his minor needs with her kind heart. Warren had told his elder sister, "Susie for me is like the rain and sunshine for my garden."

Left alone, Warren could not fathom the reason as to why Susie left him. While talking to Susie over phone he started crying bitterly. Susie comforted him sympathetically and told him that she had not broken her relationship with him but had only decided to stay separately due to the compulsions of her circumstances. They could still talk over the phone, travel together and even spend their holidays together at New York and their seaside Resort at Laguna. She continued her emotional chatting with Warren over phone. She allayed his fears by saying that they were still husband and wife; but the essence of her response was that we both have separate needs.

After Susie left him, Warren's daughter Susie Jr. came to stay with him for a few weeks. She found that her father was in a state of shock and was feeling helpless. Susie Jr. tried to console her father. Incidentally, she was also trying to get out of her marriage. She tried to dispel the loneliness in the house and assumed all the household responsibilities skillfully. She started feeding her father proper food instead of popcorn and made sure that he was dressed decently. Warren was very much impressed by his daughter's adeptness. He could not believe that she easily completed ironing of the clothes in the afternoon. Susie Jr. later told that Dad did not talk much about Mom.

"Dad was taking his time to become stable. I only remember that Dad used to keep reading, sitting in a chair and would talk about ironing of clothes. I even told him that nothing had changed. However, if you still expect being welcomed by her, the moment the door opens then it means that you still feel her presence in the house".

Warren's relations and friends who always used to praise the Warren family were surprised on Susie's departure and were also hurt. But it was not as if Warren and Susie were shattered by the separation. Even though Susie was in California, they used to talk everyday over the phone. During Christmas, they would meet along with their two children at their Laguna Beach House. During winter, Warren and Susie would spend two weeks together in New York.

The situation was becoming normal. His daughter told, "Dad had started realizing that his life had not undergone a major upheaval. In fact he had been shaken by the sudden change. He even thought of moving to Southern California, where most of his relations were settled; but he could not implement his decision. One of the reasons was that he could not manage his affairs without his longtime and loyal Secretary Gladys Kessler. Secondly, he did not want to change his daily routine. He did not want to leave his established set up and start afresh."

On the other hand, Susie was living a carefree life. Her apartment was decorated like a teenager's room. All the modern gadgets had been provided. Living alone, she tasted the joyous feeling of freedom, after a long period of time. To gain this type of freedom, she had to wait for her middle-age. There were some aspects of her personal life which she did not wish to share with Warren; she knew that Warren could not handle those aspects. The family members knew, as well as, understood that Susie had some personal needs and they could not overlook them. The family members tried to build a shield around Warren so that he could continue his work unhindered. The family members had extended such support to Warren earlier also. His younger sister Roberta even said, "We all have been concerned about Warren, I don't know how it all started, but from the very early stage the thinking has been like that."

Susie had been emotionally protecting Warren. Even while living separately she was taking care of Warren in her own style. She had the art of making new friends, at the same time; she remained worried about taking care of her husband's smallest needs. She requested several women of Omaha to take care of her husband for cinema shows and to restaurants for eating outside. One of them was Astrid Menks. Thirty one year old Astrid used to work in Omaha's French Café as a waitress. Astrid started making different types of dishes for Warren and started looking after him. Susan also encouraged her.

Astrid was much better than Warren in socializing with different groups. The rural type of locality of Market District where she used to live was undergoing changes and was getting influenced by modernization. Astrid was born in Latvia and had moved to Omaha when she was a child. Her mother had passed away when she was very young. Her father, who used to work as a waiter, had put his children in an orphanage. In simple terms Astrid was a spirited teenager. She was diplomatic and hard working. She would appear mod and attractive even in second hand attire. Her innocent round face would remind of her origins. In winter, braving the icy winds, wearing a fur coat when she used to stroll around the roads of Omaha with a red dog she seemed to appear like a character from a detective novel.

Astrid was fully familiar with Omaha's well-known people from the respected class. One of Warren's nephew Tom Rogers used to stay above the French Café. He later told, "When it started snowing and people felt the chill, in any case Omaha's residents were very spiritualistic about the snow then Astrid used to arrange dinner for Warren with enthusiasm." She wanted to be useful and helpful to others, but liked to remain in the background. When Susie had sung in the French Café then Astrid had brought tea for her. She was very alert in welcoming the guests and was always courteous.

Astrid moved in with Warren within a year of Susie's departure. Warren's son Howard was upset with this move. The others were surprised by the turn of the events. Astrid's friend from the second-hand things shop Kent Bellows an artist was astonished that she had moved with the richest man in town.

Bellow's asked Astrid, "What is cooking between you and Warren? Are you…."

It was rumoured that Warren had employed her as a cook; but in reality both of them had developed marital like relationship. Temperamentally both of them were made for each other. Both of them believed in leading a cheerful and simple life. When Warren would be busy with his stock investing then Astrid would go around the second-hand stuff sellers searching for bargains or negotiate for buying Pepsi-Cola in the Super Market. When Warren was busy in his study, she would relax in the garden. Astrid liked to stay in the house and she had relieved Warren from all the household responsibilities. Whenever Peter would arrive by a late night train, she used to go to the station to pick him up.

Possibly after having experienced loneliness herself, she did not regret her dedication in looking after Warren. She was serving Warren without any complaint whatsoever. The arrangement between the two of them was curious. Astrid had got a home and a male companion. Warren had got a female companion and a woman to look after his home. From the day she moved into the house, Astrid knew that Warren was not going to marry her because he was still attached to Susie. Astrid had decorated Warren's house, but when Susie was in town then she would watch him going to meet her in ironed clothes.

In the beginning when Warren went out of town to meet Susie, Astrid would also travel out of Omaha, instead of staying alone in the house. But after some time she did not feel any inconvenience, also her relationship with his family members had eased. She also managed to establish pleasant relations with Susie. When Susie used to come to Omaha she would take Astrid out with her for lunch. Susie did not stay in the Farnam street house. During the AGM of Berkshire Hathaway, when people saw Susie and Astrid sitting together there were many gossip talks. At that time Warren was sitting on the dais.

The relationship between the three persons had got into a curious rhythm. Astrid would take care of Warren in his day-to-day life, whereas Susie would accompany him outside Omaha. They would meet their old friends in New York and California together. They would also attend the official functions together.

For the outside world their deep love for each other was still intact. Lodge Retailer Jo Rosenfeld used to often meet Warren and Susie in California. He later told, "They both appeared to be a happy couple."

Susie Jr. told that the basic relationship between her mother and father was the same as it was earlier. Peter told that even though they were staying 1500 miles apart, their hearts were still united.

Howard Neumann, who was the son of Benjamin Graham's partner Neumann, had mocked about Warren's relationship with two women. But Warren was fully aware of his life's reality. Both the women in his life had a distinct and specific place. It seemed as if everything was pre-destined. There was a lot of difference between the personalities of Susie and Astrid. Neither were they acting their roles nor could they exchange their roles. Even though it was difficult for Warren's friends to understand their triangular relationship, they had started accepting the relationship.

The question which arises is whether Warren was content with his married life? Peter says that at the time of marriage not much attention was paid on whether Mummy had given her consent for marriage or not, though Warren denies it. Or was he weaving new relations so that he could carry on his work unhindered. Even though his friends found the new set up strange, but Warren was comfortable with the changed circumstances and was able to carry out his work. The mental support which he used to seek, he was able to secure from Susie in spite of the distance between them. Even in his youth, he used to return to Omaha to seek mental support. He was able to save himself from the pain of divorce due to the new circumstances. He was never provoked to take any revengeful action due to frustration from it. He had accepted the change of the circumstances.

He had told a reporter, "I love my life. I have woven my life in a manner which allows me to carry out the work which I enjoy the most." He was not bothered with what people thought about him nor did he have any qualms about seeking social approval. He did not feel it necessary to defend his actions. His only comment had been that none of the three persons had any problem on account of the triangular relationship.

"When you are close to a person, then there can be no problem in understanding the mutual feelings."

Warren would forcefully tell his friends that it was Susie who has chosen Astrid for him. After Astrid had moved in with Warren, his old friend, with whom he had operated the pinball machines Donald Denali toured Omaha and stayed with him. He was surprised to see Astrid and could not understand their relationship, till later in the night when he saw Warren and Astrid going to the same bedroom. Warren told that Susie and Astrid were friends. Later Denali told, "I think this statement was important for Warren. He was trying to explain that he himself had not taken any wrong decision."

On the other hand, Peter believed that the one year which his father spent without Susie had been extremely tortuous for him.

"Everything appeared desolate to him and he was in grief." A female friend of the family told that Warren felt quite lonely. But he was also trying to cope with it courageously. Except for people who were close to him, nobody else knew about his mental agony. According to Peter, sometimes Warren was not even conscious of his mental state. He kept himself busy with his work and was trying to instinctively accept the changed plan, which had happened in his life.

When he was young, he had faced a similar turmoil. Warren had to move to Washington from Omaha against his wishes. To overcome it, he had immersed himself body and soul in the job of delivering newspapers. Now he owns several of those newspapers but he still retained the same sense of anxiety which he felt when he was young. He could not rise early even though there were piles of papers waiting for his attention in the office. He used to talk loudly over phone so that the person on the other side would not get any inkling of his pain. But in the company of the two women, his will power was becoming stronger.

According to his old friend Rosenfeld, "I never saw Warren dispirited. He was always involved with Berkshire."

Saved from being involved in the day-to-day personal affairs, Warren started experiencing some kind of creative energy. In the late 70s, Warren in his own inimitable style took several important investment decisions. Delighted by the fall in the share market, he was investing funds from Berkshire Insurance Company in shares. Some of the leading companies were– Amerada Hess Corporation, American Broadcasting Corporation, General Foods, G.E.I.C.O., Night Riders Newspapers, Media General, Safeco Auto Insurance, F.W. Woolworth etc.

During that time it was said that, if there was rumour of Warren buying shares of any company, its price used to rise by 10 per cent. General Foods shares price was falling. Broker Earl Roper says, "Warren would not disclose what he was going to buy. He would wait patiently for the price to dip and then start buying."

He wanted to ink the story of his progress, but from the time of formation of the partnership firm till now, he had been silent. He started writing articles for business magazines. He also expressed his views in Berkshire Hathaway's annual report. Every year he started writing a letter to the shareholders of Berkshire Hathaway expressing openly his views on investing, management and finance.

It is not definite as to when he started penning his views. But when a collection of his letters was published, the first letter pertained to the year 1977, which was written in the beginning of 1978. Coincidently, it was the time when Susie had already left his house to live separately. In this letter he had discussed his views on several fundamental issues but it is doubtful if many people read it. He had told that before buying the shares of a company, he used to investigate the company as if he was buying the company itself. He used to be on the lookout of such companies of which he understood the working and business; its management was honest and capable. He also paid particular attention on its potential in the future. Then he would wait for buying the shares at the lowest possible price. He never invested for short-term gains.

Warren's approach and his investment strategy for buying shares in the 70s created a sensation on Wall Street. The type of shares which Warren considered ideal for investing were available; but nobody was prepared to buy them. In the summer of 1970. Dow Jones Index fell even below the level of 1969. In the middle of 70s the country's economic condition seemed precarious and all the headlines in the newspapers reflected pessimism. The Dollar was weakening against the Mark and Yen. The fundamentalist forces were on the rampage. The energy crisis had started biting. The feeling of despair was spreading in the country. Nixon's ignominious rule had come to an end and Jimmy Carter had become the President, but it was felt that his administration was ineffective. George Bush who had his eyes on the White House had expressed his concerns on the extent of the Federal Loan. Bush had promised that if he was elected President then he would first try to balance the budget.

The Wall Street was being affected by the political situation in the country. By the end of the 70s, the inflation increased drastically; it rose to 13 per cent. The investors were getting desperate and started investing in new avenues like gold, diamonds, real estate, art, other precious metals and packaged commodities and were advising to prepare for the next round of bear phase. Their message was, 'dump shares'.

Their argument against investing in shares was the likelihood of a sharp drop in the earning potential of companies on account of the downturn in the country's economy. In his letter to his shareholders written in 1979, Warren had told that pension fund managers had invested only 9 per cent of the funds in shares. He also said that whichever shares were there in the portfolio of Berkshire, we never felt despondent about the future.

At that time the share prices were down but the fund managers were not buying, they were waiting for the situation to become clear. Manufacturers Hanover Corporation had sold 60 per cent of its investment in shares in the market. A senior Investment Manager Victor Malone had said, "A lot of question remained unanswered."

Janney Montgomery Scott's Vice-Chairman, H.H. Boyle said, "In spite of the sharp drop in share prices, there is no visible enthusiasm to buy shares. People had many doubts in their minds about the future."

This uncertain scenario had been made even more scary by a special report titled, 'End of Shares', published in the August 1979 issue of, 'Business Week'. It seemed as if the article was paying homage to the share market. 'Business Week', had predicted that instead of investing in the share market people will invest in the money market, fast food franchises etc. and pretty soon investing in the share market will become history. The report had said that the shares are available at such cheap prices because no investor was prepared to buy shares. The report had concluded thus, "For good or bad, the American economy must accept the reality of end of equity. Maybe the days of equity may return but it was not going to happen soon."

He was not prepared to accept or digest such wild predictions. The very same week he wrote an article in the 'Forbes' magazine criticizing the Pension Fund Manager's ignorance and feeling of uncertainty:

"Future is never evident. You have to pay a heavy price for any kind of upheaval in the share market. On the other hand, for long-term value-based investors, the uncertainty is like a friend."

Through the article in 'Forbes' magazine he had very clearly expressed his viewpoint on shares. He mentioned that Pension Fund managers were opting for Corporate Bonds where the return was only 1 per cent; they had a simple explanation for it – stocks are not coupon and they are risk prone, particularly considering the state of the market they cannot be relied upon.

Warren believed that this kind of surmise was wrong. Since he could assess the inherent value of a share, he could confidently make such statements– like bonds, shares were also part of corporate assets and shares also could be classified as, 'coupons' because the aspect of corporate earnings was linked to it.

For example, for the companies in the Dow Jones Industrial Index the earning had been 13 per cent of their book value. This statistic can be said to be impressive. Whereas, those index shares were now available below their book value. When Warren visualised with his eyes closed, then the stocks in the Dow Index seemed like, 'Dow Bond' with a return of 13 per cent, which was many times of the returns through bonds. For a patient investor the returns could be much higher.

In spite of the bear market, his company's shares were rising. Berkshire's shares were quoting at 290 dollars per share and Warren's wealth had grown to 149 million dollars. But the interesting thing was that Warren, whose salary was only 50,000 dollars, was not prepared to sell his shares. Nor did he allow distribution of dividend, which would have reduced the capital of the company. It may have created some hindrance in his working for which he was not at all prepared.

Warren was feeling the pressure on account of bearing the expenses of two families so he told Omaha's Charlie Header, "Whatever I had received I have invested in Berkshire. So I will have to arrange some money from outside."

Towards the end of the 70s, Warren had purchased some shares in his account. He was prepared to take risk with his own money. He invested in the shares of Teledyne even though he was in a dilemma. The dilemma was that either he would lose the entire money or he would make a killing.

"It is amazing to note how easily he managed it!" An employee of Berkshire told," He had thoroughly investigated the company. In no time he made a lot of money."

When a friend suggested that he should try his luck in the real estate market, then Warren replied, "When it is easy for me to earn money in the stock market, why should I invest in the real estate market." According to Broker Earl Ravel, Warren had made 3 million dollars in no time."

In spite of becoming extremely wealthy, Warren had a simple lifestyle. He used to drive his Lincoln car himself and reach his office, where his 5 employees used to manage the corporate affairs of Berkshire Hathaway. In his free time, he liked to play bridge, read books on business, watch games and talk shows. He used to take Astrid to, 'Garrett's restaurant for eating outside. The owner of this restaurant was his old classmate.

With time Warren's circle– his friends, his companies, his articles, were spreading outside Omaha. His 40th birthday celebrations were arranged in one of the Golf Courses in Omaha. In 1980, on his 50th birthday, Susie had arranged a grand party in New York's Metropolitan Club. The party was attended by Warren's several classmates, friends and other respected people. On this occasion Susie had sung a song and dedicated to Warren.

None of the guests in the party could visualize Warren as a businessman. The way Warren was attired, his mannerism his expressions, nobody/none of the guests could visualize Warren as a businessman. He looked like a professor. Nobody could guess from his gestures that the per share price of his holding company Berkshire Hathaway had become 875 dollars.

Next year, Warren barely survived an accident. Warren and Charlie Munger's Money Manager Rick Green's wife suddenly expired. Warren went from Omaha to California to meet Green.

"I am feeling extremely distressed." Green said.

Warren replied, "I can understand the agony which you must be going through. When my father had died, I had also faced it." After being quiet for a little while he said, "You and your son take a flight and come to Minnesota Island, where Charlie Munger stays, we will spend 3-4 days together.

As per their scheduled program, they reached Charlie Munger's cabin by the side of a lake on Minnesota Island. Charlie took them for fishing in a motorboat. Seeing the extreme speed at which Charlie was driving, Green requested him to reduce the speed. Munger being short sighted suddenly applied full brakes, as a result of which the motorboat dived into the lake. Warren started drowning. Green somehow pulled him out of the water. Later they took the incident lightly, but Warren was shaken by the feeling of drowning.

Green was duly impressed by Warren's sympathetic behaviour, who had postponed all his activities to boost his morale.

Green said "He has a magnanimous heart. But people do not notice this aspect. For me, his sympathy is like a gift to me."

The popularity of Warren's letters kept on rising on Wall Street. Bankers were distributing copies of his reports. For the first time, Warren found that people were emulating him. People, who were eager to read the letters written by him, also bought the shares of Berkshire Hathaway.

Charlie Munger said that it was providence that Warren was managing a public limited company. If he wanted, he could have easily set up and managed his own company. But then it might not have been possible for him to play the role of an expert adviser. He could express himself freely through his letters. He used to pick any aspect of the operations of Berkshire and present his viewpoint, commentary on it. Even when talking about any problems related to accounts or any matters related to insurance, he used to explain the complex issues in easy to understand words. For the business world his letters were thus extraordinary. Any person who would peruse say, General Motors report would do so to find out details about its working. He was not at all curious to know about the report writer or company's officials. On the other hand, Warren used to discuss issues like human weaknesses, greed, suspicions etc. He used to discuss the issues freely. He usually presented the complex principles of investing in an interesting manner, in layman's language. He could not only teach the principles of business to the owner of, 'Washington Post', Katherine Graham but he possessed capability to teach them to Wall Street and the whole of America.

When Jack Barney, who knew Warren, used to read his reports, it seemed like adrenalin was flowing throughout his body. A 19 year old young businessman from Trinidad was overwhelmed after reading Warren's report. He said that, "God has sent a priceless gift to me; it is a copy of the annual report of Berkshire Hathaway".

The simple reason for this was that in the journey of American capitalism, no other company could match Berkshire Hathaway's success. Several capitalists and intellectuals have been born in America, one greater than the other but Warren's personality was most remarkable and singular. Warren would add humour in his articles to make them interesting and had assumed the role of a lecturer. Warren was gaining popularity because he used to explain the complex subject of investing in a simple language which even a person with average intelligence, could easily understand.

In the 80s, Warren had discussed the dangers of inflation in the annual report. He wrote – "Care must be taken to keep the prices stable, like it is required to preserve virginity; as it cannot be regained once it is lost." He had also expressed the possibility of the demise of long-term bonds on account of rising inflation. But his prediction did not materialize.

Yet Warren's foresight had alerted him and his shareholders to meet the challenges that could arise on account of inflation. His prediction on the effects of inflation on the insurance business turned out to be true. On account of the rising inflation the bond prices were falling and most of the investments of the insurance companies was in bonds. Warren could understand that the insurance business was going to suffer losses. After the drop in bond prices, the insurance companies were in a quandary to sell their assets to pay the claims. Such companies were losing their capital. Warren also believed that the money which the insurance companies had invested in bonds was not their money, but that of the policyholders. The policyholders had the right over this money.

The insurance companies could have cancelled some policies to save themselves from paying the claims. Berkshire had invested minimal amounts in long-term bonds, about which Warren had said that it was like blocking your capital at fixed rates for 30 years. In the current inflation scenario, it would have been suicidal to fix the prices of Berkshires threads for 2010 in advance.

In fact, it is not possible to save yourself by just becoming aware of the dangers of inflation. Warren told that when he had acquired control of Berkshire then one could buy half an ounce of gold with the price of its one share. In 15 years Berkshire's per share price had risen to 335.85 dollars from 19.46 dollars and yet one could only buy half an ounce of gold in that price.

At this time the only option which he had, to invest in such companies, which could face the challenges posed by inflation. He said that companies like Post Cereal and Winston Cigarettes will be able to increase their incomes at the rate the inflation rises. He invested in companies like Aluminum Company of America, Cleveland-Cliffs Iron Company, Handy and Harman, Kaiser Aluminum and Chemicals etc. However, Warren kept on reminding his shareholders that neither he nor Berkshire had any firm solution to meet the crisis.

According to Warren inflation was like a, 'Giant corporate woodworm', which everyday gobbled up humongous amounts of invested dollars and did not at all bother about the health of its digestive system.

On Wall Street, on account of inflation corporate assets were being liquidated. Companies like people were despondent and were not prepared to convert their cash holding into any other form. In the beginning of the 80s, the activity of taking over of companies intensified. Big companies like Del Monte, National Airlines, Seven Up, Studebaker and Tropicana etc. were taken over. Seeing all this, Warren became a critic of Wall Street.

Warren believed that Corporate CEOs were entering into irrational deals. According to Darwin, the breed of CEOs were very energetic and they were assessing their capabilities based on their positions. They were not taking decisions according to Warren's profit-based principle, which Warren considered as the sole logical objective. Unlike Warren, who used to buy smaller companies at discounted prices, these CEOs liked to buy big companies at premium prices. They were so much self-centered and egoistic that even after paying such exorbitant prices, they hoped to make profit. Warren wrote–

"Several of these CEOs had heard the story of the prince who was caged as a parrot and when the princess kissed it, it again turned into a prince. In the same manner, these CEOs hoped that companies will start generating profits by their magical kiss. We have seen many such kisses, but never seen the miracle.

Warren had expressed this view in the annual report of 1981, when the wave of mergers had just started. Next year he had expressed his views on the changed circumstances. Many CEOs were issuing new shares to pay for the assets that were taken over. Warren drew attention to the negative effects of this new wave, which on the surface appeared to be a normal phenomenon. He argued that the acquirers were not only buying, but were also selling. With every new share issued, the shareholding of the existing shareholders was diminishing. The CEOs were trying to cover up this fact by presenting it as something which was dear to their hearts, "Your company is acquiring another company." Whereas, the true picture would have been clear only if the truth had been revealed. It was only by selling a part of their company that the said company was being acquired.

Why was recourse being taken to lying? Most of the shares including the acquired shares were available at low prices. Then why were the CEO's of the acquiring companies getting into unfavourable deals.

Warren suggested that such Managers and Directors needed to sharpen their thought process. They needed to introspect on the manner in which they were selling part of their shares, were they also prepared to sell the entire company? If no, then why were they selling part share in the company at throwaway prices?

Warren wrote that, "The sum total of all the little bits of managerial follies will only lead to a huge folly, not any miracle."

Warren was disturbed by the CEOs expanding their own domains by frittering away the shareholders money, whereas it was their duty to take care of the shareholders interests. Warren thought that such Managers should have made their career in government jobs.

Warren was mocking the corporate abbots by comparing them to bureaucrats. Even though in his personal life, Warren had cordial relations with several CEOs. He used to attend their meetings also. In his articles, he used to refrain from naming anyone. He preferred to maintain his distance from his corporate associates. He always considered the wrong doers as white collared criminals. He wrote, "It is safer to loot huge sums of money with the power of the pen as compared to looting even small sums by pointing a gun."

Warren believed that since they were dealing with public money, the Managers bear a major responsibility. He gave examples of how in his life, he fulfilled this responsibility. In 1980, consequent to the change in Federal Laws, Berkshire had to grant the status of an independent company to Rockford Bancorp. Warren estimated that the valuation of the Bank was 4 per cent of Berkshire's total valuation. He then gave the option to the shareholders to hold the shares of Berkshire and Bank as per their choice. Warren did not keep any option for himself. He was going to hold the remaining shares. His principle was that the person who cuts the cake must be satisfied with leftoverpiece.

With a similar approach in 1981, Warren presented a Model Corporate Charity Plan. The plan was designed by Charlie Munger. Under this plan, for a million shares (at that time the share price was 470 dollars), the company would donate a sum of 2 dollars per share to the charity specified by the shareholders. That is, if a shareholder had 100 shares, then he could ask the company to donate 200 dollars to his choice charity. In other public limited companies, the decisions-related to charities were taken by the CEO and Directors, the money was taken from the shareholders also. Warren considered this as having double standards. He wrote, "Several corporate managers criticized the government for spending the taxpayer's money, on their whims; but why don't they introspect themselves for using the shareholders' money on their whims."

By such statements and actions, Warren was projecting Berkshire as a company with a unique image. He was shaping this partnership company on the lines of a public limited company. There were several of his former partners, amongst the thousands of shareholders. The purpose of his letters to the shareholders was to make them feel as if were his partners and a group could be formed. Thus, they remained associated with him.

It cannot be denied that Warren's ways were unique. Most of the CEOs did not care about their shareholders. For them the investors were faceless and changing entities. They never felt the necessity to associate with them. On the other hand, Warren believed in having a permanent association with his shareholders. In his letter to them he had compared his company to a café, where the customer liked to eat and likes to come back repeatedly.

While holidaying on Laguna Beach with his family, Warren used to write the 7800 worded letter to the shareholders on a yellow legal pad. His sister Roberta was living abroad for the last one year, while writing the letter he used to perceive that he was writing the letter to update her on his business. Carol Loomis, who used work for the 'Fortune', magazine edit his letter; but Warren's particular style, as if he was conversing with someone, was retained. His letter had a touch of humour and even serious matters were presented in an interesting manner.

Warren had gained expertise in writing annual reports as he had been ceaselessly studying annual reports. The other company's reports were more like publicity documents in which the management's capabilities were highlighted to allure the investors. They contained a brief and formal message from the CEO. Mostly these reports were written by someone else on behalf of the CEO. In these reports, the thing which most irked Warren, was the fact that the CEOs shirked from personally addressing the shareholders.

Warren used to be critical of CEOs, who kept changing their goals; and when they got disappointing results, they started seeking for lame excuses.

In Berkshire's annual report, the company's internal state was described so realistically, that the investor was able to easily understand the true picture. To achieve this, Warren used simple vocabulary. In the early days, the type of analysis which Warren used to present to his partners on the likely profit, similarly considering the shareholders of Berkshire to be his partners, he would intimately share what was in his heart. He used to honestly accept his short-comings and describe them without suppressing any aspect.

❑

Warren and Madam B

Warren used to frequently think that if instead of a public limited company, he had had to invest in his own enterprise and manage it, what kind of experience it might have been for him.

With such thoughts crossing his mind, in summer of 1983, he entered Nebraska Furniture Mart, a store built on a 43 acre plot in Omaha. The owner of this Mart was a 4 feet 10 inches tall woman named Rose Blumkin. She was addressed as 'Madam B', by the people of Omaha. At the age of 90, she used to work 12 hours every day. For Warren she was like an idol, who had set up a massive furniture empire with an initial investment of 500 dollars only.

Warren asked, 'Madam B', are you prepared to sell your business to Berkshire Hathaway?

Madam B said, "Yes."

Warren asked, "For how much."

Madam B replied, "60 million dollars."

Both shook hands and Warren took her signatures on a single page agreement. Warren had succeeded in making his life's biggest deal. After a few days Warren paid a cheque for 90 per cent of the deal amount to Madam B, 10 per cent was owned by the Blumkin family.

'Madam B' did not even look at the cheque, folded it and kept it and said, "Mister Buffett, we can drive our competitor's out ofbusiness."

The firmness, determination and understanding which was there in Madam B's personality, reminded Warren of his businessman grandfather's personality. Warren was tremendously impressed by Madam B's success story and it used to inspire him.

She was born as Rose Gorelick in 1893 in a small village called Belarus near Minsk in Russia during the Czar era. She used to sleep on the floor with her seven brothers and sisters. Her father was unemployed and her mother used to feed the family by managing a small grocery store. Seeing the hardship which her mother was facing, Rose started helping her in the store from the age of six.

There was no money for the children to attend school. Rose never attended school. She sought help from a rich family and learned to read and write a bit. She had learnt to toil and become independent from her mother. At the age of 13, she started working in a store selling dry goods in Minsk. At the age of 16, she started managing that store and supervising five male employees.

In 1914, Rose was married to Issadot Blumkin, who moved to America. Rose was to follow him later, but before she could proceed to America, war started. In the winter of 1917, when Europe was in shambles and anarchy was wide-spread in Russia, she boarded the trans-Siberian train. She was stopped by a Russian soldier; she did not have a passport. Rose told the soldier that she was going to buy leather for the army and she will get a bottle of vodka for him when she returns. She reached Japan *via* Manchester. From there she boarded a boat and reached America after 6 weeks. In 1919, she settled in Omaha with her husband. Even though she was in dire straits, she called her parents and siblings to Omaha. Rose's husband was running a, 'used clothes' shop. To help her family, Rose started selling furniture from the basement of her house. She did not know English, but her children who were studying in English medium school, taught her English.

In 1937, with her savings of 500 dollars, Rose rented a shop on Farnam Street. After a lot of deliberation, she named the store, 'Nebraska Furniture Mart.' Her business philosophy was, 'Sell cheap and tell the truth.' The big companies manufacturing furniture thought that by selling the furniture at cheaper prices, she could spoil the image of their brand, so they refused to supply to her. But she did not give up. She would travel to Chicago or Kansas by train and buy furniture from the retailers. When the shops stock was sold out, she moved the stock kept in the house to the shop. Rose approached the bank for loan but her application was rejected. The experience left her with feeling of revulsion toward banks. With an iron will, she would continue to work non-stop for the whole week, without any break. She liked to sell the furniture to the middle-income customers, who believed in paying on time.

In 1944, Mohawk Corporate Mill filed a case against her. They charged that she was violating the product pricing law. The carpet which Mohawk Mill was selling at the rate of 7.25 dollars per yard, Rose was selling the same carpet at the rate of 4.95 dollars per yard. The Judge dismissed the case stating that it was frivolous. Next day the Judge bought carpets worth 1400 dollars from Nebraska Furniture Mart.

Rose dealt firmly with her employees and her family members. Her behaviour was affectionate only towards her well mannered son Luis. On several occasions, Luis reinstated employees by sweetly counseling them after reprimanded and dismissed by Rose. Luis was adept at quelling Rose's anger.

Rose or, 'Madam B's' success formula was simple– she would buy furniture in bulk, control her expenses and pay special attention on saving. Normally, she would sell on 10 per cent profit margin; but occasionally allowed special discount to her customers. If a newly wed couple came to buy furniture, then 'Madam B' allowed a higher discount, because she knew that the couple could come again to make more purchases.

For the people of Omaha, the Mart had become an integral part of their lives. It was unlikely that there was any family in Omaha, who did not have furniture bought from the Mart. Ageing had not diminished 'Madam B's' enthusiasm or working-capabilities. Once storm demolished the roof of her store but she continued selling the furniture. On another occasion, the store caught fire. 'Madam B' gifted a TV set to the fire brigade employees. She was never on holiday. She used to say, "I do not lie. I do not deceive anyone. I do not promise anything which I cannot fulfil. Sticking to these principles has helped me to attain success."

After buying the store, Warren did not want to manage it himself. He wanted a manager, who would manage the store according to his style of functioning. Warren felt that he could not get a Manager, better than 'Madam B.' He appointed, 'Madam B' as the store's Manager on an annual salary of 300,000 dollars per annum. He always used to refer 'Madam B', as one of his great idols.

❑

Most Prosperous Period of His Life

After Susie's death when her Will was read, everyone was surprised, even though most of the clauses were not unexpected. Susie had willed most of the shares of Berkshire, valued at approximately 3 billion dollars to Susan Thompson Buffett Foundation. This Foundation was now being managed by her daughter. She left approximately 50 million dollars to her children's charity, while each of her children received 10 million dollars and each grandchild received 100,000 dollars.

She was generous towards people whom she liked, even though it was not evident on account of her husband's influence. She also left a number of friends and employee's substantial sums including $8 million to John McCabe and $1 million to Ron Parks. The names of Cathleen Cole and her husband's names were also included. Before her death, she had made changes in her Will through a new lawyer. The changes made by her in the Will had surprised everyone.

Susie had never accepted the split in her life and had left this aspect undefined till the end of her life. She used to live for others but this reality was not expressed in words till her end.

Warren considered his wife as his idol and was in love with her for a very long time. She kept him in touch with the outside world and kept the family bonded. After her death, whenever Warren looked at her photo, tears would roll down his eyes. In spite of this, he did not break down; nor did he isolate himself or think of committing suicide out of despondence. Though, Susie had earlier expressed the possibility of occurrence of such actions. However, Warren continued to grieve and for next two months; he appeared extremely weary. After that, as it happens with most of the people, he gradually fell into his normal routine. With loving memory of his departed wife in his heart, he started his life anew.

His elder son said, "His relationship with mother was sincere and there can be no doubt about it. He depended a lot on mother. But my father is a fighter. People, who had thought that he would be shattered by mother's death, apparently did not know him very well. My Daddy's will can never break down, he is inherently strong, even though it may not be evident on the surface. The heights which he has attained are due to his strong determination."

Warren was able to recover on account of his mental perseverance and was successful in overcoming the fixation that, "Susie will take care of everything." He was ready to face the ground realities. As time passed, he began accepting the reality of Susie's death and started bonding with his children on new grounds.

According to his sister Berta, "At the time of her death, Susie had handed over her inheritance of strength, emotional attachment and generosity to Warren. Unexpected changes had started occurring in Warren's personal life. He had started tackling those emotional issues which he had left for his wife to tackle. He had become sensitive towards his children's feelings and had started taking care of them.

His daughter, Susie Jr. had promptly assumed the responsibility of her mother's legacy and taken over its leadership. She liked philanthropic activities and for past several years had been preparing for such work. She engaged herself in expanding the philanthropic activities. She did not consider managing two foundations a burden, but considered it as a challenging opportunity.

His musician son, Peter was presenting his musical production 'spirit the seventh fire', in Washington's National Mall. The program had been organized during a function of 'National Museum of American

Indian.' Over phone he told his father, "Dad our presentation is going to be an amazing feat." After telling this to his father, he realized that had his mother been alive, he would have told it to his mother, who would have informed his father. He felt happy that he had communicated with his father directly. Warren grouped his friends and they departed for Washington to see the program. Before the presentation of 'Spirit', Peter had released 13 Albums. While enjoying the program, Warren felt a distinct attachment towards his son. This feeling was arising not only because of Peter's success but also on account of the fact that they were making efforts to share their lives.

When 'Spirit' was presented in Philadelphia, it was declared as a historic presentation.

Warren's elder son, Howard had published two books on photography, 'On the Edge' and 'Tapestry of Life'. He had also organized several exhibitions. His foundation office still appeared like a teenager's bedroom, a museum filled with odd things. But his business sense had improved. He was a member on the Boards of Lindsay Manufacturing and Connemara. He had dismissed two CEOs. He believed in saving and he had invested in Berkshire. Howard was emotionally attached to his mother and used to yearn for his father's shield over him from the very beginning. Now he had got an opportunity to establish a distinct relationship with his father. He, along with Devon bought a house in Omaha so that he could stay close to his father.

The events after Susie's death had deeply affected Astrid. She had lost a close well-wisher. She then realized that Susie's life was running on parallel tracks in which a particular type of life had been out of sight. After maintaining a cordial relations with Susie for many years and tied to an unconventional marriage, was living like a role model, suddenly felt that everything was collapsing. She knew the manner in which Warren had been emotionally tied to Susie and this was disconcerting her. However, gradually Warren was also realizing that by following Susie's arrangement Astrid had paid a heavy price and for the past several years both of them had been overlooking it. He blamed himself for it and began improving the relationship anew. After recovering from his grief Warren started making Astrid a part of his public life.

In the month of December Warren used to gift cheques of substantial amounts to his grandchildren for Christmas. He also used to bear their education expenses but he did not like to pay for any wasteful expenses. He always counselled everyone through a covering letter on how they should spend the money. He would write, "Use some of it on entertainment, pay off your debts but I would not like you to spend it on unnecessary things. You will get your next cheque next year."

Warren did not send the gift cheques for Peter's adopted daughters – Nicole and Erica. But Susie used to like Nicole and Erica. Both of them had attended Susie's cremation. Susie had left a sum of $100,000 for each of them in her Will. But just 10 days after the cremation Warren told Peter, "I do not consider them as my grandchildren. I am not going to leave anything for them in my Will."

Peter could not believe it. He asked him," Are you really going to do so?"

Warren was undeterred on his word. Since Susie's Will had conferred the status of grandchildren to those girls. It seemed that Warren had developed a sense of attachment towards money. Peter was under the impression that if his Dad excluded the girl's from his Will or did not send the Christmas cheque, the girls will not come to know of the reason.

Warren and Astrid celebrated the New Year's Eve with Sharon Osberg and her husband David Smith at Warren's house in Marine County in California. He was playing bridge with Sharon, David and Gates, while Astrid was busy in shopping. In the beginning of November, Warren's fears that Berkshire's Board would be suppressed under Gates imposing personality were allayed. He had invited Gates to join the Board of Berkshire.

Sharon and Gates were discussing the challenges which the Buffett Foundation was likely to face. The possibility of a dramatic change seemed likely after one year of Warren's death on donating billions of dollars. There was no history of any Foundation having succeeded in bringing about such a change because no other foundation had tried it. Gates Foundation was an exception; otherwise no other Foundation had received such a massive donation.

Warren had also been pondering over this issue. In winter, he had arranged for a video recording of a question-answer session with the Foundation's Trustees. He wanted to ensure that the Trustees clearly understood his wishes. He wanted to eliminate the possibility of any fraudulent action after his death as it had happened in the case of Walter Annenberg.

In the beginning of 2005, Sharon had met Warren in Omaha and after praising Gates had asked if he would consider making a donation to the Gates Foundation after his death. Warren did not promise her anything at that time, even though before Susie's death, he had thought about donating some amount to the Gates Foundation.

Charlie Munger was also in agreement with this thought. He believed that like Warren, Gates also believed in staying away from the beaten path. He was only 50 years old and he would utilise the money properly.

Warren's long standing belief was that he could best serve the society by continuing to maintain the pace of his earnings and there was no need to distribute it. He had planned to return the money to the society after his death; but he was also apprehensive that if he died before finalizing the donation, it may not be utilized properly. He had been changing gradually over the years. From a child who had stolen his sister's bicycle and selling barbells; a father who refused his children's request for money; a person who gifted thousands of dollars to his children on their birthday after every five years; a father who had bought a heart shaped pink diamond ring for his daughter. In spite of all these things, he had definite ideas about money but after Susie's death he started re-evaluating the ideas. He had made up his mind to take specific action now itself to resolve the apprehensions of the future. It did not mean that it was easy for him to overtake time.

It was his birthday, nearly a year after Susie's death. He could not believe that he had been through 75 springs. He started thinking about people with long lives and good health. His mother had lived for 92 years; his aunt Cary had lived for 97 years, 90 year old Walter Schloss was still playing tennis and his idol Rose Blumkin was still enjoying life.

His 75th birthday was celebrated at Sharon and David's house. In the party Astrid, Bill Gates and his sister Berta were also there. The birthday cake was prepared with white chocolate and it was shaped like a 100 dollar bill. David had invited an American girl of Chinese origin on Saturday morning to play ping-pong with Warren. Sharon had invited an artist who was going to teach the basics of drawing to Warren and Gates. The drawing which Warren had made depicted trees-shaped liked lollipops. The ping-pong competition was declared as the most exciting event. It was decided that the ping-pong competition video be shown in the next share-holders meeting.

Before 2003, Warren's desire to publicise himself was fulfilled through interviews and shareholders' meetings. Warren was cautious while dealing with the media. He used to adopt a diplomatic attitude. But when Susie fell sick, for whatever reason, he tried to draw their attention. His attachment towards TV cameras heightened. It became difficult for him to stay away from publicity for long. He assisted in the making of several documentaries. He would extend interviews with Charlie Roe for hours. He was appearing on CNBC regularly.

On one hand, he appeared to be obsessed with the media, on the other hand, his mind was completely focused on Berkshire. He was capable of rapidly switching his roles. After the induction of Bill Gates in the Berkshire's Board, he had introduced a monitoring system in his organization – the system allowed any employee to report any kind of short-coming. He also wanted to ensure that Board of Berkshire became self-reliant in taking decisions even in his absence. To achieve this end, he organized several board meetings in which he did not participate. Even today, he participates in the investment activities of the company with the same concentration and devotion as he used to do in his youth.

After the 9/11 incident, the Federal Reserve had dramatically cut the interest rates and the share market had started showing signs of weakening. In his letter to the share-holders, written in 2004, Warren had stated "I had expected new investment of several billion dollars, which would have created new avenues of earning. But I am surprised, I see only very few attractive securities which can be bought. Next year Berkshire made four small investments and one large investment. The large investment was in the renewable energy sector. The company's name was MidAmerican Energy. The oil prices were continuously rising so the importance of renewable energy was growing. This company's CEO, David Sokol was being rumoured to become Warren's successor, even though Warren never said anything about it.

Warren had in his report expressed his doubts on the strengthening of the dollar and believed it was going to weaken. After his first report, dollar kept on becoming stronger and his views were criticized in the financial papers-magazines. He reduced his hedged positions to buy foreign stocks but maintained his stance. On derivatives he wrote–

"Long time back Mark Twain had said that if somebody wants to catch his cat's tail, then he cannot experience the feeling without actually doing so. I discuss derivatives every year for two reasons. The first one is personal and disturbing. At the time of buying General Reinsurance (Gen Re), Charlie and I knew that it will create problems and we had told its management that we wanted to exit from this business. It was my responsibility to ensure it. Instead of tackling the issue, I wasted several years in trying to avoid the operation. It was a futile effort. Because we could not find a fitting solution for the crisis, which had been in existence for decades, it was not easy for me to exit the business." Warren was referring to the period when he had appointed a new Director and allowed him sometime to expand the business. But later this turned out to be a loss-making proposition.

He wrote: "Whenever problem arises, may be in personal life or in business, it must be tackled immediately."

"The other reason for referring to these problems regularly is that our experiences can help the directors, auditors and regulators."

Warren suspected that like the decade of the 70s, the investment sentiment was not likely to improve soon. In spite of this, he kept his search open and continued evaluating new ideas.

In 2004, he borrowed a voluminous book from his broker which appeared like a compilation of several telephone directories. The book contained a detailed record of South Korea's stock market. He had been tracking the world economy. He was on the lookout for a country and market, which had not drawn much attention and was relatively cheap. South Korea's stock market fitted the bill. He spent a lot of nights and studied the book in-depth. He was finding it difficult to understand the numbers and other details. He felt that it was necessary for him to learn a new business language through which he could properly understand a different business culture. So he got another book and tried to understand the important details of Korean accounting. It thus became simpler for him to understand the riddle of numbers.

When he fully understood their shares listing procedure, he started comparing the accounting details of their companies and selecting them. While doing this he recalled the days he had spent under Graham-Newman, when he used to sit near the ticket machine wearing a grey jacket. From the hundreds of pages accounts of different companies he was trying to identify the important numbers and checking for their sequential consistency. He was successful in selecting the cream shares from the thousands of Korean shares. He was regularly noting all his comments on a yellow pad and was able to prepare a brief list.

The list was so brief that he was able to record it on a single sheet. He discussed the list with a visitor. It contained the names of about a dozen companies. A few of them were well-known companies but mostly they were smaller companies.

Warren said, "Please see how I have prepared it. These companies believe in winning. If you check for these companies on the Korean Stock Exchange site, on the net, you will find that instead of ticket symbols they use numbers. In case it is not a blue-chip stock, then they place a zero at the end of the number. You can see such statistics every night. I can name five brokerages who are big buyers and five brokerages who are big sellers. You will have to open a special account in a Korean bank and it is not easy to do so. I am trying to learn the procedure. For me it is like picking up friendship with a new girl. These are good companies and their shares are still cheap. They are only priced equal to their next 5 years earnings, whereas their business can be relied upon. Though half the companies names sound like porn films. These companies produce basic things like steel, cement, flour and electricity. People will continue to buy these things for the next 10 years. These companies have a good presence in the Korean market, which is unlikely to change. Some of these companies are also exporting to China and Japan. Due to certain factors these companies have till now not come in the limelight. I am not an expert on foreign currency, but I think that buying these shares will be a profitable investment."

"The main reason why these share are cheap, is North Korea. In case North Korea attacks South Korea, the whole world can be affected. China, Japan and the other Asian countries can be involved in the conflict. The outcome of the war cannot even be imagined. North Korea seems to have developed capabilities to produce nuclear weapons. I think that it is the most dangerous country in the world. In spite of this I am prepared to take the risk, because I know that China and Japan will be able to stop the devastation ofwar."

"When you invest in shares, then there is always a risk. The future is uncertain forever. I think that for the next few years these share will continue to perform and I am prepared to hold them for that duration."

Warren had found a new game to play and a new puzzle to solve. He immersed himself in the search of new investment opportunities with the enthusiasm of his younger days.

During his visit to Harvard Business School for a lecture, he was asked how Buffett Foundation, which was the world's richest organization could benefit the society. He replied "I, am not doing any good to the society by multiplying my wealth so I am thinking of donating my wealth for the benefit of the society."

Nobody said anything. Though nobody realized that through his reply had clearly hinted of making a directional change in his life.

After his lecture, he had talked about Gates Foundation. He had praised the welfare work being done by Bill and Melinda Gates. He had said that Gates Foundation was working wisely and its principles were being followed in the best manner. He said that he liked their style of giving charity without any publicity. They never wanted their names or the foundations name to appear anywhere.

A clear plan had started evolving in his mind in the beginning of 2006. He was satisfied with his children's work, who were managing their own Foundations. But now he could not even find any sense of security which he felt in the presence of his wife Susie. Emotional power worked at a level higher than consciousness. When he had given Susie the liberty spending money for charitable activities, he had not assessed her ability to serve mankind. After living together for decades with Susie, they had developed a relationship of trust which had generated his faith in his wife's wisdom and ability to take decisions. Everything had changed after her death. He told about his change of heart to Tom Murphy, during his daughter's marriage. He also told about the change in him to Sharon Osberg. He wanted to donate his wealth at the earliest. But this decision was still a thought; he did not have a plan.

It took several months to prepare a plan because it was vast and complex.

He started telling about his plan to people, who might be affected by it. His sisters were pleased by his plan. Bertie told him that it was his best decision. Doris, who was managing Sunshine Lady Foundation, also said that it was a superb decision, because she knew that it was a very difficult task to donate billions of dollars wisely.

On 26th of June, 2006, Warren announced that he will donate 83 per cent of his share in Berkshire Hathaway, which was valued at 37 billion dollars at that time to a group of foundations within a few years time. In the history of service towards mankind, such a massive sum had never been donated earlier. The biggest charity in the world, 'Bill and Melinda Gates Foundation', was to receive 5 shares out of every 6 shares, which he personally owned. This was going to unite two great personalities and benefit the entire world. Warren desired that his donation be used in welfare activities according to his wishes but at the same time the foundations had freedom to decide on the amount they wished to spend on those activities. Fully understanding the impact of his decision, he allocated the balance shares valued at 6 billion dollars to his children's and his wife's foundations. His three children's foundations were allocated 1 billion dollars each and Susan Thompson Buffett Foundation was allocated 3 billion dollars. His children never imagined that their personal foundations could get such huge sums and that too while Warren was still alive. In the first annual instalment, Gates Foundation received shares worth 1.5 billion dollars, his children's foundations received shares worth 50 million dollars each and 'Susan Thompson Buffett Foundation' received shares worth 150 million dollars. There could be variations in the amounts deemed to be paid, based on the price of the Berkshires shares prevailing at that time, in all probability amounts would continue to rise. The second richest man in the world was donating his entire wealth, and he was doing it without registering his name anywhere. He continued to earn money throughout his life but he did not set up any foundation in his name i.e. Warren Buffett Foundation, nor did he open any hospital, college or university in his name or get his name inscribed on any structure. While donating, he was not bothered about highlighting his name or controlling the donated amount. He was donating to a foundation that he had selected after considering its expertise and merit. He had not set up another empire to donate and thus shown a new way to donate; very different from the customary convention. Till today not a single big donor had taken such a step.

Rockefeller Foundation's advisor Doug Bauer said, "It was a momentous moment in the field of service to mankind. A new milestone has been laid."

Even though Warren's action was surprising but considering his attitude possibly it could be considered normal. A person who was an unconventional thinker and crisis handler wanted to stay away from vain display and wasteful expenditure. Gates Foundation had received the funds but they had to use the first instalment quickly. This decision was uncharacteristic, highly personal, an extraordinary example and as expected attracted attention. But on the other hand, it could be considered as an unerring decision taken by Warren in his own exceptional style.

He had astounded the entire world by donating most of his wealth; but his donation *modus operandi* was such that he retained the funds till the time he physically transferred the shares. At the same time in a single move, he had announced donation of most of his life's earning and had initiated the process of distributing millions of dollars. A boy who would not allow even his family members to touch his piggy bank, in which he deposit his coins had today become the world's greatest donor, who was donating billions of dollars for philanthropy.

While announcing his decision to donate Warren had said in his speech, "Fifty years back I had a meeting with seven people. We had formed a small partnership company with an initial sum of 150,000 dollars. They had thought that I would be able to manage their money better they could do so themselves.

Fifty years after that event, on a particular day it occurred to me that I was myself the best person to give away the money appropriately. This argument is entirely logical. Often people do not get the opportunity to think. They are often heard wondering – who will be able to take care of my money? Such people usually give the responsibility of taking care of their money to the people whom they consider capable. But they overlook the persons who are active in the field of philanthropy. They handover the responsibility one of their trusted friend or colleague to take care of their money but they are no longer there to see how it is being utilized.

So I consider myself fortunate as the job of serving the mankind is more difficult than doing business. One has to find solution for vital issues, which have been solved in the past by applying wisdom and with aid of money. So it is more important to search talent in field of philanthropy as compared to searching talent in the investment field.

I have been lucky. I was born in America in 1930 and have been lucky from my birth. I got wonderful parents, good education and I was brought up in such a manner which enabled me to succeed in deriving benefit from the society. Had I been born earlier or in some other country, it's possible that I might not have been so lucky. In a market-based economy it is essential to learn the art of wealth allocation and this ability can yield desired results.

I always thought that wealth is something which must be returned to the society. I don't believe in dynastic wealth, particularly when we see the 6 billion people, who face hardships. We get opportunities to serve the people with our wealth. My wife also supported this thinking.

"It was obvious that Bill Gates had a brilliant mind and his target was correct. He was wholeheartedly serving the mankind, rising above sex, religion, colour or geographical boundaries. So when I was faced with the question—to whom should I donate? It became easier to decide."

Warren was impressed by the Gates Foundations Mission statement which stated, 'Every life is equally precious.' The foundation's objective was to eliminate the inequality in the world and improve the life of mankind. The organization was focusing on providing health care and education. The Gates couple considered themselves as organisers, who were trying to find permanent solution to the countless difficulties being faced by mankind in consultation with persons with brilliant minds.

Even though after Susie's death, Warren's thinking had undergone many changes but in certain matters his beliefs remained unchanged. Allen Greenberg, who was, managing the 'Susan Thompson Buffett Foundation' learned that foundation was only going to get 6 million dollars and not 45 billion dollars. He was expecting the larger amount. Warren sent him a message through Susie Jr. that he should prepare the future plans after proper consideration and he should not consider himself any slighter because of the smaller amount. Susie Jr. was Allen's new Boss and his former wife. Allen realized that even with 6 million dollars, his foundation will be considered as one of the top 10 richest foundations in the world and he heaved a sigh of relief.

All the people associated with the donation were satisfied. Even though Warren had announced the donation, its disbursement was spread over many years.

Warren's donation announcement had a deep impact elsewhere also. Hong Kong's Cinema Star Jackie Chan announced that he would donate half of his wealth. Asia's richest man Li Ka-Shing announced donation of one third of his total wealth of 19 billion dollars to his charitable foundation. Mexico's richest man Carlos Slim initially made mockery of Warren and Gates philanthropy, but after a few months changed his mind and announced that he would also donate his wealth. Gates set up a new department in his foundation which communicated and followed up with persons who were desirous of donating. A 7 year old girl donated her entire savings of 35 dollars to Gates Foundation.

Gates Foundation's influence was spreading all over the world and funds were pouring in. The objectives of this foundation were similar to Warren's objectives. According to which, carefully selected serious hardships were being funded to solve them. This foundation was distinct from the other foundations in the world. In most of headquarters of foundation, money was wasted. The workers were whimsical and the philanthropic activities were neglected. By the end of 2006, foundations like the Rockefeller Foundation, impressed by the working of the Gates Foundation brought about changes in their working styles.

After Warren's announcement to donate to Gates Foundation, 3000 letters from needy persons were received in his office. Everyday the letters were piling up. From—sick people, who did not have health insurance and could not afford their treatment; people injured during work and were unable to take care of their families; people whose children were suffering from incurable diseases and did not have sufficient funds left to carry on the treatment; helpless single mothers who had been left stranded by their lovers, at the mercy of God. Warren was sending all such letters to his sister Doris. For the last 10 years she had been managing the, 'Sunshine Lady Foundation' and helping persons affected by domestic violence. The foundation was being funded by, 'Howard Buffett Foundation'. The foundation had been aiding helpless families. Warren had also sent $ 5 million along with the letters.

Doris gave the responsibility of screening the letters to few women who more than 50 years old. Persons who had suffered due to bad luck, rather than by their own folly were given preference and due care was taken that it would possible to improve the circumstances of the affected persons with normal funding. She only offered advice to gamblers, debt ridden and lethargic persons. Also persons, who had alternatives to solve their problems, were not helped. Doris was also not in favour of fulfilling all needs. She said, "I don't want to become their mother." She also taught the people to write letters expressing their gratefulness. Who had received help, She wanted to inculcate the feeling of gratitude and self-esteem in them.

Warren was busy in managing billions of dollars of wealth. He had been donating $ 5 million every year to Ted Turner's campaign, 'Nuclear Threat Initiative' (N.T.I.). He believed that this was America's most powerful body, which working to strengthen global security by reducing global threats from nuclear, biological and chemical weapons. Warren wanted to give more help to this body. N.T.I. was being managed by former Senator Sam Nunn, who had suggested setting up an international bank for storing low-enriched uranium to address nuclear proliferation risks. Warren had liked the idea and offered to donate 50 million dollars and hoped that sufficient funds would be arranged for this campaign. Warren was ever ready to donate funds for nuclear non-proliferation campaigns. He was in favour of finding a permanent solution for this crisis.

Warren had extended financial help to the former US President Jimmy Carter to manage the activities of 'Carter Centre.' Carter, who departed from White House as an unpopular President, did not look back, nor was he discouraged. His contribution in the fields of health, democracy and human rights were considered remarkable and he was honoured with the, 'Noble Prize for Peace.' After receiving the donation from Warren, he wrote to him, "If you come to Ghana from 6th to 8th February, 2007, we shall be delighted. You can see the work being done by us." Warren considered Carter as his friend, but even his son and Gates could not convince him to undertake the plane journey to Ghana.

It was the 3rd time that he avoided travel to Africa. Some things do not change, but as time passes some things do change.

In the programs arranged outside Omaha, Astrid was accompanying Warren as his official life-partner. She had not changed at all, a frank person, idol of simplicity; but her life's circle was expanding rapidly. She regularly attended social functions along with Bill and Melinda Gates. In the winter of 2005, she travelled to Tahiti along with Warren, where Gates 50th birthday was going to be celebrated. It was being celebrated on Paul Allen's famous ship 'Octopus.' The ship had a movie theater and recording studio, two helicopters and a small submarine. Astrid and Warren's stay had been arranged at Allen's mother's magnificent house.

Overwhelmed by the hospitality extended by the world's 6th richest man, Astrid had remarked, "It was an amazing experience. I have never had such a magnificent experience earlier and maybe I shall never have it again in my life time."

According to Warren, the arrangements at sea were far better than they would been at home. They had returned after enjoying the bridge game.

Two years after Susie's death, on his 76th birthday, Warren married Astrid, in his daughter Susie Junior's house in a simple ceremony. In this function, only the family members were present. Astrid had worn a blouse and white pant while Warren was attired in a business suit. When Warren adorned Astrid's finger with a large sized diamond ring, tears trickled down from her eyes. After this they went out for dinner. Thereafter they reached San Francisco, where the marriage party had been arranged. The conventional marriage cake had been prepared at Sharon Osberg's home. The Gates couple was also present in the party.

Even though he was not an unsophisticated person, he started living a simple life. He had always wished to live a simple life. He had a wife, a car, a house which had not been renovated for years and a business. He started spending more time with his family.

Warren always used to say that a tree can never grow to reach the skies, but it can create new plants.

Warren's shareholders were wondering as to whom he will appoint as his successor. Warren used to make fun of this matter. It was definitely being felt that there can be no alternative to Warren. On one occasion he had said, "My ideas are fully ingrained in Berkshire." And people working with Berkshire and its investors were also ingrained with Warren's ideas.

Warren had once said if Berkshire continued to earn profit for its shareholder even 30 years after his death, then he will be happy. This was his thinking. The foundations of the organization which he had laid could service the next generation even in his absence. In fact, Warren was the soul of the structure and without him there could be a vacuum, which could not be filled up. Only Warren could take the decisions of the organization in the best way and an alternative to him could not even be imagined.

After Warren's death, the manner in which the shareholders of Berkshire will miss their CEO, perhaps in history no other group of shareholders will miss their CEO. No other group of shareholders must have considered their CEO as their mentor and friend, the way in which Warren's shareholders thought about him. The person who earned billions of dollars also won the hearts of thousands of persons. Such countless people used to consider him as their well-wisher, who had never met him personally. In spite of receiving countless letters from his admirers and signing autographs for them, Warren could not understand how much the people admired him or praised him. He would be elated like a teenager after receiving each letter. He would also be filled with happiness when someone asked for an autograph.

Even though trees could not reach the skies, Warren believed that they could help plants to grow. He retained his earlier focus towards his business; the moment he achieved would lead an ideal life, the preacher in him was awakened. He had started lecturing college students in America. He used to visit colleges or establish contact with them from Omaha. He liked to talk to students because they were like unbaked earthen pots, who could be motivated in the right direction.

He used to tell them that he had started making money very early in life. If he had delayed it by 10 years, then possibly he might not have attained such success. He advised them to start early and stay away from the credit card mentality.

In 2002, he increased his interactions with students. The students were coming from MIT, North Western, Iowa University, Nebraska University, Chicago University, Indiana University, Michigan University, Houston University, Missouri University, Tennessee University and many educational institutions. He used to tell the students that the aim of becoming rich overnight was not important for living.

In 2008, he was declared as the richest man in the world. At that time students from Asian, Latin American and other countries started coming to Omaha. These students were extended excellent hospitality in Omaha.

The students asked more questions on subjects other than business, like what is the objective of life? The mathematical precision with which he replied to the questions related to business, he also replied to the other questions with the same adeptness.

When Susie was recovering in the hospital after her operation, then he had told the students from Georgia Institute of Technology about the purpose of life – "The purpose of life is to gain the love of the maximum number of persons from whom you wish to seek love."

To the question, how to get a perfect life-partner? He says, "Get married." To the question, what is right? He says, "Trust your heart." To the question, in which field should I make my career? He says,

"The field is which you are passionate about." I work with people whom I like. The field in which you cannot apply your mind is not right for you."

Warren would say to the students, "Consider your body like a sole car which you have got for your entire life. Look after this car, park it in the garage in the night, remove all the stains, change oil regularly and so on." Then he used to take the students to a restaurant for lunch. After lunch, the students would have their photographs taken with Warren. Some day, maybe after 40 years, they could tell their grandchildren about their meeting with Warren and having lunch with him. Warren was teaching them the mantras of life based on his lifelong experience.

During these discussions, he would accept that although he had great aspirations but he had made no plans from beginning to achieve them.

When Warren was very young and used to collect the crown caps, he had no inkling of what he was going to become. He distributed newspapers and he always ensured that they were delivered to the customers on time. If at that time had someone asked him whether he wanted to become the richest man in the world, then his heart would have replied, "Yes."

This dedication prompted him to study the world of share market. For hours, he would peruse such records in the library to which no one paid any attention. He would stay awake for nights and examine thousands of numbers to which no one else would have liked to pay any attention. Every morning he would read several newspapers thoroughly and would digest every word of, 'Wall Street Journal.' He would study the information on companies and would talk to their employees for hours. To understand the finer points of stocks, he would read magazines like *'Progressive Grocer.'* When he went for his honeymoon, he carried copies of *Moody's Manual* and Lesotho on the back seat of his car. For months he studied newspapers dating back to the last 100 years to understand the ups and downs in business, Wall Street's history, history of capitalism, history of modern Corporation's, etc. He kept a close watch on the political events and tried to correlate its impact on business. He studied the economic parameters till he completely understood its implications. From his childhood, he had been studying the biographies of his favourite persons and kept learning lessons from their lives. He liked to be associated with people who could help him. He liked to keep his attention focused on the business world.

He had developed several skills to avoid making mistakes. He continuously thought about the different aspects of doing business – how to carry forward a good business? Why do businesses fail? What is competition? How to gain the trust of customers? He had a different way to find solutions for problems. He set up a network of loyal people who were always ready to help him with dedication. Whether the circumstances were favourable or adverse, he never stopped thinking about ways to create wealth.

Warren loved money. The game of accumulating wealth was into his blood flowing through his veins.

While celebrating his 77th birthday, he realized that possibly he has spent more than two thirds of his life on American soil. His age had started showing. It was now not possible for him to study for the whole day. The visibility in one eye was becoming hazy. His hearing was also getting impaired, so he agreed to wear hearing aids. He had also started speaking rapidly. He used to get tired soon. In spite of all this, he was still capable of taking business decisions quickly and competently.

Warren's life's philosophy can be gauged from the following sentences – The snowball just happens if you're in the right kind of snow, and that's what happened with me. I don't just mean compounding money either. I did not wish to only expand my wealth to undreamed of levels, but wanted to explain it to the world and wanted to have a group of friends. You have to choose when the time comes. That's the way life works.

❑

Charlie Munger and Warren Buffett

Charles Thomas Munger had been working as the Vice-Chairman of Berkshire Hathaway along with Warren Buffett. Warren has often referred to him as his right hand man and partner. Warren had been telling that the extraordinary contribution made by Charlie, behind his success. He had an estimated net worth of $ 1.3 billion today.

Charlie was a lawyer earlier. He was given admission to the Harvard Law School without a Bachelors degree, which was not an easy thing. Charlie was an exceptionally brilliant student and could easily answer complicated questions.

Warren met Charlie when he was practicing law in Omaha. Impressed by his personality, Warren asked him to leave his law practice and take up financial investing. Charlie consented. Time proved that Charlie's decision was correct.

Charlie was also the CEO of Wesco Financial Corporation, an associate company of Berkshire from 1984 to 2011. Like Warren, he also wrote annual letter to his shareholders through which one could learn useful tips of investing.

Charlie is not only a successful investor; he is also a famous thinker who has been writing valuable quotes about business, investing and life in general.

Like Warren, Charlie is also from Omaha, Nebraska. After studies in Mathematics from University of Michigan and service in the US Army Air Corps as a meteorologist, trained at CALTECH, he entered Harvard Law School.

Charlie is known by the world as Warren's associate; but he independently managed an investment partnership from 1962 to 1975. During this period the partnership generated compounded annual returns of 19.8 per cent, as compared to a 5 per cent annual appreciation for the Dow Jones Index.

Though Warren and Charlie are friends, there are lots of differences in their personalities. Charlie supports the Republican Party, whereas Warren is known to support the Democrats. Warren spends most of his time in managing the business, whereas Charlie likes to keep himself aloof from the day-to-day activities of the company. Charlie has been associated with different missions of philanthropy.

Charlie's principle is – "Good businesses are based on ethics. Businesses based on trickery are doomed to fail."

❑

Warren's Ten Formulas to Earn Money

1. Invest the Profit

Drops make an Ocean. Even saving small amounts can turn into a big fortune. If you learn to save your profits then the magic of compound interest will keep on making you richer.

2. Don't Fall into a Groove

Develop innovative thinking. Don't join the herd. Use your own wisdom for any investment. Don't invest on hearsay.

3. Avoid Doubt

People, who remain entrenched in doubt even loose golden opportunities. Take the decision to invest quickly after examining the available data.

4. Understand the Deal Before Deciding

Before taking any decision, understand the deal properly. Think carefully how it will profit you. It's like you must carefully read any document before signing.

5. Keep Minor Expenses Under Control

It's not as if only major expenses impact. Even minor expenses can prove to be detrimental. Before incurring any expense, consider if it is justified.

6. Keep Debt Under Control

If you get into the habit of living on debit and credit card, then you can never become rich. By taking loan you can try to improve your living standard, but under the burden of debt, you will never be able to improve your financial state.

7. Maintain Continuity

If you think that the work being done by you is important and correct, then continue it. Keep advancing towards your goal with confidence.

8. Distance Yourself from Loss

If you feel that any investment is turning into a losing proposition, dispose it quickly. Sitting on it would lead to more loss.

9. Assess Risk

Before you decide to invest, think about the future consequences. You can take the right decision, after assessing the risks.

10. Understand the True Meaning of Success

For every person the meaning of success is different. Only accumulating money is not success. The things which give meaning to life, paying attention towards those things also as they are important components of success too. Out of those people whom you wished loved you and how many actually loves tells you the true meaning of success.

❑

Warren Buffett's Seven Formulas to Success

1. Happiness Comes from Inside

"In my business career, I never felt the need to differentiate between professional and personal life. I get absorbed in my work and this gives me immense pleasure."

If you do the work of your choice, then your productivity also become better.

2. Look for Happiness in Ordinary Things

"I look for happiness in ordinary things. I play bridge online for 12 hours in a week." While playing with children, while wandering in natural environment, while talking to relations-friends, in all such small things, we can look for happiness.

3. Live Simply

"I only want to do such tasks, which have some significance. In my personal life I don't care about how other rich people are living in royal style. I don't want to buy a 405 feet long boat because some rich man has a 400 feet long boat."

4. Think Easy

"I am ready to accept my mistakes. This means that I undertake only those tasks, which I understand fully."

5. Invest Simply

"The best way to buy stocks is to invest in index funds."

6. Have a Mentor in Your Life

"I was lucky to get capable mentors. You tell me about your idol and I will tell you the direction in which your life will move. The persons whom you consider as your idols, practice their merits and imbibe them in your personality."

7. Earning Money is Not the Primary Objective of Life

"Earning money is not the primary objective of life; it is the by-product of your primary objective. If you love doing some work then you should get involved in it with full dedication. The process of earning money is also like that. Money should not be an achievement but a means."

❑

Warren's Interest in India

The world's well-known investor Warren Buffett is quite impressed by India's fast growing economy. Warren feels that India offers unlimited business opportunities. He even believes that India's advancement can greatly benefit America. Keeping this in mind, he says that India can no longer be considered as a developing market. In other words, Indian market has developed to a large extent and it has become capable to provide new momentum to the economy of even a country like America.

In March 2011, Warren came to India for the first time. After his arrival, he told the reporters that he is looking for investment opportunities in large countries like India. He also said that he feels very happy, even if only one big investment idea succeeds in a year. So it does not matter that such an idea came from India or America or any other country. He thinks that the 26 per cent foreign investment limit in the insurance sector is not correct. Though there is a proposal to increase the investment limit to 49 per cent; not much progress is happening in that direction.

Warren only expressed his intention to invest in India but did not specify his plans. Warren, who is considered as the greatest warrior of investing, has invested in countries like China, Japan, Israel and South Korea in the past few years.

As far as India is concerned, Warren's company's presence is very small. His company Berkshire Hathaway has entered into an agreement with Bajaj Allianz to distribute motor insurance schemes. Recently they have formed a company called, 'Berkshire India', which has been appointed as their corporate agents for general insurance.

Even though Warren had come to India for expanding his mission's philanthropic activities, but he also perused at the possibilities of investing in India.

While touring India, he told the journalists that donating is harder than investing. The owner of $ 52 billion said that his needs are fulfilled with an annual salary of 100,000 dollars. I have no use for the rest of it, so it will be given back to the society.

Indicating the possibility of appointing an Indian as his successor, Warren said that he is thankful to India for giving him Ajit Jain. He said that Ajit Jain is more capable than him.

❑

References

1. www.google.co.in
2. www.goodreads.com/
3. www.thestreet.com
4. www.marketwatch.com/
5. www.thestreet.com
6. www.fortune.com/
7. www.cheatsheet.com/
8. www.goodreads.com
9. www.finance.yahoo.com/
10. www.suredividend.com/
11. www.time.com/
12. www.ruleoneinvesting.com/
13. www.brainyquote.com/

Success Secrets

Author's Note

Warren Edward Buffett is a renowned American business magnate, investor and philanthropist. He is the chairman and CEO of Berkshire Hathaway. Also, known as the "Oracle of Omaha", Buffett is one of the most successful investors in the world. He was born on 31st August 1930, in Omaha, Nebraska. Born to congressman Howard Buffett, Warren had a keen interest in business and investing from a young age. He was only 11 years old when he first started investing in the stock market. While at the age of 14, he made his first real estate investment.

Being business-minded, Buffett spend almost all of his childhood in various entrepreneurial ventures. From selling chewing gums, Coca-Cola, newspapers and magazines to working in his grandfather's grocery store, there was maybe any venture that Buffett hadn't used to earn money in his early days. His father was responsible for the young Buffet's interest in investing and the stock market because when he was just 10 years old, his father took him to visit the New York Stock Exchange.

After completing his studies, Warren Buffett went to work with his mentor and professor Benjamin Graham at Graham-Newman Corporation. There he worked as a securities analyst. Later, he worked as a general partner at the Buffett Partnership, Ltd. Eventually, he became the chairman and CEO of Berkshire Hathaway Inc., which is an American multinational conglomerate holding company headquartered in Omaha, Nebraska.

From such an exceptional and successful person, one could learn many lessons that could help one become successful in their concerned field. In this section, 100 Sucess lessons from Warren Buffet, we are going to learn and understand lessons that helped Buffett become successful both in his professional and personal life.

Here, you will learn about how to do business, how to deal with customers, how to have a work-life balance, how confidence in oneself could change everything, how to deal with bad decisions, standards of living, the value of hard work, the power of habits and so much more.

I hope it serves as a guide to its readers so that they could bring about positive changes in their lives. It would be my immense pleasure if this could have an optimistic influence on the lives of its readers.

– N.Chokkan

❑

1

Innovators, Imitators and Idiots

We see innovation in the market all the time. Many companies (and individuals) claim that to be their lifeline. Hence, new thoughts, products and services are regularly being introduced.

However, when we look beyond the quantity (number of innovations) and focus on the quality of those innovations or their long-term results, only a few of them turn out to be transformational and sustained. Others create an initial impression, but later they slowly fade from the market and people's minds.

Warren Buffett explains this phenomenon with 3 I's: Innovators, Imitators and Idiots:

- As the name suggests, innovators are the ones who spot an opportunity that didn't exist before. They look at the existing products and services, constantly think about making them better, ask the all-important 'why not?' question and imagine something new.
- Once these innovators find something new, try it and see some success, these imitators jump in. This is why a fantastic, original best seller book on a certain niche topic is always followed by a series of cheap imitations with similar-sounding titles and

wrappers. These people just imitate what the innovators are doing and see some success. After all, it is already a proven idea!

- Finally, we see idiots in the market. These people are worse than imitators because they are here only for the benefits. Their greed spoils the original intention behind the innovation and the whole premise on which it was created.

In our field of expertise, which tag fits us? Are we the innovators who find unique things which solve a real problem or imitators who are happy to go behind a recent success or trend or idiots who only see 'what's in it for me?' in others' creations? It is obvious that innovators are the ones who are going to have maximum satisfaction and fulfilment and the thrill of finding something totally new is priceless!

☑ **The Warren Lesson: *Be an innovator.***

❑

2

Tools and their Value

When Warren Buffett talks about modern gadgets and technologies such as mobile phones, computers and the internet, he makes jokes about his lack of understanding about these things and creates an impression that he is too old for these and would never use them right. We also tend to believe this impression because he belongs to a different generation and hence we assume that using modern tools would be difficult for him.

However, a careful look at how he uses some of these new gadgets and tools gives us a totally different picture. Suddenly, he doesn't look like an anti-technology old man, he doesn't look like someone who hates modern creations, instead, he looks like someone who attaches a premium to his time and would only use these tools in the right way. He refuses to jump to a modern tool just because it is new and everyone else seems to be using it. Instead, he looks at it, analyzes it, understands how it can fit in his way of thinking and working and then he decides to adapt it the way he wants.

For example, Warren uses his computer for researching, reading and playing bridge online. He feels these are the main purposes of this gadget for him. Others around him might use computers for trading online or for sending emails. But, Warren has a different set of needs and adapts his computer usage to suit them.

On the flip side, Warren once stated that he doesn't consume podcasts. This is not because he doesn't like that technology, but because he can read faster than he listens.

If you want to know about a certain topic and there are two information sources, an article and a podcast, you don't have to pick the latter one just because it is a modern tool. If you read faster than you listen, picking the old-styled article and reading it is a good use of your time. Instead, if you read slow or if you are driving and can't read, a podcast may be appropriate.

Thousands of people around Warren, even those in his age group, may be consuming podcasts. But, Warren doesn't go by such trends, he looks at podcasts (and other technical tools) from the value perspective and makes the right choice, even if it is old-styled!

☑ **The Warren Lesson:** ***Customize gadgets and tools according to your needs, not the other way around.***

❑

3

Read and Analyze the Raw Data

Let us say for example, you want to learn a topic. How do you go about doing it?

Of course, we research, we read, we understand, we form an opinion and this is the best way to learn. But the question is deeper than that: what exactly do you read? Do you read the source material or the raw data which helps you understand that topic or do you read someone else's analysis, findings and thoughts about it?

When you search for any topic online, you get both kinds of results. It is very easy to read the second category of articles or watch a Video where someone talks about the topic and learn it. Compared to this, articles and sources in the first category are hard to read, digest and make sense. However, when done right, these are the sources that will give you the real knowledge or the exact knowledge you are looking for.

When Warren Buffett researches about a company, he does it the long (and hard) way: he reads their annual reports, understands their business; current state, strengths, weaknesses and future outlook; he then reads about their competitors in the industry to get a complete picture. This is how he understands companies and makes his investment decisions.

According to Warren, we need not read others' reports to understand about a company. Others won't do it for us. We need to absorb information, decide what is important, what is not, relate various items we read about and see patterns. Others can't do this because their views, needs and perspectives about the same data might be entirely different. Our unique information needs can only be satisfied by our unique research.

We can extend this to any topic we want to know about: don't be lazy; read a lot of first-hand information, decide on the important points and use them for better understanding. Others' reports (and speeches) might be easy to consume, but they may not satisfy our requirements most of the time.

☑ **The Warren Lesson:** ***Read the raw data; decide what is important to you; analyse and understand.***

❑

4

Dealing with Gaps

Today, when Warren Buffett speaks, the world listens. If he gives a piece of advice or asks people to invest in a certain company, everyone does it immediately. His word has such a superpower.

But, this was not always the case with Warren. In his early days, he was talking to a lot of people and told them to do certain things. Those instructions were not random, they were based on his research and analysis and he trusted them. Unfortunately, others didn't. They listened to him, but they were not convinced that they should follow what he says.

In this situation, instead of blaming others for their lack of insight or understanding, Warren looked inwards. He started asking, 'What do I need to make sure these people listen to me?'

Note that, Warren's analysis focuses on the gaps on his side, not those on the other side. It is very easy to point fingers at others (or external factors) for our failure and sometimes we may be right too. But, most of the time those things are not in our control. Hence, analysing our own weaknesses (or room for improvement) helps, as we can get actionable insights from those questions.

Back to Warren. His early day self-analysis told him that he lacks sales skills. He took a step back and analysed why he lacks sales skills.

He found that he lacks public speaking skills. He decided to act on it and enrolled in a course.

Joining a course is just the first step. Warren dutifully followed the course, applied those principles, got better at public speaking, which in turn improved his sales skills. All these were possible only because he was not afraid of asking that first question and pointing a finger at himself.

☑ **The Warren Lesson:** ***Understand your own gaps and work towards filling them; become a better person every day.***

❑

5

Are you the Smartest Person in Every Room?

If you are the smartest person in a room, in any room for that matter, how cool is that!

Of course, being the smartest person in a group is a fantastic feeling and you get a lot of respect for that. Your views are respected and you may even get a chance to lead the crowd in the right direction.

However, if this continues in every place you walk in, it can only mean one of these two things: you are the smartest person on earth or you carefully decide to hang around people who are not smarter than you.

Warren Buffett advises us to surround ourselves with people who are better than us, because, "you are going to move in the direction of people whom you associate yourself with."

For example, if you are a computer programmer and want to get better at this art (or science), you should start hanging out with better programmers than yourself, you should read their code, you should understand why they have done certain things in a certain way, you should have conversations with them about coding, you should ask them to review your code and share feedback… This applies to every field. People better than us provide us with an opportunity to learn and improve. If this becomes a regular habit, the world becomes a continuous learning platform and we constantly improve from where we were earlier.

On the flip side, if you decide to surround yourself with people who are inferior to you, there is hardly any learning you can get from your interactions with them. Of course, it will feed your ego and make you feel important, but you never know what you are missing.

Hence, there is value in seeking the friendship of people who are better than us in any aspect: they may be quicker in thinking, they may be better in analysing, they may be well-read, they may come with a multicultural experience, they may be more empathetic, they may be good with words, and communication, they may ask better questions… Whatever be the reason, if they are better than us, we can learn from them and constantly improve!

☑ **The Warren Lesson:** ***Surround yourself with people who are better than you.***

❑

6

A Great Deal, Rejected

When people say they don't like the environment they are in, who is the reason for their problem?

Some of the life decisions are forced on us. This means, we don't have a say in them or we don't have enough control to change them. Hence, we need to accept them and move on even if we don't like them. But, many other decisions are made by us. For example, we decide to work with a person or a company, we decide to do business with a store, we decide to accept (or reject) a certain position, we decide to get married, we decide to move to a new city and so on. If these decisions result in a bad environment, we should understand that we are the primary reason for the mess we are in.

But, what do we do with this information?

Next time when we are making a new decision, in addition to considering the data points on the table, we should also think about our previous decisions, their results and map them to the current decision, visualising the possible future. We can't be 100% right, but we can see glimpses of the future and if we don't like what we see, we should either reconsider that decision or do something to ensure that the future is different from what we see now.

Warren Buffett says, he has denied good business deals because, he has to work with people he doesn't like. In other words, he sees a future where he may be working with people he doesn't like and makes a decision in the present so that he needn't be in that situation ever.

Notice the term "good business deals" in Warren's statement. This means those are good decisions when seen from the business perspective. But, when seen from the people perspective (who you will be working with and what energy they bring to the table), they become bad decisions and Warren doesn't hesitate to say no to such deals because for him working with the right people is important.

What if money is more important to you and you don't mind working with people whom you don't like?

In that case, your viewpoint of "important things" is different and you will be making a different decision unlike Warren. That's perfectly fine. There are no rights or wrongs here, as long as our decisions are in line with what we consider as important.

This means, every decision has to be analysed from multiple perspectives and we need to look at the possible future from many lenses (things that we consider important). If we believe something is important and not negotiable, it should reflect in the decisions we make now.

☑ **The Warren Lesson:** ***While making decisions, always consider what is important to you.***

❑

7

Knowable and Urgent

Deciding, whether to invest in a certain company or not, is a tough decision. You need to consider multiple factors, measure them, analyse them, form an opinion and decide based on that. However, while analysing those factors, Warren Buffett says that he only looks at things that are "knowable and important".

For example, the industry in which a company operates, its business, products, services, management team, partners, competitors, possibilities of international expansion etc., are important factors and you can know them with a bit of research. Hence, they come under the "knowable and important" category. We should strive to know these details as much as possible and make our investment decisions based on them.

On the other hand, possible interest rate changes during an investment period may be an important factor for an investment decision, but it is not knowable as no one can accurately predict the direction in which interest rates will move and by what percentage. We can make an intelligent guess, nothing beyond.

Hence, Warren advises us to worry only about knowable and important factors and use them for decision making. This way, we will still be following a scientific approach and not enter any guessing game.

Warren's approach can be extended beyond the investment world too. For example, when selecting which college degree to pursue, a student may consider knowable and important factors such as curriculum, university details, credentials of teaching staff, lab facilities, availability of practice opportunities, higher study options, campus interviews, etc. Focusing on these is better than worrying about important but not knowable factors such as the job market when he or she graduates. Of course, students can keep a watch on such factors and course correct if required, but worrying too much about not knowable factors won't get them anywhere.

Hence, when you have to make a decision based on certain factors, try classifying them as important or not and knowable or not. Suddenly, you will see additional clarity that will help you in decision making.

☑ **The Warren Lesson:** ***Focus on the Knowable and Important Things.***

❑

8

Is Time a Friend or an Enemy?

One of the common aspects you find in the websites of great companies is a section called "Timeline". It provides the history of that company from its early founding days till today, with a specific focus on milestone years and events. They could've provided it as a series of paragraphs, but this timeline view provides a unique perspective and understanding about why this company is where it is today and what made it great.

According to Warren Buffett, time is the friend of good businesses and the enemy of bad businesses. This means, if you have good fundamentals, systems, team, product or service over time, you are likely to succeed. Time will help you make the best use of those strong basics and achieve great things. On the flip side, if your basics are weak, time will only expose them further and make your mediocrity public.

We can see this in every field: when a new idea clicks, hundreds of businesses emerge trying to cash in. But, not all of them survive and taste success. Over time, only a few companies emerge as leaders and others slowly fade away. That's the effect of time. It clearly shows who is strong and who is not.

This is true for individuals as well. When we have a strong skill set over time, we will have multiple opportunities to showcase them, make changes as per the situation and succeed. On the flip side, if someone starts with a weak skill set and is not willing to improve it, time will only make things worse. They may try to fake intelligence or success for some time, not forever.

Hence, we (as individuals or as companies) should constantly observe what happens to us over time. We should strive to use time as our friend and improve, achieve bigger and better things. If time happens to make us worse, it is a signal that we must introspect and find out how to get our basics right. Once this is taken care of, time will suddenly become our friend.

☑ **The Warren Lesson:** ***Time is your friend if you have good basics.***

❑

9

Income and Consumptions

Personal Finance is an essential skill that everyone needs. But, it is rarely taught to individuals in a structured manner. Everyone learns it in different ways, mostly by trial and error, making expensive mistakes and learning lessons from them.

For example, living within our means looks very obvious but it is not that easy. There are lifestyle choices that have increased the number of our needs and the corresponding salary or income is not able to catch up with them. As a result, people use tools such as loans or side hustles to somehow fill this gap and pay their bills.

While these are useful tools, they come with a cost. People can easily fall into the debt trap or have no time to spend with their friends and families, on their passions and hobbies due to overworking.

Warren Buffett gives one simple rule for personal finance: you should always adjust your consumption to your income, and not your income to your consumption. This means, always look at what your inputs are and decide on your outputs accordingly and don't let your outputs decide what your inputs should be. This helps in setting the right expectations for ourselves and avoids disappointments.

This lesson is applicable for individuals as well as companies, organisations, and even countries. All these have income streams and consumption streams and it is important that they are not out of sync.

What if you want to improve your consumption? For example, what if one wants to drive a better car or live in a better house or have an expensive vacation every few months?

These are fair demands and people can always get there. But, instead of using shortcuts and hurrying to these large consumption goals, it makes sense for them to watch the current state of their income and arrive at scaled-down consumption goals. Now, these will be met comfortably without any pain as they have already matched income and consumption. As their income grows, corresponding consumption goals can get larger and larger. This is a healthy pattern that ensures the best of both worlds.

Of course, this doesn't mean people should consume everything they earn. There is also a need for savings and intelligent investments which made Warren of today.

☑ **The Warren Lesson:** ***Always adjust your Consumption to your Income, not your Income to your Consumption.***

❑

10

What does a Leader Really do?

Every company has two kinds of people: leaders and workers.

As the names suggest, leaders lead and workers work. But, such a one-dimensional view can hide us from the fact that leaders also work. They perform an important task that others in the organisation don't (and many times can't): seeing where their company or team should be and boldly taking other people there.

Why does this need boldness?

Many times, the path seen by the leaders (in their mind) is not easy or already tried. However, they see a reason to walk that difficult path and lead others there so that the benefits can be realised. When they are bold, others trust them and follow them.

Warren Buffett says, a leader should have visions and goals for a company for a long time horizon. But, this is only the first part of the puzzle, just having the right vision is not enough, they should also achieve them through other people. They should influence others to walk in the direction they take them and use their skills for the greater benefit of everyone.

Hence, true leaders will never feel insecure about their subordinates being more skilled or intelligent than them. In fact, they will make it a habit to hire such people in their team because accomplishing the vision is an equally important task and you need more hands and brains to make it happen.

Organisations typically have a hierarchy of leaders. Someone at the top thinks about the whole group's vision and future; a few people under him/her think about the vision and future of individual companies; more people under them think about the vision and future of specific groups or teams. Irrespective of level, all of them have a common aspect which is seeing into the future and leading others. In addition, they also spot leaders in their teams, coach them to do the same at a different level. This is how companies grow.

A small version of such a system runs inside all individuals too. We all have a vision or goal for ourselves and we get them accomplished through our own performance. This means we are our own leaders and our own workers. It helps in our personal growth.

☑ **The Warren Lesson:** ***Leaders should have Visions and Goals, and they should achieve them through other people.***

❑

11

Best Salespeople

Businesses deploy a variety of sales and marketing techniques to inform and attract potential customers. They go door to door talking about their products and services, demonstrate their creations to customers, give huge discounts and offers, use huge billboards to talk about their features and benefits, publish multicolour advertisements in newspapers and magazines, run cool video advertisements in television channels and websites, use affiliates to bring new customers and so on. There are sales, marketing experts all over the globe and these fields are constantly growing and thriving.

However, when it comes to truly winning a customer, "Satisfied customers are a store's best salespeople", says Warren Buffett. Treat your customer well, give them a high-quality product at the right price, service them right and ensure the customer gets the full value and they will automatically become your salespeople. They will happily go and tell others about the great value you provided and people trust such feedback much more than the paid advertisements.

Of course, this doesn't mean other sales and marketing efforts are useless. Many of the companies, where Warren has invested, spend millions of dollars every year on advertisements and other ways to bring in a customer to their store or to make them pick their products.

But, all those are useful only when the store or the product satisfies their need. That's the core advantage that actually converts someone interested to a real customer.

Similarly, when Warren appears in stage shows and television interviews and talks about his company and the businesses where he has invested, he also acts as a great advertiser and salesperson. However, it works only because what he does (value investing) works and creates wealth for others. People who invested in his company are happy and they act as salespeople and tell others.

Whatever be our business or industry, the focus should entirely be on our customer's needs and expectations. Understanding them, solving their problems and satisfying them, should be our first priority. When it happens, they go and tell others and success follows naturally.

☑ **The Warren Lesson:** ***Satisfied Customers are the best Salespeople.***

❑

12

The "Easy" Way to Make Mistakes

When you look at a viral tweet or video, there are hundreds (sometimes thousands) of comments. Some of them are genuine appreciations or criticisms. But some of those comments don't seem to make any sense. Many people just seem to be adding all sorts of things in their mind as comments, whether they are relevant to the current discussion or not. If those people faced the same tweet or video situation in real life, they probably wouldn't react like that. But, while they are online, they do it not once, not twice, but multiple times. They repeat the unusual behaviour again and again. What could be the reason?

"Ease of doing something makes people do things that don't make a lot of sense", says Warren Buffet. When something has a low entry barrier and can be done easily without thinking, people just seem to do that: they shake their shoulders with a casual 'why not?' and do it!

On the flip side, when something is slightly difficult or has a higher entry barrier, it makes people stop and think. That brief pause filters out some nonsense habits.

For example, if money grows on trees and can be earned by anyone easily, people are less likely to have saving habits or disciplined spending habits. But, if one has to work hard to earn it, he/she will think twice before spending it away on something useless.

Being a great investor, Warren uses a stock market example to explain this, "Buying businesses on wall street is so easy. You can buy one at 10:00 and sell it at 10:05. But most of the fortunes were made in relatively few securities and ones that were held for a very long time and one that the buyer understood."

In this example, Warren shows both the easy way and hard way of owning a business. The easy way happens with a click of a button and you don't need to know anything about a company. As long as you have money, you can buy a business without thinking.

But the hard way involves understanding the business before making a decision. You may still click a button to buy this business too, but you are not doing it because the button exists, you are doing it after careful analysis.

The modern world with its technical innovations is making things easier than ever. Just because we can e-mail or text anyone anytime, we shouldn't let that low barrier of entry make us do things that don't make sense. An easy tool needs tremendous self-control on the part of the user.

☑ **The Warren Lesson:** ***Just because something is easy to do, don't forget to think before doing it.***

❑

13

Being a Complete Leader

Everyone knows Warren Buffett is a great investor. But, what does he invest in?

Of course, he buys stocks of companies, sometimes buying entire companies. However, 'company' or 'business' is a very generic term and it becomes meaningful only when we consider what value it brings to the table: it may be a great product or a service or a brand recognition or a social impact or a wonderful team that understands the industry and runs the business well.

When making his investment decisions, Warren always looks at the people behind the business. This is because almost all the time he lets those people continue running their business as always, even after it changes hands. As he has a variety of businesses under his investment umbrella, he needs such experts and gives them a free hand to operate.

In one of his shareholder letters, Warren describes what skills his team looks at when hiring directors for their companies:

- Business-savvy
- Owner-oriented
- Strong specific interest in our company

- ❖ Actions guided by thoughts and principles, not robot-like processes
- ❖ Seeking managers who delight their customers, cherish their associates and act as good citizens to communities and countries.

This list shows the holistic expectations that Warren has in an executive: they should understand business, care for the owners and bring them value; they should be truly interested in the company and not just be motivated by money or other extrinsic motivations alone; they should be original thinkers; they should build a team of managers who keep customer satisfaction, employee satisfaction at the centre of everything they do while doing their bit to people around them.

Some may consider this to be an "impossible list". But, these expectations are not items that you study in a college or learn by working in a company for many years. They are solid foundations that make people complete leaders, they drive their thought process, controlling every decision they make. This culture fit is important and can take the company (and individuals) to great heights.

☑ **The Warren Lesson:** ***Be a complete leader.***

❑

14

Margin of Safety

Let us say, you have a truck that weighs 9,800 pounds. You are driving this truck on one side of a river and your destination is on the other side. You are looking for a bridge that can help you cross it.

Suddenly, you see a bridge. It says, "Capacity: 10,000 pounds."

Now, will you drive your truck over that bridge?

Technically, the bridge's capacity is above the weight of your truck. So, it should be safe to drive the truck over it. But, you normally don't do that. Instead, you will continue driving until you find another bridge that says, "Capacity: 15,000 pounds". Now you happily drive your truck over that bridge.

If you go purely by the numbers, the first bridge is as good as the second bridge because your truck's weight is lower than both their capacities. Yet, the second bridge gives us additional comfort because it has a higher "margin of safety". This means, if something goes wrong in the first bridge and the capacity calculation is wrong by a small margin, you are likely to face a problem. This is less likely to happen in the second bridge because it has a higher margin of safety.

When Warren Buffett analyses a company, he looks at two important factors: the price at which he might buy the company and the company's value estimate. If there is a small gap between them, he normally doesn't invest in that company, unless and until there is some other strong reason to do so. This is because the margin of safety is so low, it doesn't accommodate possible errors in his analysis.

The margin of safety is an important factor not just in investment decisions, but in our everyday decisions as well. For example, if you are preparing for a 15 minutes speech, you must have enough material to cover 25 minutes, because it will take care of possible errors in your "number of words per minute" calculations.

When observed carefully, almost every decision can be enhanced by identifying the equivalent of those two magic numbers: the truck's weight and the bridge's capacity. If the gap between them is small, better find another bridge (or switch to a smaller truck).

☑ **The Warren Lesson:** ***When making decisions, have enough Margin of Safety to accommodate unknowns.***

❑

15

Be Your Own Compliance Officer

Large organisations have their own compliance departments. Officers in this department look at various operations of that organisation and ensure that they are always complying with the applicable laws. If they see a problem, they immediately raise an alarm and ensure that it is corrected.

But, what drives this process? Are companies doing this because they are afraid of the law and possible punishment for misbehaviour? Are they doing this because the government will be angry if they don't? Or, are they doing this because they genuinely want to do the right thing and are not interested in making money by the wrong means?

Warren Buffett asks his employees and associates to ask a simple question before engaging in any act: if this appears in the local newspaper tomorrow and is read by everyone I love, will I still do it?

This question can convert each one of us into our own compliance officers. We will think about the act from a new perspective and will start skipping shortcuts. It will motivate us to do the right thing even when no one is watching and it will make us feel good.

For example, these days we hear a lot about cheating in online interviews. Some people do all sorts of tricks to land a job that they may not deserve. They may even consider themselves clever for doing so and laugh at their friends who are failing.

But, while the result is important, the means used to arrive there, are equally important. Someone cheating their way to a great job opening or a business deal or an election victory breaks this natural law. They may feel happy at that moment and enjoy the glory, but their own heart won't forgive them for getting there using unfair means.

"We've got all the money we need. [But,] we don't have an ounce of reputation beyond what we need and we can't afford to lose it", declares Warren. "We never will trade reputation away for money."

That's why Warren and many other leaders insist on integrity as an essential value. If you can't look at the mirror and say 'I did the right thing today', all the success in the world is meaningless.

☑ ***The Warren Lesson: If your actions appears in a local newspaper tomorrow and is read by everyone you love, will you still do it?***

❑

16

Tails and Legs

Joseph was eating a chocolate bar which surprised Nancy. "I thought you were on a diet", she exclaimed.

"Yes, I am", answered Joseph.

"But, now you are eating a chocolate bar."

"Yes. But, Chocolate is made from cocoa beans. Hence, I call this a Salad", told Joseph, taking a big bite.

We all know a chocolate bar is not a salad. Joseph also knows it. But, he decides to call it a Salad so that he can stick to his diet. It may make him happy but won't get the results one expects from a diet.

Warren Buffett uses a riddle from Abraham Lincoln to explain such a thought process, "If you call a dog's tail a leg, how many legs does it have?"

Contrary to popular belief, the answer is not five. Just because we call a tail a leg, it doesn't become one. A dog still has four legs and one tail, irrespective of the different labels you use.

Warren quotes this example to laugh at questionable practices from some organisations that cleverly label their costs as something else so that the final numbers look 'good'. But, this is just an illusion and doesn't become a fact.

When we are facing difficult problems which can't be solved, an easy way out can be labelling them in a different way. For example, someone who spends a lot of time on Facebook may call it "relax time" or "me time" or even declare that the Facebook feed is an information source. Such a change in the label is convenient because we don't have to change the status quo, yet, claim that we have achieved what we wanted to. But it will be a false victory.

Hence, it may be a good practice to question our beliefs. We may be under an illusion or we may be believing something because that's how it was always presented to us by our parents or teachers or seniors. Just because we always called a tail as a leg or a chocolate bar as a salad, it doesn't become one. Asking this question and understanding reality can make us see the world better and improve our thinking and actions.

☑ **The Warren Lesson: *Face Reality.***

❑

17

Circle of Competence

Warren Buffett may be one of the best investors the world has seen. But, that doesn't mean he spotted and made use of every great opportunity in the stock market. There are many companies where he didn't invest, but they went on to become great successes. Does that bother him?

Yes and No. If a company is outside his circle of evaluating competence and he missed to spot its potential success, he is not worried. But, if something is within his circle of competence and he missed spotting it, he realises that as a big mistake and learns from it.

This term (circle of competence) may be new to many. But, it is familiar to us and we all have our own circles of competence in various matters. Let us understand this with an example.

Warren is an expert in understanding businesses in certain industries. If there is a company that he wants to invest in and it falls in one of those industries, he can read about the company and understand it better to make the right decision. He may decide to invest or skip the opportunity. His decision may be right or wrong. But in either case, it will be a calculated move because he understands this business.

However, there are other industries that Warren doesn't understand well. When there is an opportunity in one of those industries, he sees it as falling outside his circle of competence because he can't understand the business to make a decision.

We need to remember that this circle needn't remain constant. Warren can always learn about new industries and expand his circle of competence. But, his success is not determined by the size of this circle. Even if he has a small circle, he can still be a big winner by taking the right calls within that small circle, ignoring the areas outside.

The circle of competence is not specific to the share market or investment world. Every individual creates his/her own circle of competence in certain areas through education, experience and interest. They should understand the boundaries of this circle very well so that they can always play to their strengths.

☑ **The Warren Lesson:** ***Understand your circle of competence, especially its boundaries.***

❑

18

Views of Others

Some people like hearing their own voice in any forum. They may have other experts and subordinates around, but their love for their personal thoughts prevents them from hearing the views of others and considering them before making a decision.

When seen logically, one person cannot be the expert on every topic and it is practically impossible for that one person to have all the skills, knowledge and experience. There is huge value in the diversity of thoughts that come when we listen to others. It gives us new perspectives, helps us form new connections in the brain. In addition, it also makes those other people feel good about their contribution in the decision-making.

However, Warren Buffett asks us to be careful about whose advice we listen to. He explains this with a piece of humorous advice, "Don't ask the barber whether you need a haircut."

As the barber benefits from every person who decides to go for a haircut, their opinion about whether someone needs a haircut or not is likely to be clouded by this interest. They may be honest people and tell you the truth most of the time, but why take that risk?

Hence, when we are thinking about a problem and want to explore it from multiple dimensions, collect various possible solutions, analyse them and arrive at the best course of action, we should expand our toolkit by speaking to others. But, we need to select them carefully in such a way that there is no conflict of interest and their views are likely to be balanced.

For example, if we want to buy a car, we can speak to an expert who analyses cars from various brands and can give us a balanced view. But, going to a particular brand's showroom and asking the salesperson there, is less likely to give us the right details. As this salesperson has a personal motivation to sell that car (or another car from that brand) to us, he is likely to exaggerate the benefits and downplay the issues. This doesn't mean we shouldn't talk to salespersons at all, but they shouldn't be the only sources for our decision-making. We need to take their views with a pinch of salt or verify them with facts.

☑ **The Warren Lesson:** ***Carefully select your advisors depending on each topic or problem.***

❑

19

A Car you can't Replace

Everyone has a dream car. They may not be able to afford it immediately. But, they start from somewhere and progress towards their dream car steadily.

Hence, when it comes to buying a car, people may not hesitate to experiment. They tend to pick the car that they like at that moment and something they can afford. If things don't work well, they know they can sell it and go for a different car later.

Warren Buffett brings a twist to this usual habit and asks us to imagine that we can only buy one car in our lifetime. This means, there is no option to change it for another (hopefully) better car, and we need to drive it forever. If we lose it, we can't buy a new car. In such a situation, imagine how much care we will show towards that single car and how gently we will take care of it!

Through this interesting thought exercise, Warren teaches us an important lesson: Our Body and Mind are not replaceable. They are not cars that you can change if you are unhappy with them or if they have some problems. They are like the only car that we will have forever. Hence, we need to take good care of them so that they serve us well into our ripe old age.

In today's use and throw culture, we attach very little sentiment to any object because they can be easily replaced as long as we can afford a new one. Hence, we tend to mistreat or misuse them without thinking. Unfortunately, the same habit gets in even in the way we treat our body and mind: we don't think twice about eating unhealthy food or compromising on necessary sleep to get something done. These may look like good choices now, but if and when we need to replace the car, we will come to know that it can't be replaced. At that time, we will feel bad about our life choices. That's precisely the point Warren makes: don't wait till the point of no return, take good care of your body and mind now as they can't be replaced; give them the attention that they deserve.

☑ **The Warren Lesson:** ***Your Body and Mind are precious assets. Take good care of them.***

❑

20

The Perfect Choice

In 1986, Warren Buffett interviewed someone for an insurance-related position. He asked the young man, "What experience do you have in the insurance domain?"

He replied, "None."

Usually, such an answer will result in a rejection. After all, the position needs insurance domain experience and what is the point in hiring someone who has no experience in that domain?

But, for some reason, Warren didn't consider it as a strong reason to reject this person. He saw some other qualities and decided to hire him with the note that 'Nobody's perfect.'

That young man whom Warren hired in 1986 is Ajit Jain, currently the Vice Chairman of Insurance Operations for Warren's Berkshire Hathaway. Someone who had no experience whatsoever in the insurance domain, went on to become a great asset for Warren's organisation and an industry leader driving big growth and profits.

Today, Warren calls Ajit the 'perfect choice' for that position and openly praises Ajit in multiple forums. But, many human resource experts may not agree with him. They might argue that this is a lucky selection and it could've easily gone the other way. Hence, they conclude that hiring should be strictly based on factors such as skills and experience that the candidate has.

Agreed, hiring someone shouldn't be a random process and it helps if the candidate has the right skills and experience. But, this focus shouldn't result in a machine-like selection process that expects perfection ignoring many other strengths that the candidates might be bringing to the table. For example, Warren saw something in Ajit which made him ignore Ajit's lack of experience in the insurance domain and trust him to do that job well. You can't teach this to a machine and expect it to take the right call. We are human beings and we see other human beings holistically and make decisions. This is true not just for hiring decisions, but also various other decisions such as whom to interact with, whom to do business with, where to study, whom to marry and so on.

Hence, when interacting with someone new, we should keep both channels open: the brain channel which looks at data and matches them with our needs and expectations as well as the heart channel which looks beyond data and thinks what else is important and useful in working with that individual. Balancing these two during decision making and constantly learning from the results of such decisions can help us become better thinkers and decision-makers.

☑ **The Warren Lesson:** ***Look at People Holistically.***

❑

21

Dealing with Bad Decisions

When we buy a pack of biscuits or a cool drink, we don't have to think much about the price to pay. Manufacturers of those products clearly specify their retail price and we need to just pay it, minus any discount. Easy!

But, buying a business is a different story. No business comes with a price tag. It has to be calculated based on various factors, including but not limited, to the value that the business brings. Hence, investors do a lot of calculations before arriving at the right price. Even then, there is no assurance that the price is right. Only time can tell, that is, only the future performance of that business will indicate whether they have paid too little or too much for it.

Warren Buffett is known as an expert in assessing companies. But, he too makes mistakes and talks openly about them. His letters to stockholders regularly contain such revelations.

But, when Warren talks about paying too much for a business, there is no regret in his voice. This is not because he wants to throw away money. In fact, he is one of the biggest advocates of paying the right price (or better, a discounted price) and calls himself a bargain-hunter. Still, he is not worried about paying too much for a business because such things get adjusted over time even though there are some short-term impacts.

For example, he might have paid too much for a business which can result in an immediate bottom-line impact for his company. But, over time, the business performs well or other businesses where Warren has invested hit gold and things get balanced. As this is always a possibility, there is no point in getting worried too much about a single bad decision.

Of course, we should give every decision the attention it deserves. But, if things don't go well, despite this, we needn't be too hard on ourselves. Either accept it as an error, take the learnings and move on or wait for the time to balance out things. Chill!

☑ **The Warren Lesson:** ***When you have a structured thinking process for decision-making, don't worry about decisions that go wrong now and then. Don't be too hard on yourself for them and move on.***

❑

22

Possibilities: Good and Bad

Let us say someone is telling you about a potential problem that might occur a few years down the line. If it happens, it is a big problem and can create huge issues for yourself and the people around you. But, if it doesn't happen, you can relax. Unfortunately, you don't know whether it is going to happen or not with any certainty because you are not an expert in that domain. In such a situation, what will you do?

Warren Buffett faced a similar situation when someone asked him to consider the Climate Change problem and its possible impact on his insurance business. Will he do anything differently now because Climate Change can cause some disruptions in the future?

"I have no scientific aptitude", responded Warren, "However, it would be foolish for me or anyone to demand 100% proof of forthcoming damage to the world if that outcome seemed at all possible and if prompt action had even a small chance of thwarting the danger."

This means, even though we can't say for sure that a dangerous situation is going to occur in a certain number of years, we still need to take action now because of a simple calculation: magnitude of benefits that can occur if we act now Vs magnitude of losses we might face if we don't act now. "If there is only a 1% chance the planet is heading towards a truly major disaster and delay means passing a point of no return, inaction now is foolhardy", declares Warren.

We may not face Climate Change level problem possibilities in our everyday life. But, we regularly come across "important, but not urgent now" tasks that we tend to delay in favour of "urgent" tasks. When doing so, we need to remember the thought process Warren teaches us when thinking about Climate Change: is there a slim chance that this delay (or a series of such delays) can cause a point of no return in future? If yes, is this delay a wise decision?

For example, someone might regularly delay starting an exercise routine because they are constantly busy with many other things. When they think about the slim (no pun intended) chance of a big health issue in future, they may understand that not acting now is unacceptable. Instead of arguing 'what is the exact probability or proof of this health issue occurring to me?', they will think about the benefits of assuming, that is going to happen in future and taking concrete action now.

☑ **The Warren Lesson:** ***If there is a small chance of a big problem occurring in future, opt for 'action' against 'inaction' now, as long as the benefits of 'action' are considerably large.***

❑

23

Best Person for the Job

Every year, hundreds and thousands of people are entering the job market with the belief that the system respects their talent, looks at their potential and gives them the right opportunities to grow. In return, they are ready to work hard and help the organisation that trusts them with the opportunity.

While 'best person for the job' is rightfully the norm that is driving any industry, there are instances where we see people using back doors to enter a job position. They may use their relationship with one of the existing team members or any other influence to get there. When such a route is taken by someone unqualified, other qualified candidates waiting for an opportunity are disappointed. In addition, this also hurts the organisation because the best person is not selected for the job which will reflect in the quality of work and results. It can spread negative energy in the team because talented people will start questioning whether they will have a fair chance to grow in this organisation.

"Meritocracy is important", says Warren Buffet. He explains this with a beautiful example: when a country is picking people for its Olympics team, they go for the best athletes and players, not sons or daughters of previous medal winners.

Of course, sons or daughters of previous medal winners may be great players and they can enter the Olympics team by showing their skills and talent; they can enter there by consistently winning many competitions and showing that they belong to the country's topmost players list. As long as no one enters there for just being the child of a previous winner or by knowing a senior official, the competition is fair.

Similarly, when someone is selected for a job, whom a candidate knows or who recommends that candidate should never be a category. Even someone with no connections whatsoever should be able to get that position as long as he/she is best qualified for that position. This keeps a level playing ground and helps the organisation also by creating a healthy environment for everyone to contribute and succeed.

☑ **The Warren Lesson*****: Respect Meritocracy.***

❑

24

The Selection Criteria

Warren Buffett's Berkshire Hathaway owns many businesses, some of them fully and many others partially. These companies range from candy makers to insurance providers to railway lines. A casual look into the list of companies owned by Berkshire Hathaway may make one wonder if there is any logic at all in that compilation. They may even conclude that Warren and his friend and partner, Charlie Munger just buy businesses randomly.

But, the truth is far from this assumption. Berkshire Hathaway is so successful because the companies it owns, are not selected randomly. Warren and Charlie carefully pick them based on various rules. In fact, they don't even keep those rules a secret. They have published it as an open "Berkshire Hathaway Acquisition Criteria", inviting businesses to come and talk to them if their business meets the given criteria:

1. Large Purchases
2. Demonstrated Consistent Earning Power
3. Good Returns on Equity; Little or No Debt
4. Management in Place
5. Simple Businesses
6. An Offering Price.

When we read this acquisition criteria, the first thing that strikes us is its simplicity. There is no ambiguity in which acquisitions Berkshire Hathaway is interested in and which acquisitions they are not interested in. Any business can easily tick (or not tick) these six boxes and conclude whether they should call Warren's office or not.

Similarly, when someone calls Warren's office about a possible acquisition, it is very easy for the office staff to decide whether this is a conversation worth pursuing or not. For example, as Warren himself explains, if a transaction's price is unknown, Berkshire Hathaway is not interested in any further discussions, even preliminary ones.

Hence, a simple criteria definition helps both parties think clearly and avoid unnecessary wastage of time. Bringing such clarity to a complex topic such as acquisition, teaches us the importance of keeping the rules simple: when everyone knows the criteria, there is no ambiguity and a lot of progress.

This lesson can be applied in multiple scenarios such as hiring someone for a job (or applying for a job), picking the right projects to focus on, identifying the right social cause to donate money or time etc. When we make the criteria clear, decision-making becomes easy and less error-prone.

☑ **The Warren Lesson: *When you have to make a decision, first clearly define your selection criteria.***

❑

25

Making People Listen to You

A stranger approaches you at a party. He extends his hand with a warm smile and introduces himself. You don't know him, but still, you talk to him because he looks friendly. After all, parties are places where you make new friendships, isn't it?

However, within the next few minutes, you lose interest in this person, looking around the room for an excuse to move away. Why? He starts talking about his company or the new product that he sells and directly or indirectly asks you to buy from him. This makes it clear that he originally contacted you not for friendship, but only for business.

The same behaviour can be seen online too. Many of the new people who friend you or follow you on social media approach you with a business proposal in no time. When this happens, your fingers immediately rush to the "unfollow" or "block" button.

In general, people are not afraid of new friendships, they are not even against the idea of giving business to someone. But, they dislike fake friendships created with the only purpose of selling something to them.

Warren Buffett owns many companies whose products and services he is proud of. In his interviews, he frequently mentions these companies, their products and services and encourages people to go and buy from them. In fact, he himself is a walking billboard of his companies.

Yet, people listen to Warren; they take his advice seriously. Every interview, every stage appearance of him is followed by thousands and thousands of people eagerly. When he hosts a Q&A session, people are lining up to ask their questions and hear his opinions. What could be the reason?

"I am not selling them anything", says Warren Buffett, "[What I am giving them is] just an unbiased advice from somebody who's been around a long time. It worked for me. I try to talk their language. I think people can tell when you are saying what you believe versus talking points."

This is a fantastic advice on how to talk so that people listen. While Warren explicitly talks about his companies, products and services now and then, he doesn't let this bias the opinions he shares or his genuine advice to someone. He believes in telling the truth, telling them something that he himself tried and succeeded (or failed). He only shares what he truly believes, and doesn't carry talking points that generally focus only on pleasing the audience. This means, he may even share unpopular opinions sometimes, but that's only because he believes them. When someone is truthful, others can see it and they respect it.

So, if you run a company and approach someone new, should you not talk about your business to them?

Of course, you can. But, make it a genuine consultation which benefits both the parties. First, understand their problem(s) and see whether your solution is suitable to solve their problem(s). If yes, explain why you believe your offering will work for them, along with its possible weaknesses. Finally, let them take the call based on the suitability, quality and price of your offering. By doing this, you are moving away from a blind sales pitch to unbiased advice which helps both of you.

☑ **The Warren Lesson:** ***Give unbiased advice and people will listen.***

26

Don't Teach a Fish How to Swim

When Berkshire Hathaway acquires a company, they usually retain the same senior leadership to run the business exactly the same way they did before the acquisition. Warren Buffett doesn't believe in giving 'instructions' to those managers and leaders on how to run their business, because they were doing it for many years and were successful, why interfere with that?

Given Warren's stature and track record in running successful companies, leaders of those companies may want to listen to him and give serious consideration to his thoughts. But, this can also backfire as they might attach too much value to his opinions because of his position. In addition, it can affect scalability as Warren can't be focusing on every business, trying to give high value strategic consulting or advice to all his leaders. Instead, by giving them the freedom to operate in their areas of expertise and providing an opinion only on matters where they need support, Warren sets up their individual organisations and the Berkshire Hathaway group for success.

As a bonus, the trust, Warren keeps in these leaders, acts as tremendous motivation for them to perform better than ever. He openly praises them in multiple forums and acknowledges the value they bring to the table. He is one of those rare leaders who will be happy to say, “I don’t know much about this particular business, it is totally handled by our leader of this company.”

“If my job were to manage a golf team and if Jack Nicklaus or Arnold Palmer were willing to play for me, neither would get a lot of directives from me about how to swing”, says Warren. We can see that this strategy works because many of the companies acquired by Berkshire Hathaway continue to remain successful, some of them growing multifold and getting better value than ever for shareholders.

Recognising talent, expertise and giving people the freedom to operate is an important trait for any leader. This attitude comes only when they are humble and accept the fact that they can’t be experts in everything just because they have a large title. Different people come with different skills and a combination of all those is valuable for a company or a group. Everyone contributing with their thoughts is acceptable, but interfering with someone’s job with our limited (or even amazing) knowledge can cause unnecessary friction. When a leader recognises this and trusts everyone to bring their best to the table, everyone gets the satisfaction of doing their best for the organisation.

☑ **The Warren Lesson:** ***Trust your leaders and give them the freedom to excel.***

❑

27

Watch the Puck

Wayne Gretzky is a famous ice hockey player and coach from Canada. Warren Buffett quotes one of his sayings as a piece of investment advice, "Go where the puck is going, not where it is."

For the benefit of those who might not know, a puck is a hard rubber disk used in ice hockey games. Players constantly chase it so that their team can control it better. Hence, knowing the exact location of the puck in the ice rink at any given point of time is valuable information for every player.

Average players may just look at the puck and try to reach there so that they can play it. But, by the time they reach there, some other player might have moved it to a different location, forcing them to rethink their strategy. If this happens throughout the game, they will keep moving (to the place where the puck is), but will not impact the result of the game much.

Instead, if they invest in careful observation of the field, other players (from both teams), their positions, movements and the puck's current movement itself, they can stay a step ahead of everyone else and can reach where the puck is going. Of course, there is no assurance that they will be right every time, but this approach is better than reaching the current and transient location of the puck.

Warren considers Wayne's advice to be a useful tip when picking the right companies to invest in. But, the scope of this strategy moves beyond the investment world. Irrespective of the field we are operating in, we need to constantly invest in understanding the current way things are working, trends and the future direction where they are going. These predictions may not be accurate. But, by consciously thinking about where the puck is going, we are in a better position to handle various possibilities, including those that need course corrections from our side.

For example, a student learning to code can look at the current programming languages, their usage patterns, newly introduced technologies, languages, their pros and cons, adoption rates, success and failure of these in the hands of various small, medium and large companies etc which improves their chances of understanding where the programming puck goes. This knowledge will then lead to them investing time in the right technologies instead of being dependent on what everyone around them is learning.

But, this can't be a one time process. They should continue watching the trends to understand if the original assumptions they made are still valid; if they see some mismatches, they can quickly readjust the path to ensure their understanding of the puck's new location improves their chances of success. In today's constantly changing world, it pays to regularly understand where the puck is going next.

☑ **The Warren Lesson:** ***Instead of focusing on the puck's current location, go where the puck is going and invest your money or time there.***

❑

28

Clear Boundaries

In today's world, most victorious individuals seem to give away something in return for their success. It could be health, sleep, exercise, family time, personal interests or something else... These are seen as costs of success that must be paid.

Once Warren Buffett was discussing a business deal and shared his proposal. He asked the other party to call him with their thoughts and indicated that they can proceed with the next steps if they show interest.

However, Warren asked this other party not to call him regarding this deal for the next few hours. Why? Because on that day he had plans to go out with his grandchildren and didn't want to be disturbed while he was spending quality time with them.

This incident may be dismissed as too old-style by modern entrepreneurs and leaders. They may argue, "if it is such an important deal, why make the other party wait? Just have fun with your family and when the call comes, excuse yourself, spend a minute or two to discuss the matter with the other party and close it. Easy!"

While multitasking is seen as an essential skill in the workplace and some people even use it to mix personal and official tasks together, multiple researches show that humans can't really multitask. It is just an illusion. Every time we think we are doing multiple things in parallel, we actually stop one and start the other rapidly. This stop, start process has its own cost which nullifies the effect of multitasking. We may be better off handling one task at a time to get maximum efficiency.

Similarly, Warren's example also shows the need to draw the boundaries between personal and professional time. It is okay to make an exception here and there in some circumstances; but, the moment we relax the rules too much and start allowing any sort of interruption anywhere, we will not enjoy both worlds.

Another important point is the message Warren sends to people around him by saying 'don't call me when I am spending time with my family'. It stresses the importance of work-life balance and encourages everyone to take it seriously. When a leader acts that way, others follow and it helps them excel professionally, while having a healthy personal life.

☑ **The Warren Lesson:** ***Enjoy your personal time fully. You can pick up business tasks when you are back!***

❑

29

Don't Keep Scores

When two teams play a game, someone carefully keeps the score and updates it regularly. Hence, at any given point of time, you will know which team has scored how much, what the gap is and who is winning.

Even outside the sports world, people keep scores. For example, students may keep a score of the number of lessons they have studied, the number of topics they have revised, etc. Mountaineers may keep a list of mountains they have scaled and haven't scaled.

We should remember that not every score is noted down on a piece of paper or electronic scoreboard for everyone to see. Some scores may just be registered in the minds of people; yet, they remain as strong indicators of their performance and success, at least to themselves. They may also guide their next step as different kinds of scores will need different kinds of actions.

Keeping scores is good and many times motivates us to do better. However, the problem starts when people bring the same habit in a relationship, trying to keep a running score with their friends, family members, business partners, co-workers, etc.

For example, let us say a husband and wife are arguing about a certain decision to be taken. If both of them openly discuss the merits and demerits of the given options based on the available data, it will lead to a better conversation. Alternatively, what if one of them goes like this: "Your suggestions on these matters are always bad; let me give you a few examples where you made these stupid decisions…"

Such a comment is the result of a mental 'score' the husband (or the wife) has kept all these years. He/she has seen this relationship as a sports match and has noted down instances where they won and instances where the other party won. If the other party also kept a similar score, this becomes a faster downhill journey.

"You cannot keep score [in a relationship]", says Warren Buffett. "It just doesn't work with the best of human relationships."

What if we keep score in our minds and never express it to the other party?

According to Warren, it still doesn't work. We may implicitly indicate to the other party that we keep the score and that doesn't help enhance the relationship. "It shouldn't be even suppressed. It should be something that doesn't even exist."

This means that both parties should be open and understand that all of us make mistakes. Instead of keeping scores such as who said what, who's idea was finally selected, etc. The focus should be on having the right conversation considering all options so that the best option is arrived at collaboratively. Irrespective of who gave an idea, other people can enhance it with their thoughts, experience and expertise. In the short term, it improves the idea; in the long term, it strengthens the relationship.

Hence, when we work with other people in our personal or professional life, it is important to remember that it is not a game with a single winner and there is no use in keeping score. When we approach people with this mindset, we don't try to win or dominate that relationship, it becomes a two-way street where both people contribute happily.

☑ **The Warren Lesson:** ***Don't keep scores with people. Instead, have open conversations and help each other.***

❑

30

Standard of Living

Cost of living is typically defined as the cost of maintaining a certain standard of living. For example, if you want to live in a comfortable house in a safe society, you need to spend a certain amount to buy or rent such a house. If you want a certain quality of food three times a day for all your family members, you need to pay for the ingredients, cooking fuel and energy to store food items safely. If you want to travel to your office with certain comforts, if you want your children to go to a private school, if you want to have an annual vacation in a foreign location, etc. all these add up to your total cost of living. Depending on whether your earnings/savings match or exceed this cost or not, you can enjoy all or some of them.

However, some people get this relationship wrong and assume that getting a very high income or accumulating a lot of wealth or assets automatically gives them a better, satisfying life. While this is true to some extent, many researches suggest that once the basic needs are met, additional money doesn't increase life satisfaction. In fact, in many cases, the race and grind to earn that money can even reduce the feeling of satisfaction and happiness.

"Your standard of living is not equal to your cost of living", says Warren Buffett. Instead of calculating how much money we are able to bring to the table, we should start looking at what value it brings and what difference it makes.

For example, driving a cool, luxurious car to the office is wonderful. But, that doesn't mean those who use public transport or drive a smaller, less comfortable, less stylish car are having a rough life. They may be happy with their mode of transport and that's what matters.

Warren's life itself is a testimony to this advice. Even though he consistently features in the lists of richest people in the world, he is frugal, spends wisely and doesn't believe earning and spending money is the way to happiness.

☑ **The Warren Lesson:** ***Good standard of living doesn't mean spending a lot of money on everything. It comes from inner satisfaction.***

❑

31

Working with Smart Customers

When Warren Buffett was young and looking for a job, he applied for an investment consultant job opening. During the interview, the interviewer asked him, "If you get this job, what kind of customers will you look for?"

"Smart customers", answered Warren. "They will understand what I'm talking about and they'll make money eventually [by the investments I am suggesting them.]."

"Wrong answer" declared the interviewer. "You should look for rich customers."

This interviewer's expectation is typical of conventional investment advisors of those days. They will look for rich people who can afford to spend money on large investments so that these advisors can make a lot of money through their commission for such investments.

But, Warren, even at that young age, didn't believe in this. He felt he should attract those customers who are smart, who can understand what he is doing, what he is suggesting and why he is suggesting it. Those customers tend to invest not because they have a lot of money, but because they believe in the strategy suggested by Warren. Hence, such customers tend to stick with him for the long term.

This is exactly what Warren did when he started his own business. Even today, those who invest in Berkshire Hathaway shares understand and trust Warren's methods and those are the kinds of customers he wants to work with.

Today's business world uses the term 'Velvet Rope Strategy' to describe the process of creating exclusivity with services or product offerings. In Warren's case, 'being a smart customer' and 'understanding my strategies and believing in them' were his velvet ropes. Those customers who crossed those velvet ropes benefitted the most. Warren also enjoys working with them.

In addition, Warren also managed to attract a large group of Smart Students. These students from all over the globe study Warren's methods so that they can understand them, customise them and use them in a way that makes sense for them. Warren may not get to work with all of them directly, but he has created these Smart Investors in every generation which continues even now.

When we trust in the intelligence of our customers, we are forced to provide something of true value. Fake promises won't work with them simply because they are smart. So, we need to work hard, improve our processes, offerings and as a result, we grow and succeed. It is a true win-win for everyone.

☑ **The Warren Lesson: *Work with smart customers.***

❑

32

Products that Travel Well

One of my friends wrote a great business guide. It was accepted by a publisher and released as a beautiful paperback book. It sold well and got nice reviews too. This made my friend very happy.

A few months later, my friend got an email from a foreign publisher. They heard about the book and wanted to publish the same in their native language. My friend gave the necessary permission and within a few months, the book was released in a foreign language which my friend doesn't even know.

The story didn't stop there. The second language publication of the book made it even more popular and it got published in two other languages, all within the first year of publication.

I asked my friend whether he expected such a success for his book in four languages spoken in different parts of the world. He just laughed, "Well, I didn't. But, when I think retrospectively, it makes sense. The topic I chose was not a local one. It was understood and appreciated by people of different cultures and hence, I could use my one-time investment (researching and writing a book) to get multifold returns. If I chose a local topic, this wouldn't have happened."

When investing, Warren Buffett applies similar thinking and looks for products that 'travel well.' This means products that are not restricted to a specific market but can be successful in other markets too. For example, a soft drink or a chewing gum will travel well and can be manufactured, marketed and sold to a variety of markets and consumers. He likes investing in those products and in companies manufacturing such products because their market can grow beyond geographical boundaries and they can bring in more money than products that are locally successful but don't travel well.

We can apply Warren's idea when picking our projects or when deciding where to spend our time. If there are two tasks and one will have a larger, wider impact than the other, it may be wise to spend time on it so that we can maximise our returns. The other task can be either dropped or delegated or improved in such a way that it too has a wider impact.

☑ **The Warren Lesson:** ***Focus on products that travel well.***

❑

33

The Path to Expertise

Every field has novices and experts. Both their behaviours and results are entirely different. After all, experts have years, sometimes decades, of learning experience with best practices embedded in all their actions. They seem to look at patterns that others totally miss; their decision-making is (usually) flawless, and even if they make a mistake, they are able to recover from it and course-correct smoothly. They learn lessons from those mistakes, implement those learnings and ensure it strengthens their overall performance. Hence, it is not easy for novices or even mini-experts to match them.

However, this shouldn't be a reason for non-experts to avoid entering that field altogether. Even those experts would've started somewhere and got here. Hence, they should remove the hesitation and enter the field, learn and improve. As the famous saying goes, you can't edit a blank page!

Warren Buffett is an investment expert. But, he tells others that "you don't have to be an expert in order to achieve satisfactory investment returns". In such scenarios, that is, when we are not an expert in what we are doing, he advises us to follow two simple rules:

First, we should recognise our limitations. Just like we know what we know, we should also know what we don't know. When this understanding is clear, we will look for ways to bridge this gap and minimise our damage possibilities.

"Unsophisticated investor who is realistic about his shortcomings is likely to obtain better long term results than the knowledgeable professional who is blind to even a single weakness", says Warren. Even though his observation is about the world of investing, it applies to every field and knowing our weaknesses is key to making the right decisions.

Second, we should identify and follow a course that is certain to work reasonably well. No one can predict the future accurately, but finding a path that has the maximum possibilities of things going well is doable and that's something a non-expert should look for.

These two rules may not guarantee success. But, they minimise risks and send us in the right direction. We should continue to observe, learn and improve. This smart path will make us experts in our chosen field.

☑ **The Warren Lesson:** ***When you are not an expert, recognise your limitations; follow a course certain to work reasonably well.***

❑

34

Learning from Friends

How do we pick friends?

Some friendships start very early, from school days or even earlier. They may be people with whom we like to play or study or work or simply to talk nonstop. After that, we keep adding friends to our list as we grow. We may also remove friends from this list, but new ones keep coming to ensure a steady supply. These friends share our dreams, goals, feelings, anxieties, disappointments, expectations and secrets. From a small kid to an elderly person, everyone seems to need friends and enjoy their company.

But, is there any common thread that connects all these friendships?

"I learn from all my friends", says Warren Buffett. "It is difficult for me to be friends with someone from whom I don't learn something. That's the fun of having friends."

While we have a good time with our friends in a playground or classroom or office or theatre, we constantly learn from them. Some of them teach us good habits, best practices to be followed in different circumstances. A few others teach us what habits to avoid for us to succeed. They do this by talking, by sharing their experiences, by expressing their views about things they saw or heard, by demonstrating values through their behaviours and by openly providing us feedback on our actions.

Feedbacks coming from friends are most important because they are more likely to tell us the truth instead of sugar-coating it. They do this because they want us to succeed, they want us to grow, they want the world to look at us with awe and they want to enjoy that pride of being "the best pal of a successful person". When such feedback is shared reciprocally, both friends benefit and the bond between them strengthens.

Warren has explained in multiple forums how he enjoys working with his long time friend Charlie Munger. This is not because they always share niceties and agree with each other. They do have disagreements and some of Warren's decisions are challenged by Charlie. However, he doesn't take it personally because he knows that Charlie is a true friend and he respects his intelligence. This makes him reevaluate his original thought process and apply the perspective from Charlie. Hence, every disagreement becomes a learning opportunity.

When we have friends with varied skills and talents, we can constantly observe them and learn from them. This will be more effective than the learnings we get from classrooms, textbooks and preachings because it comes with fun and from people whom we love.

☑ **The Warren Lesson:** ***Learn from your friends.***

❑

35

Prescriptive Approach vs. Descriptive Approach

Howard Buffett, the father of Warren Buffett, was a Congressman. He gave his son a terrific gift.

What was it? Money? Stocks? Lessons on Personal Finance? Contacts of his wealthy friends? Recommendation letter to a famous company?

All these would've been great gifts. But the gift Howard gave his son was even better and long-lasting: He told his son that he cared only about the values he had, not the particular path he chose.

This means Howard was not concerned about Warren trying something different from all others. He didn't want his son to follow a certain path simply because everyone else was doing it or because the chances of success are higher there. Howard believed that Warren will be successful in life as long as he has the right value system.

Warren says that his father told this to him both verbally and by behaviour. Howard informed his son that he had unlimited confidence in him and he should follow his dreams.

A typical parent today might be horrified to hear this. They may wonder what the kids know about life and its different paths and the things they would need to be successful. This may make them think that they need to instruct their children and guide them in the right direction, carefully watch their progress and do the necessary course corrections until they are ready. This would in turn lead to them pushing their own dreams on their children, influencing their choice of college or degree or job or anything else.

However, all this 'guidance' doesn't guarantee success or happiness. Even if it does, the children will only be living their parents' lives, not their own.

Compared to this, the route taken by Howard is pleasant and gives complete freedom to children, as long as their value systems are right. After all, it is their life and they should make the decisions. Parents can be there to give support if necessary, otherwise, set the basics right and let them explore the world.

This might apply even in a professional setting. When seniors start using a prescriptive approach (telling people what to do and how to do it) instead of a descriptive approach (telling people what needs to be done and letting them decide how to do it), their subordinates tend to become their poor copies or get frustrated and leave. Instead, if seniors give the right guidelines and give freedom to juniors to perform in a way they feel right, they may make mistakes, but will learn from them and grow to be better individuals.

☑ **The Warren Lesson:** ***Give your children (or subordinates) a terrific gift: care about their values, not the path they select.***

❑

36

When it is Raining Gold...

Opportunities don't follow a regular pattern. They tend to arrive at a time when people least expect them, and they tend to vanish very fast, giving no room for those who hesitate.

Hence, everyone in any field should make 'looking for opportunities' a daily job. They should find systems and sources to search for opportunities, build intelligence to spot them early and act fast.

For example, a business owner operating in a certain field should continue watching the local and international markets, trends in customer behaviour, the performance of his/her competitors, partners and complementing services etc. If possible, they can have their own think tank which enhances their chances of spotting the right opportunity at the right time.

"Not using a right opportunity is a mistake", warns Warren Buffett. "Using it on a small scale and not grabbing it fully is also a mistake."

For example, if the business owner spots an opportunity for a great business relationship, he/she should also understand its full scale. It could be the dollar value of the opportunity or the number and depth of relationships it can create. While even a partial involvement will get great returns, if it is clear that the opportunity is a good one, it makes sense to use it fully. Warren explains it with a beautiful illustration, "when it is raining gold, reach for a bucket, not a thimble."

Another important aspect of using opportunities fully is being ready for them. Starting our preparation after the opportunity is spotted might be too late and the opportunity may not wait until we are fully ready. Hence, we should be ready to grab great opportunities when they arrive and this needs preparation of skills and resources. A business owner willing to use an international opportunity to expand his/her business should already have the right systems in place to discuss, close and get started with the necessary formalities even before the opportunity is spotted. While doing so, we need to make sure that we prepare a bucket for the gold rain, even though there is not a single drop in sight yet.

☑ ***The Warren Lesson: Spot the right opportunities, and use them fully.***

❑

37

What Makes a Product Great?

There are hundreds of thousands of product companies all around us. Starting from the toothpaste we use in the morning to the mobile phone we carry everywhere to the car we drive, we use and endorse multiple products and companies that make them.

But, except for the fact that they all make products, these companies are not the same. Their size and degree of success vary a lot. Some products attract customers (and repeat customers) easily, selling in large numbers, while other products need to struggle, make some noise before they can make any sale.

If you are an investor (or a business owner), companies making the first category of products will be your dream companies. You would want to design, make and sell products that customers love and buy again and again. This will ensure sustained growth and great returns for your company.

But, picking such products or companies is not easy. Is there a formula that guarantees product success?

"[Warren] Buffett buys companies with products that fill the basic needs of society, appeal to human emotions and evoke highly favourable images", says Author Nikki Ross, providing a few examples from some of Warren's investments: Gillette (fills a basic need, associated with grooming), See's candy (satisfies chocolate craving), Coca-Cola (quenches thirst).

Basic needs and emotional needs might be different for different people. But, we can look at the majority and arrive at the set of needs that they typically want to be satisfied. Then we can look at the brands that have got highly favourable images to satisfy those needs. For example, there may be hundreds of candies, but what are the few brands that come to people's minds when they think of their need for candy? This line of thinking provides the clue into those products and brands that have long term potential.

What if a great basic or emotional need exists, but there is no single brand that has captured people's minds in that area?

That's great news. We have a wonderful opportunity to build a product and a brand to fill that void!

We can use Warren's product-company-selection mechanism to also enhance our communication. If we have an idea and we want people to see it favourably, we can tie it to one of their basic or emotional needs and ensure that our idea satisfies those needs. Once this is established, they will favourably look at our idea and we can seize that moment to establish its benefits further!

☑ ***The Warren Lesson: Look for solutions that fill a basic or emotional need of society.***

❑

38

Every Employee Contributes to the Success (or Failure)

The success of a company is usually linked to its chairman or CEO. At best, we might give credit to the next level of leaders who report to this top boss. Anyone below their level is considered part of the organisation, but not directly responsible for its success.

In fact, the same rule is followed when crediting people for the failure of a company. Top leaders are blamed when the company doesn't perform well. In the case of extreme flop shows, they may even lose their job.

Warren Buffett reminds us that the success or failure of a company is rarely a function of a few individuals. He feels every activity done by an employee (at any level) can strengthen or weaken that company.

For example, Warren wants us to think about the sales clerk behind the counter of a candy shop. When a customer walks in to buy some sweets, he or she may either smile and give a great experience to this customer or speak to them angrily and act as if they don't care whether the customer buys sweets or not. Depending on this clerk's behaviour on that day, the customer leaves the shop in a happy or angry mood.

This reflects in the customer's feelings about the shop or the brand itself.

We may think of this as a single transaction that has no impact on the overall scheme of things. But, when we add thousands of such transactions performed by hundreds of staff members with thousands of customers, the impact adds up. In addition, the customers can also tell their friends and relatives about their experience. A positive word of mouth can help the company progress and a negative word of mouth can destroy it.

Hence, people working at every level of an organisation must understand the importance of doing the right things. In addition, their leaders and management team should also understand their importance, train them, respect them and treat them fairly. Such a company will grow fast as people give their best.

☑ **The Warren Lesson:** ***Every activity done by employees at all levels can strengthen or weaken a company. Hence, set the right message to employees, treat them well so that they can treat your customers well and the company can grow.***

❑

39

Addressing Self-Doubt

Every year, the world is producing thousands of talented individuals. They start their career with limited experience, talent, tremendous hope and ability to work hard. As they progress, they gain experience and skills which help in their further growth.

However, this journey is not always smooth. They face roadblocks in their path now and then which they need to fight against. Many times these roadblocks are placed by other people or market situations. But, sometimes, they are placed by these individuals themselves.

A talented person won't put a roadblock for his/her own success knowingly. Some of the habits they had earlier or acquired during their work-life are responsible for this. One best example is self-doubt.

"I've never had any self-doubt", says Warren Buffett. "I've never been discouraged."

This may not surprise us because we know who Warren is today. But, his statement talks about his entire career which spans many decades. He was not the best investor in the world on the very first day of his career. He faced many hurdles and worked hard to win against them and reached the pinnacle of success. Even during those hard days, he didn't have self-doubt.

Not having self-doubt benefits someone in two ways: it doesn't pull them back, instead, it pushes them forward. So, the impact is 2x when compared to someone else with similar talents, but has self-doubt. Not being discouraged about things not going as per our plan and not blaming ourselves for the same are important mindsets that give us the enthusiasm to face the world and think of the next step. They tell us that the current state or the results of our earlier action don't define us and with a different approach, we will be able to produce a different result.

In addition to spotting and addressing our self-doubt, we should also be watchful of this habit in others. Many times, people move ahead and succeed because of the trust others show in them even when they doubt themselves. If we can play that role to others and encourage them to move forward, someone else will do the same to us when we need it the most.

☑ ***The Warren Lesson: Don't have self-doubt; don't feel discouraged; act with confidence.***

❑

40

Meeting Obligations

Let us say there are two ways to run your business. The first way is to run it in a cautious way that allows you to get decent profits on a continuous basis, even when the conditions are adverse. The second way allows you to get great profits under normal conditions. But, if the conditions are bad, it may produce poor profits (or even losses). Which one will you select?

People who are comfortable in taking risks are likely to select the second way after doing some analysis. They would argue that the results will match the risk taken. When things go our way, we will make a lot of money, which will balance the poor performance during bad weather.

Warren Buffett says that he will select the first way in these circumstances because 'we do not wish it to be only likely that we can meet our obligations; we wish that to be certain.'

This means if a business runs for many years and has obligations to take care of, Warren's first priority as its leader is to ensure that those obligations can be met with certainty, even when things go wrong. To ensure this happens, he is okay to compromise on some additional profit which might be the prize for risk-taking.

"We adhere to policies that will allow us to achieve acceptable long-term results under extraordinarily adverse conditions, rather than optimal results under a normal range of conditions", says Warren. Notice that he doesn't talk about the percentage of times normal conditions occur because that calculation will simply tease the leader to think of the Risk Vs Rewards balance. Such a thought process will make it likely that in some years their business won't be able to meet its obligations. Warren feels it is not a worthy risk to take.

These obligations may differ from company to company. But, all of them have some obligation or other which they must meet on a consistent basis. For example, providing the best products or services to our customers, extending great support experience to them, bringing value to our stockholders, creating opportunities for our society, paying back loans, being a responsible corporate citizen and many others. When you keep these obligations as your priority, then 'acceptable results even under adverse conditions' looks better than 'optimal results only under normal conditions'.

Similar obligations exist for individuals too. They drive each one of our decisions. Meeting our obligations consistently makes others trust and respect us and improves our business and personal relationships.

☑ **The Warren Lesson:** ***Meet your obligations with certainty; That's an important priority for everyone.***

❑

41

Short Read, Long Read

A few years back, one of my favourite newsletters introduced an interesting new feature: before beginning every article, they started stating the typical time it takes to read that particular article. For example, a short article might start with "Reading time: 2 minutes", while a long read might start with "Reading time: 12 minutes". Readers can look at this data and decide whether they want to invest this time or not, even before they start reading it.

Soon, many other publications such as websites, blogs and newsletters started announcing the reading time ahead of their articles. Readers expressed their pleasant surprise and many others followed this trend. In fact, Readers understood the value of this data in their decision making or article selection process so much so that they started mentally calculating the reading time even on those articles which didn't publish them explicitly.

Similarly, some people have the habit of announcing the time before starting a discussion. For example, they might ask, "I need to discuss something with you which might take 10 minutes. Are you available now?" This helps the other person decide whether they want to start that discussion at that time or not.

Warren Buffett advises us to think in a similar manner before starting any task. "Understand the natural time horizon of the task you are set out to do. If you can't stand that time, do not do it."

For example, if someone wants to be an entrepreneur, he/she should be prepared for many months, if not years, of hard work. That's the typical time horizon of that task. If this understanding is not there and someone enters there expecting a quick win, they will be disappointed.

But, some entrepreneurs win quickly. Don't they?

Yes. But, are there rules or exceptions? We should always look at a larger sample set and understand what is the typical time it takes for a certain task. Then we should be mentally prepared to give that effort and not give up in between. If we can't, it is better we don't enter there at all. We should find another task that matches with our time expectations and that is likely to be a better fit for us.

☑ **The Warren Lesson:** ***Understand the time each task takes; if you can't invest that time, don't start that task.***

❑

42

Necessary Prudence

You are walking on a busy road. Many people are walking along with you or coming in the opposite direction. All of you are walking at a normal, gentle pace and it looks like a usual day.

Suddenly, a bell rings and everyone (except you, of course) go wild. They start moving in unpredictable patterns in whichever direction they think of. Some of them even run and jump. The road has become a dangerous place.

In such a situation, what will you do? Remember that you are still not going wild and can think and decide!

When everyone around us is acting in a strange way, we needn't (and shouldn't) join them. In fact, that's the time we should be extremely careful because irrespective of what we do, someone else can cause damage to us. So, we should act in such a way that we protect ourselves and others, if possible.

A similar responsible thought process should come to our mind whenever we see trends around us. If the majority of the people act in a certain manner, that doesn't mean they are right. In fact, if those people are acting without thinking, it is better we break the chain and think before we act. This might help us and others too, who might look at our behaviour and understand that there is a different way to do things and they don't have to follow the majority all the time.

'The less the prudence with which others conduct their affairs, the greater the prudence with which we must conduct our own', says Warren Buffett. This means, when others are not being sensible or careful and taking unnecessary risks, we should pause and watch. We should be extremely careful and trust data and our analysis before proceeding.

On another occasion, he conveyed a similar message using a casino analogy, "You are dealing with a lot of silly people in the marketplace. It's like a great big casino and everyone else is boozing. If you can stick to Pepsi, you should be OK."

Being prudent is always a great skill to master. However, Warren's comments ask us to also observe whether others around us, especially our industry peers, are being prudent or not. When the majority of them are being less prudent, we should bear the responsibility and act with extreme caution, educating everyone about the benefits of such a thought process. It helps us stay on the right course while helping others.

☑ **The Warren Lesson:** ***If others are not prudent, we should be more prudent in our actions.***

❑

43

A Successful Day

What is the definition of a successful day?

Some people tie the success of a day with the tasks completed or the goals achieved during the day. For example, they might have closed a large sales deal or written a fantastic program to solve a major customer problem. These would make them feel very happy and proud when they go to sleep that night.

However, there is a flip side to this thought process. If you consider achievements as the mandatory requirement for a day to be successful, a lack of achievements or the presence of a mistake will immediately make it a "day of failure". Such a black and white approach can put tremendous pressure on us as we will be seeking achievements every day, becoming more and more anxious if we can't find something. If everyone thinks like this, the work environment can become a continuous race where only a few can win on any given day.

Warren Buffett gives us a different yardstick to measure a successful day: being smarter at the end of the day than at the beginning of the day. If every day can be like this, we will grow in any field.

Compared to the race to achieve things continuously, this is a refreshing change and gives us a learning mindset. We may start with no knowledge or limited knowledge and follow this process every day to become a little bit smarter and all those add up to give us big gains.

For example, an employee or a manager or an entrepreneur does various activities throughout the day, meets people, gets feedback, reads articles, watches training videos and so on. If he/she constantly looks for learning opportunities in all these interactions, every day will add something or other to his/her skillset. Even a complex topic can be learnt bit by bit by following such an approach.

This is where habits become very important. If we can form a habit of continuously learning things and connecting the dots, we can learn anything and everything and stay ahead of others without participating in a daily race. We will have more happy and successful days and that will contribute to our mental health as well.

☑ **The Warren Lesson:** ***Become smarter at the end of the day than at the beginning of the day.***

❑

44

The Win-Win Deal

Every financial transaction has two parts: a credit and a debit. A credit entry represents a transfer of value from an account and a debit entry represents a transfer of value to an account. This means each transaction transfers value from a credited account to a debited account.

In common terms, this means that every transaction involves someone losing value and someone else gaining value. For example, if you pay $10 to a shopkeeper, your account loses $10 and the shopkeeper's account gains $10.

We can see such transfers of value in various real-life scenarios as well. For example, when someone joins a company, they agree to transfer a value (their experience and expertise) to the company they are joining. In return, the company agrees to transfer a value (their salary and other benefits) to them.

Even when two companies or individuals are discussing a possible deal, the question of transfer of value applies. Both parties ask the important question, "What's in it for me?", in other words, "What will you (the other party) transfer to me?" If both parties can answer this question satisfactorily, there is a balance and they agree on a deal. Else, one of the parties may walk away from the deal because it is one-sided.

"Try to come up with deals that are good for both sides", says Warren Buffett. "Both sides should walk away thinking they won."

This means Party A should give something that Party B needs and vice versa. This makes both of them feel good about the transfer of value and a deal is signed.

Even individuals can use this advice from Warren effectively. When we need something from others, we can try to create this balance by offering a transfer of something of equal value immediately or in the near future. This makes it likely that they agree to give us what we need now. A similar question can be asked when others need something from us, making sure that the deal is good for both us and them.

☑ **The Warren Lesson: *Deals should be good for both sides.***

❑

45

Value of Hard Work

When someone wants to write a book, he/she starts by doing deep research on the topic. They may read hundreds of thousands of pages of written material, meet experts in that domain or those who have first-hand experience working with the subject, analyse the available data and related research to connect the dots so that they can perfect their message, and take extensive notes. All these need to be done even before the first word can be written.

Many months or years later, someone might pick this book from a shelf and read it casually. They may not even realise that the author went through all these hardships to get this work released. But, it remains a fact and will be the guiding principle for others who may want to write books in the future. There are no shortcuts to hard work.

This is not restricted to books and authors. Every field has its own version of hard work necessary to produce something meaningful. This is especially true for those who are entering those fields as freshers; they may have to consume a lot of information before they can use all that knowledge to make the right decisions.

When Warren Buffett was getting introduced to the world of share market and stocks, he realised that no one is going to tell him the right thing to buy. In fact, such a piece of knowledge was not readily available anywhere. Hence, he figured out that he needs to go where the raw data is and start processing it however large it might be.

Warren says that during this time he was reading bulky manuals running hundreds of pages. He was reading them to find out more details about the potential items he could buy and used those details to make those decisions. This is how he spotted his early opportunities.

When we face large challenges, the sheer volume of work might overwhelm us. During those difficult times, we need to remember that if we work hard enough, we will find something of value. It may be searching for a needle in a haystack, but that's the only way we can progress and looking at the volume and getting surprised is not going to take us anywhere. Get started and get going, you will find your way.

☑ **The Warren Lesson: *Work hard, find your path.***

❑

46

The Right Seed

Which one is more important: the destination or the path taken to reach there?

For example, a student scoring top marks and a sales representative winning a big deal have achieved great feats. But, if they used unfair means such as copying or bribing to get there, suddenly their achievements look flat. Even if no one knows the wrong methods employed by the student or the sales representative, it is against the universal laws.

Integrity is an essential element in any individual or organisation. Warren Buffett explains it beautifully, "Don't cut corners. You won't like it when you look back."

This reminds us of the proverbial, "answering the person in the mirror". He/she always knows that we have cut a corner and won't let us forget that. The world may praise us for our achievements, but this thought or knowledge that we have taken the wrong route to get there will continuously make us feel bad which won't be worth the effort.

In today's competitive world, success is respected and sometimes, means to achieve the same are ignored. Students are encouraged by others, even by some teachers and parents, to take shortcuts when they see them so that they can achieve greater things faster. Even if they feel bad about it, they are shown examples of others taking similar shortcuts and messages such as 'in the larger scheme of things, these shortcuts are nothing' try to comfort them.

If someone goes against this advice and firmly refuses to take a shortcut, they are immediately labelled as impractical. Slowly and steadily, society seems to take a view that winning matters, not the methods. We are trying to normalise wrong-doings as long as the result is favourable.

Mahatma Gandhi calls means as seeds and ends (results) as trees. Just like there is a strong connection between seeds and the trees that come out of them, means are linked to the end. As a poisonous seed will only give a poisonous tree, you can't achieve a good win with bad means. We need to remember this always, especially when faced with tough situations that present opportunities to take a shortcut. They are the times we should firmly say "No". This is not because we are afraid of someone finding it or putting us in jail, but because it is the right thing to do.

☑ ***The Warren Lesson: Don't cut corners. You won't like it when you look back.***

❑

47

Talk and Action

"Talk is cheap", they say. This means anyone can lecture about the great things they are going to do or the wonderful principles they are going to follow. But, it is harder to put them into action. Until this is done, there is no value to all the things you say.

For example, a businessperson may say, "I will never cheat my customers or the government and I will always go by the rulebooks, even if it results in a loss to me." This tall talk about integrity is true only if he/she follows it in every situation.

What will happen if one doesn't really follow what he/she says?

The world is listening and watching. It attaches limited value to things people say, but tremendous value to things people do. If someone says something and does something else, it immediately results in a loss of reputation. On the flip side, those whose words and actions are in line get great respect.

This is especially true for parents. If they advise their children to do certain things and they themselves don't follow them, their children will never respect or follow them in this aspect. When they stop advising and start living the life they want their children to adapt, immediately they see their children following them, without the need for a single word of advice.

"It is not what you say, but what you do", says Warren Buffett. Instead of wasting words in describing the right behaviour, one can start following it or doing it, which is easier for others to follow. This applies not just to kids, but to everyone.

For example, if managers want their staff to prepare reports in a certain way, paying special attention to careful verification of facts and data, they can actually use the same method to write a few reports on their own. All their staff, especially those who want to improve and grow, will watch this and start following it. This is better than a lecture on how to write an effective report.

☑ ***The Warren Lesson: Instead of telling others what to do or how to do it, start doing it the right way and they will watch and follow.***

❑

48

The Orangutan Effect

Warren Buffett wants to be remembered as a good teacher.

Yes, you read it right. When such a question was asked to him, he mentioned that he wants to be remembered not as a good investor, not as a good corporate leader, not as a good philanthropist, not as a good family person, but as a good teacher. While his other roles mentioned here are important and he respects his contributions in those roles, Warren wants to excel as a teacher so that he can help others grow and succeed.

Agreed, Warren is not a traditional teacher. He doesn't go to a university, lecture children or adults on various subjects, give them tests, correct their test papers or grade them. But, he has met hundreds of students from various educational institutes and taught them his life lessons. Hundreds of thousands of people have attended his sessions, read his articles and letters and learnt the art of investing and other topics. From this perspective, he is a great teacher.

Warren says that in addition to the benefits his students get from him, he too gets benefited from teaching. "Like writing, [Teaching has] helped me develop and clarify my own thoughts."

In other words, when we agree to teach something to others, we need to gather our thoughts, fine-tune them, identify and fill the gaps, read the counterarguments, analyse them well to understand the overall picture. All these add clarity and we understand the topic better even before we start teaching.

Warren's partner Charlie calls this the Orangutan Effect. Let us assume you are sitting with an Orangutan and trying to teach it some complex science lesson. The Orangutan may not learn anything from your teaching. But, your act of teaching it something will make you understand that topic better.

That's why we should eagerly grab any opportunity to teach any topic to anyone. While it might benefit others, it will definitely benefit us by giving more clarity on that topic. If we keep doing it, our thinking improves, the way we present facts improves and we become better communicators.

☑ **The Warren Lesson:** ***Teach Others; It will help you too.***

❑

49

Good Decisions and Bad Decisions

Life gives us numerous opportunities for decision making every day. We keep making small, medium and large decisions on a regular basis which take us on different paths. This means that taking right decisions on a consistent basis can set us up for success.

Hence, decision-making skills are seen as a strength for any leader. They are trained to identify various options, weigh their pros and cons, analyse them and make a decision objectively. Some leaders even maintain a decision journal that records all the situations, their context, information considered, decision made, its eventual result and retrospective feedback on whether the decision was right or wrong. A regular review of this journal can help them make better decisions by using the power of experience.

There are many leaders who are expert decision-makers. But, even they can't claim all their decisions were right. It is a continuous learning process and their skills improve over time.

While we can feel happy about our good decisions, Warren Buffett advises us to give a careful look at our poor decisions regularly.

"Knowing your poor decisions and knowing why they were poor is part of good decision-making."

For example, let us say you are responsible for deciding which products need to be stocked in your company warehouse and their respective quantities. A new product has emerged in the market and its manufacturer asks you to stock it in a good quantity so that you can fulfil the customer demand. But, you feel it is not mature enough to deserve a place in your expensive warehouse space. So, you decide not to stock it for the current month and make a mental note to relook at this product next month.

But, during that month, the product becomes a big hit among consumers and stores are asking for it in huge numbers. Unfortunately, you don't have the stock and it results in a big opportunity loss for your organisation.

Agreed, this is a bad decision. But, it won't make you a bad decision-maker. In the same month, you might have made 99 other good decisions that resulted in millions of dollars of additional revenue for your company. However, those 99 decisions can't teach you lessons that this 1 decision can. By carefully analysing it and by asking tough questions such as "why did I feel this product won't have high demand?", "what other information I could've reviewed before arriving at a conclusion like this?" etc. you can learn a lot and avoid a similar mistake in future.

Hence, when it comes to teaching us lessons, bad decisions are our best pals, including the bad decisions of others.

☑ **The Warren Lesson:** ***Look at your bad decisions; learn from them; it helps you make good decisions.***

❑

50

The "Because" Test

Very often, people buy stocks because of inputs from others. These might be their neighbours or colleagues or relatives or friends, who may not even be stock market experts. But still, people listen and respect their inputs mainly because many of them lack the ability to do their own analysis about a company. Hence, listening to others and hoping for the best looks like the right thing to do.

Warren Buffett argues that buying a part of a business is a serious decision and one should do it only after careful analysis. He encourages people to take a piece of paper and write a statement like this: "I am buying the stocks of XYZ company at this price because….."

Imagine you are writing a similar statement for your grocery purchases. It is very easy to write it because we know why we are buying milk or fruit juice at a certain price. The same logic should apply to stocks as well and "my friend asked me to buy" can't be that reason.

Even if we don't invest in stocks, Warren's advice can still be used because we do various things on a regular basis and not all of them are based on a clear thinking process. Taking a minute to form a sentence such as "I am doing X because…", will help us ensure that we have a strong reason for doing those things. This can make us avoid unreasonable activities.

For example, let us say you are planning a meeting for 1 hour and inviting four people. You can take a piece of paper (or open a text file on your computer) and answer questions such as these: Do we really need this meeting? Can't this be resolved in an Email or a phone call? Why 1 hour? Can't this be discussed in 30 minutes? What about 15 minutes? Why do you need these four people in the meeting? Are they the right people? Are you missing anyone? Can it be done with less number of people? Why should this meeting happen this week? Can't it be moved to next week? What decisions do you expect to take in this meeting? What if this meeting is postponed for a month?

The "because" word in Warren Buffett's statement looks small. But, it opens a big set of questions and answering them is not easy. However, if we learn to answer them for everything we do and pass the "Because" Test, we are more likely to focus on the right things and drop the weak, ambiguous things.

☑ **The Warren Lesson:** ***Why are you doing this? List down your reasons; make sure they are strong reasons.***

❑

51

Average Office, Amazing Portfolio!

Major league games get great media attention. People watch them regularly and follow their favourite teams and players. From stadium ticket sales to sponsorships to live telecast fees, these events bring a lot of money to the respective leagues.

Compared to these, Minor league games are not very popular. But, you still see the same passion, if not more, in the players. Why?

The first reason is that they love the game and want to play it well no matter whether it is a major league or minor league. In fact, a good player will show his/her skills even if it is a practice game not watched by anyone.

But, there is a second reason which makes minor league games interesting: they help junior players build a record of achievement. This acts as proof of their skills and consistency and can become their entry ticket for the major league selection.

Similar examples can be found in other fields also. A programmer can join an online coding challenge and build a repository of great works. Later, when he/she attends an interview, this repository can be used as proof of all the good work they have done in their field.

"I operated out of a small set-up for years", says Warren Buffett. "It was not set up to impress people. My numbers impressed people and that's how money came in. If you are a new person, try to get an auditable record of your achievement."

When we start operating in a field, we won't need a flashy office or a fancy website. Many freelancers start with their own home office and a free email address. However, they invest in building a great portfolio, which Warren calls an auditable record of achievements, so that they can use this as the real set-up which impresses future clients.

For example, a designer might work out of a small desk in her kitchen. But, if she has 20 high-quality designs made for a variety of clients and requirements, it can be used as the basis for inviting future work from her clients and prospects. The world will respect talent and we need to make sure we collect the proof of our talent in one place and present it right.

☑ **The Warren Lesson:** ***Build an auditable record of your achievements.***

❑

52

Lunch with Warren

In 2007, Value Investor Mohnish Pabrai paid $650,000 for an opportunity to have lunch with Warren Buffett and Charlie Munger. The proceeds went to charity and Mohnish had a rare opportunity to discuss with and learn from these great investors.

When Mohnish spoke to author Morgan Housel about his lunch with Warren, he told that Warren put him at ease, making him think he is having lunch with his grandfather. This is a great gesture. But, Warren didn't stop there. He went ahead and gave a wonderful experience to Mohnish by answering his questions in a manner that gave him tremendous learning. Why?

Mohnish feels this is because Warren understood that this lunch was very important to the other person at the table. They have paid a huge sum of money not for the food items that are offered, but for the opportunity to speak to him personally. Agreed, the money goes to a good cause. But still, they will expect to get some value out of lunch with Warren. Hence, Warren wanted to ensure that the guest doesn't feel disappointed about the conversation.

This incident not only demonstrates Warren's humility but also shows his great skill in seeing every interaction from the other person's view as well. Being a celebrity, he may have many items on his calendar, but still, he didn't treat this lunch as a usual transaction. He ensured providing the best value to the other party.

As our daily calendars are full of meetings and discussions, we tend to move from one conversation to another with minimal preparation and try to manage depending on the situation. While this may be seen as a smart hack, it doesn't do justice to other participants in the meeting for whom it may be a very important meeting and they may expect us to be there with deserving preparation. When we see meetings from this perspective, we won't see our calendars as a collection of 30-minute slots to be used for all sorts of meetings. We will learn to respect other participants and spend time on our preparation, we will be fully present (instead of "multitasking" on an e-mail or Document), we will listen carefully, ask the right questions, provide value in our responses and ensure the other participants have a great experience.

But, what if we are very busy and don't have the time to prepare well or to be present fully?

In that case, we should be upfront in asking for more time, stating the reason for the same. It is better to be well prepared and fully present than provide a less than perfect experience to other participants. They deserve better.

☑ **The Warren Lesson:** ***Give the best value and best experience to the other person at the table.***

❑

53

Difficult Problems don't Need Difficult Solutions

Once upon a time, a soap company had a big problem: some of their soap boxes were empty which frustrated their customers. They felt cheated and complained loudly, which hurt the brand's reputation.

Hence, engineers working in that soap company gathered for a discussion, "how can we find those empty boxes and remove them before they reach stores?"

Within the next 30 minutes, the whiteboard in the meeting room was filled with diagrams. More than twenty solutions were captured. They involved electronic scanners, accurate weighing machines, robots and artificial intelligence software.

At that time, a junior staff member asked casually. "Instead of all these complex solutions, why not install a large fan in the conveyor belt which sends our soapboxes to the outside world? If a box is empty, it will be removed from the conveyor belt by the wind from the fan."

This imaginary story teaches us a valuable lesson: complex problems don't need complex solutions. Sometimes, even simple things can help us resolve complex issues. As Warren Buffett says,

"You are awarded no points in business endeavours for the degree of difficulty."

That doesn't mean we will always get a simple solution to any problem. We should expect a mix of solutions. Some of those solutions could be so simple and easy that anybody can understand and even implement them. However, a few other solutions will be in a medium or large complexity/difficult level which might need a deeper understanding of the context and technologies before we can move towards a solution. All these solutions need to be analysed before the best one is selected. Sometimes, the best solution could even be a combination of two or more solutions of various complexity levels.

While doing this solution analysis, some of us have a bias towards complex solutions (and a negative bias towards simple solutions). We somehow feel complex problems need complex solutions and hence look down on solutions that might be too simple. In reality, "degree of difficulty" or "complexity" is not an important part of such decision making. As long as the solution solves the problem well, it should be adapted. As every computer user might know, even the most complex problems can be solved by closing and reopening a window!

Hence, when we are analysing possible solutions to a problem, we need to remove the bias towards complex or difficult solutions and focus entirely on solving the problem. Hard work is good, but if some easy work solves the issue, who would say no to it?

☑ ***The Warren Lesson: There are no points in business endeavours for "degree of difficulty".***

❑

54

The Need for Immediate Help

A friend calls you with an urgent request, "Hey Buddy, one of my business decisions flopped and I need to do some damage control. Can you help me with this?"

"Sure, I will be happy to do that", you reply enthusiastically. "Let us meet over a cup of coffee and discuss it. I am sure we can sort the problem out and you will be back to normalcy soon."

Within a few hours, you both meet in a cafe and your friend explains his decision and its current state. He proposes the next steps he has identified and asks for your inputs and help.

Now, your friend has acknowledged his error and made it clear that he is expecting your views and support on the next step. Instead of that, if you start with strong criticism on why he shouldn't have taken that business decision in the first place, how will he feel?

Unfortunately, many of us make this mistake when working with people who are in desperate need of support. We like pointing out their mistakes (which they might have realised by now) instead of focusing on the next steps. This puts them in a disadvantaged position to correct the error which has happened.

Notice that no one is denying their error. A good friend or guide will point it to them and help them avoid similar mistakes in future.

However, there is a time and place for it. When there is damage control to be done to ensure normalcy, discussing the past is not the optimal use of our time.

Warren Buffett uses the example of someone ill to describe this process. At that time, the expectation is not to criticise them for not following healthy habits or for not testing earlier. We should only look ahead to the treatment required to cure them.

Even when thinking in that direction, Warren advises us not to worry or argue too much about the accurate treatment. Instead, we should focus on what needs to be done immediately with the best information and resources in our hands. As we start this first aid, slowly more data emerges and we can move towards the right solution.

After the issue is resolved and the person in front of you can smile comfortably, you can gently remind them about some of their earlier wrong choices and ensure that they have learnt their lesson. They are more likely to listen to you now because they are not anxious about the issue and can understand and take action with a clear mind.

☑ **The Warren Lesson:** ***When someone has a problem, instead of criticising them or worrying about the right solution, get to the best action according to what you know at that time.***

❑

55

Earning and Spending

Every person on earth does a balancing act of income and expenses almost daily. They do some work or run a business and earn money which acts as their money input. On the flip side, they have bills to pay, items to buy and services to use which cost money. These act as their money output. Depending on which one is higher and by what amount, they may save some money or they may have to borrow some money from others.

When people don't realise the importance and value of saving, they tend to spend whatever they earn and live paycheck to paycheck. Even if their salary or income increases, they tend to increase their spending and still manage to live paycheck to paycheck. The increased income is seen as a licence to spend more and enjoy more.

Warren Buffett encourages people to spend only when necessary, even when they have a lot of money. This can be done by carefully analysing our spending, ensuring that each expense is justified for both its purpose (is this required?) and the amount (is this the right amount to spend?).

We can see many examples of this habit in Warren's life itself. While other rich people live in large mansions with fancy facilities, he is famous for living in the same house for decades. His children attended normal schools attended by other kids in the neighbourhood. Just because Warren had money, he didn't throw it on unnecessary stuff.

Spending wisely reduces our expenses and allows us to save more. These savings can then be invested in something right, like what Warren did. In addition, it also provides us with a useful life skill: being conscious about where our money goes. Those who don't have this skill will constantly complain about losing everything they earn and won't even realise that they are the prime reasons for this issue. Even if their income doubles or triples, they will still have the same problem because they automatically increase their expenses in the same ratio. On the other hand, those who spend wisely will watch their expenses and will be able to adjust them as per the need.

☑ **The Warren Lesson: *Spend Wisely.***

❑

56

Facing Pain

A driver in a new city misses spotting a red light at a traffic signal. Only after jumping the signal does he realise his mistake and say, "Oops! I am in trouble."

He is a good citizen and doesn't want to run away from his mistake. So, he pulls over to the side of the road and waits for someone to come and give him a ticket. He mentally prepares himself to seek an apology and pay the necessary fine.

But, surprisingly, nothing of that sort happens. Even after many minutes of waiting, no one comes over and gives him a ticket. So, he moves away from the place, full of guilt.

A few days later, he faces a similar situation. Once again, no one noticed and no one blamed him for the error. Next month, the same pattern repeats once again and he gets away from yet another traffic violation ticket.

Now, imagine what impact this will have on that driver's mindset towards respecting traffic rules. He has made three mistakes already and got away from them. So, he is likely to press his luck more and make more such mistakes. On the contrary, if he was punished for his first offence itself, he would've become extra careful in his driving and would've followed all traffic rules dutifully.

Warren Buffett reminds us that such behavioural patterns can be observed even in our offices. When we make a stupid decision and no one notices or tells us that we could've done something better, we tend to underestimate the effect of such stupid decisions. Instead, if we feel some pain (of hearing tough feedback or even a few harsh words from our superior) immediately after the stupid decision, we are likely to use it as a lesson to improve our future decisions.

Hence, our attitude about feedback should change dramatically: hearing 'you are doing good' from everyone all the time is not necessarily good news and hearing 'you did something really stupid' is not necessarily bad news. In fact, the pain we feel ourselves, or the pain which is given by others to us for doing something wrong acts as an effective guide in guiding our future decisions in the right way.

☑ **The Warren Lesson:** ***When you make a bad decision, face the tough feedback, feel the pain and use it to improve your future decisions.***

❑

57

Success, Guaranteed!

A company can win a customer's business in many ways: providing a high-quality product or service, keeping their price competitive, offering world-class support, advertising in the right channels, reaching out to the customer in their own spaces, being environmentally responsible and so on. These are great techniques and are likely to help the company succeed. But, there is another way that combines the power of all these and almost guarantees its success: deserving the customer's business.

GEICO, one of the major companies in Warren Buffett's empire, has a long history. It has served multiple generations of people and many things about this company have changed over time: leaders, managers, products, sales channels, support channels, marketing channels, advertising platforms, payment methods and so on. But, Warren states that its core goal has remained unchanged: saving Americans' substantial money on their purchase of auto insurance. By doing this, they deserve the customer's business and make it a very simple and straightforward choice for them. By focusing on this objective, GEICO grew its market share and became one of America's largest auto insurers.

When a product deserves the customer's business, its makers don't have to explicitly convince them about it. There won't be any need for fancy marketing literature listing down the product's features and benefits; comparison charts showing its superiority against competitors won't be necessary. Even if these materials exist, the customer will simply say, "I am already convinced because you deserve my business."

For many, this may look like an unbelievable, unachievable dream. But, it is possible. History is rich with examples of many companies building such products and customers welcoming them with open arms giving their unconditional loyalty. This magic happened because those companies focussed entirely on their customers. They understood their customers' needs, pain points, expectations and feelings and built something which takes care of these and becomes an automatic choice for customers.

This doesn't mean those companies neglected other factors in product/service development. They are important too; but addressing the customers' problems and giving them a satisfactory solution should be their core objective. When a product or a service is made with such care and love, it shows and customers will understand it readily!

☑ **The Warren Lesson:** ***Build something that deserves the customer's business.***

❑

58

Heroes won't Let you Down

Who was your childhood hero (or heroine)? What about school days? College days? Early career? Now?

These heroes and role models may not be the same people. As we grow, our interests change, our definitions of success and achievement change, we start looking at nuances that we missed earlier and these changes help us look up to different people at different ages and it is quite normal.

Also, these heroes needn't be big achievers or people with special skills. They may be ordinary individuals whom we respect due to various reasons; they may be people whom we want to become because we admire certain great qualities in them.

"Having the right heroes will help you manage tough times in life", says Warren Buffett. "If you tell me who your heroes are, I can tell you what you will become to some extent."

Warren had some great heroes in his own life: his dad, his wife and his professor Benjamin Graham. He feels these terrific heroes never let him down throughout his life and that took him a long way, especially when facing tough times in life.

This is where obsessing over a few people we like becomes a strength. We may read books about them, hear stories from others, we may read their own works and understand how they think, we may even be lucky enough to speak to them and learn from them directly. All of these form a picture in our mind which acts as a guideline whenever we face issues. We don't have to compare ourselves with people around us, who may be good folks, but work-in-progress like us! A simple question like, "how will my hero face this situation? what will he/she do?" can help us think straight and arrive at a better decision. Even if that hero or role model lived a few centuries back, he/she is still able to guide us and help us become better people.

☑ **The Warren Lesson: *Having heroes helps you!***

❑

59

Use the Available Interstate

Until a few decades back, libraries were the largest sources of knowledge. If someone wanted to know about a topic, he/she had to go to the local library and patiently go through many books on that subject. It took a lot of time, but there were no other better options.

Today, this problem is solved with the help of technology. A student can access all the books, videos and audios about almost any subject with a few clicks online. Reading every book, every chapter, every paragraph, every line won't be necessary as a quick search will give them the information they need. They can even directly reach out to experts in that field from all over the globe and clarify their doubts without leaving the comforts of their homes.

Now, if a modern student refuses to use all these facilities and insists that he/she would research using the good old library method only, will it be the right use of his/her time? If some materials are not available online, they can always use an older method. In all other situations, they should use the available new technologies so that the saved time can be used for some other useful purpose.

Warren Buffett uses the analogy of a country road and an interstate road to explain this difference. If our current location and the destination are connected using a modern interstate road, we wouldn't be using an old country road to reach the same destination. Using the modern road saves us time, energy and fuel.

However, all these savings are possible only if we are aware that such an interstate road exists. Else, we will still be using the old, inefficient road. Similarly, we should keep our eyes and ears open to understand the latest and modern developments in our field and equip ourselves with the right skills as necessary. This gives us the best chance to use those advancements and get things done in a faster, efficient manner.

For example, there may be an online forum where experts from our domain usually discuss interesting topics. If we are aware of the existence of such a forum, we can read those conversations regularly and improve our knowledge. In addition, if we have a question or a doubt, it can be posted there for a quick and detailed response. This will be more efficient than posting the same question on Facebook and hoping that some expert would notice that and answer our question. We will know the presence of such forums and other tools only if we keep ourselves updated about the latest happenings in our field.

☑ **The Warren Lesson:** ***Use the most efficient tool available to perform any activity.***

60

Focus on Positivity

Certain online and mobile apps allow us to capture our mood on a regular basis. You can do it daily or every few hours or even every hour. Idea is to capture how your mood changes over a period of time, analyse it and determine corrective actions, if any.

Let us say someone uses one such app for a few weeks to dutifully record all his/her emotions. Later, he/she looks at the dashboard to understand the trend or pattern. It gives him/her a shocking truth: you are feeling negative most of the time.

More than the shock, he/she is surprised because "I never considered myself as a negative person. Of course, I feel down now and then; but didn't realise that it is affecting me so much."

This situation might look simple or amusing to some. But, it needs to be understood and addressed before it becomes a larger issue. They should focus on understanding various reasons that can cause this problem and handle them with the help of a professional, if required.

For example, they may be holding grudges against others which they may not even remember, but they stay deep inside and make them feel negative whenever they see those other people or related triggers. Similarly, they may feel negative things and have negative thoughts about how things will happen, "What if this fails?", "What if that doesn't work?"

Sometimes people around them may have continuous negative thoughts and spread negativity to others. In those cases, even if someone is usually optimistic about life, these thoughts will come and bother them unknowingly.

Warren Buffett advises us not to keep grudges or negative feelings about any people. He also encourages thinking of positive things and working with positive people. While this looks like an old styled solution, he assures us that it works.

In many interviews and letters, Warren continuously talks about the people he works with and how great they are. Whether it is professional associates or personal friends, he likes to spend time with positive people and it keeps him energised.

This doesn't mean we shouldn't think of risks or take necessary steps to mitigate them. While doing so, we should remember that thinking of these risks and mitigations early puts us in a better position to complete the task at hand successfully. Having a healthy environment where the focus is on progress, growth and making things happen shifts the spotlight from the possible negativity and allows us to stay happy.

People generally give a lot of importance to physical health and staying fit. But, mental health doesn't get the attention it deserves. Feeling good and positive about work and life in general is a non-negotiable aspect we all deserve.

☑ **The Warren Lesson:** ***Avoid holding grudges or negative feelings; think positively; work with positive people.***

❑

61

The Pricing Power

Pricing a product or service right is an important skill. It depends on various factors such as the raw materials used to manufacture the product, cost of producing each unit, profit margin and so on. After considering all these, the company makes a pricing decision and regularly reviews it to ensure they stay competitive while continuing to make money.

Hence, when a product's price is increased, it can't be attributed to the company's greed by default. Sometimes, greed or making more money can be the reason for such decisions. But they are rare cases and companies usually increase the price because other input parameters have changed. They normally resort to this as the last option and try to avoid it as much as possible. When it becomes inevitable, they go for it with an apologetic mindset, "Dear Customer, we tried to avoid this as much as we could. But, now we should increase our prices. We understand this is inconvenient for you. But, we have no other option. Please understand and cooperate. We value your business."

This message shows the humble attitude with which companies approach a price increase because customers' reactions to it can make or break a company. Sometimes, they accept the price increase and continue to be loyal to the company. Some other times, they reject the price increase and move to a competitor who offers something similar at a lesser price. Whether they continue to stick around or jump depends on various factors such as product quality, how important or necessary is its need, the quality of competitors, the gap between the new price and the competitors' price and the corresponding quality gap, if any. Customers think about all these before making their final call. If customers do that analysis and accept your price increase, it indicates that your company has something called "Pricing Power", which means, you have the power to determine the right price for your product, not others.

"The single most important decision in evaluating a business is pricing power", says Warren Buffett. "If you've got the power to raise prices without losing business to a competitor, you've got a very good business. If you have to say a prayer before raising the price, then you've got a terrible business."

We must remember that the decision always lies with the customer. But, we have many factors in our hand which can be used to control their decision: building a world-class product, making it rightly priced and increasing the price only when necessary, being so ahead of other competitors that customers won't even consider them as alternatives, creating a loyal fan following etc. These are the raw materials that give us the Pricing Power and the success.

This can apply to individuals as well. When someone interviewing for a job can show all the required skills, but can't command the right salary, it shows a lack of Pricing Power. They should do a self retrospect and understand what it takes for them to get the salary they deserve and fill those gaps. Being able to control their own price is an ultimate power that differentiates great companies/people from others.

☑ **The Warren Lesson:** ***Do you have the power to price your product right? If not, what can you do to acquire that power?***

❑

62

The Game of Liked and Disliked Qualities

Sometimes, Warren Buffett plays an interesting life game with his audience: he asks them to take a sheet of paper, draw a vertical line and split it into two parts. Then, they should think about people they know and list down all the qualities they like in those people on the left side of the paper. They should repeat the same process for the qualities they dislike in those people and write them on the right side of the paper. Finally, he asks them to analyse both the lists and see if any patterns are emerging.

For example, on the left side, we may have qualities such as hard work, humility, eagerness to learn and so on. The right side may be filled with qualities such as anger, not being able to complete things on time, disrespect to others etc.

Warren's theory is that the qualities on the left side (those we like in others) are not difficult to get. It won't have items like scoring 99% in every exam or being able to run a 100 metre race in 9 seconds or being the most beautiful person in the office. The real things we like in others are qualities that are achievable to anyone and everyone if they want them and try sincerely.

Similarly, the qualities on the right side are not things people can't get rid of. They are not must-have qualities. If someone has those qualities and wants to remove them, they can do it with practice.

When we admire certain qualities in people and know that we can have them too, why not make an attempt? When we dislike certain qualities in people and know that we too can get rid of them, why not make an attempt? A combination of these will make us much better than where we are today and doing this continuously will help us mature, grow and become the best we can be.

☑ **The Warren Lesson:** ***Think about the qualities you like or dislike in others. Then, compare those qualities with what you have and don't have. Such an analysis helps you improve and grow.***

❑

63

Compounding Value of Learning

Constantly educating ourselves is an important skill today. As the world around us moves and changes, new things evolve and we need to unlearn and relearn so that we can make use of the new opportunities that emerge. People who are rigid about their past learnings score less when compared to those who are flexible in their approach.

This means that education doesn't have a full stop. You can't throw away books after you graduate from school and college. In your work life or entrepreneurial life, no one may publish a syllabus and give you a set of reference books to read. Instead, you decide your subjects and lessons on your own, by careful observation of your field and the trends. Then you can use a combination of books, videos, podcasts, talking to experts, working on new domains etc. to learn. Every professional should set aside certain hours for their self or guided learning.

But, how to make the best use of this time? How to determine the right things to learn that provide us maximum value?

Warren Buffett recommends that we start learning early (at a young age) to ensure the knowledge has an opportunity to compound over a long period of time. Hence, we should invest in learning things that have long term value and have the potential to compound.

For example, let us say a person spends 200 hours learning a specific programming language or a business tool. They are able to make the best use of their learning and get some immediate benefits. But, two years later, this language or tool becomes obsolete. No one in the market uses it or the original company which made it shuts it down. In this case, they have to restart the learning process again by focusing on a newer language or tool which is the market's favourite at that time. As this process repeats every few years, there is hardly any opportunity for their learning to compound and give multifold benefits.

Instead, let us say the same person spent 150 hours learning the basics of programming, logical thinking, high-level design, low-level design, optimised performance, etc. and only 50 hours on the programming language-specific details. The first part of their learning is going to compound for decades as those basics don't change very often. They can simply relearn programming language-specific topics every few years and use the solid basic understanding as the basis for their growth.

Hence, continuous learning is important; continuous learning of things that can compound over time is smart.

☑ ***The Warren Lesson: Invest in education early; Learn skills that can compound over time.***

❑

64

Win Some, Lose Some, then Win Some More

When kids play a game, every win makes them happy and every loss makes them unhappy. Depending on the age and maturity level of the kids, they may even start laughing or crying when they face these results.

Thankfully, adults who face similar successes and failures on a regular basis don't react like that. However, there is no denying that we feel happy when things go as planned and unhappy when they take a different direction. We may not express it, but the inner ups and downs are always there.

People in leadership roles face this problem almost every day. Whenever they think about a problem and make a decision to solve it, they do it with a lot of care and expect it to be the right one. But, only a certain percentage of their actions and decisions turn out to be right. This means, they face successes and failures all the time.

"If every decision is perfect, it won't be fun", says Warren Buffett. He uses the analogy of a golfer who manages to get every ball hit in the right place. It may make the player extremely happy. But will it be an interesting game? Viewers certainly won't enjoy it. Actually, after some time, the player himself/herself may not like it. A game is fun only if it has those ups, downs and dramatic turning points.

For example, think about the most interesting sports event you ever watched in person or on television. Chances are high that it won't be a game where your favourite team or player won every point. They would've faced failures here and there and pushed hard to succeed. Those successes are more satisfying to players as well as viewers because we all understand bad things happen and what we do to them differentiates average people from extraordinary people.

Hence, Warren feels failures or mistakes are part of the game and they shouldn't discourage us from moving on. Every error or wrong call teaches us something. Once the lesson is internalised, we should try to focus on the next steps. Later, when a similar situation emerges, this learning can be used. Hence, we shouldn't let failures discourage our progress. They actually make the game more interesting by giving us additional motivation to push for success.

☑ **The Warren Lesson:** ***If everything goes perfect, the game won't be fun. Enjoy the ups and downs and move on.***

65

My Luxury

How do you define Luxury?

For some, it is the number of houses one owns, the size of those houses, the number of workers attending to their needs, the number of cars, the number of foreign vacations, the ability to wear costly suits, send kids to foreign universities, donate to causes they believe in etc. A few others measure luxury with not having to work or not having to worry about how much money is there in their wallet or bank account.

While these are practical definitions of luxury, its dictionary definition goes like this: a state of great comfort or elegance, especially when involving great expense. Notice that the expense part comes later and the focus is entirely on comfort and elegance which may even be achieved at a lesser cost. This seems to suggest that we don't have to spend a lot to live a luxurious life.

Warren Buffett, one of the world's richest people, lives a simple life. He looks at others showing off their wealth and understands them. But, he feels it is not for him, "If it [Showing off wealth] makes them happy, it doesn't do anything for me."

Does this mean Warren doesn't live a luxurious life?

He does. Just that his definition of luxury is different. "I'm happy when I can spend every day doing things that I like to do. That's my luxury."

Of course, Warren is not against spending. He owns a private jet. Many of his companies and other companies where he has invested depend on people spending their money on various products and services. His letters to Berkshire Hathaway shareholders regularly request them to buy things from Berkshire Hathaway owned firms.

However, houses, jewellery, cars, private boats and hefty bank balances are only expressions or external indicators of wealth. If they make one happy, great. But, being able to do what one likes every day without any restrictions is an important result of being wealthy. If someone has all the money, things in the world and yet is forced to spend a certain number of hours in front of an office desk they don't like, they may not be living a luxurious life after all.

Another important lesson from Warren's quote is his emphasis on the "My" word. One person's definition of luxury may not match another person's definition and hence a blind copy of someone else's lifestyle is less likely to give us happiness. True happiness and the feeling of luxury which comes with it are unique to each individual and they should look for them within themselves.

☑ **The Warren Lesson:** ***Do what makes you happy; That's luxury.***

❑

66

The Unsalaried Employee

Do you know Warren Buffett once worked for zero salary?

It was before his Berkshire Hathaway days. He was managing money from many individuals (and all of his own funds) through a series of partnerships. Not one, not two, more than 10 partnerships. He didn't even have a secretary to run them. He was writing all the cheques, picking the right investments, getting personal delivery of all shares and so on. For all this hard work, he was not paid a salary. Instead, he was compensated if his partners secured returns above a threshold of 6%.

But, in a particular year, if their returns fall below 6%, Warren needs to take care of that shortfall against his share of future profits. Thankfully, Warren managed to get a "better than 6%" return every year and didn't face any such situation.

However, the strange policy of "you get paid only when you earn a decent return for everyone" would've made Warren a better analyser because his regular income and returns from his own investments in those partnerships are directly linked to his performance. Probably, that's where he learnt important lessons in not losing money and selecting the right investments which provide consistent returns.

Another instance where Warren agreed to work for almost no salary was when he worked under Benjamin Graham, one of his heroes. He didn't do it to learn something new from Benjamin Graham; instead, he wanted to be inspired by the master on a regular basis.

Sometimes, especially in the early part of our careers, we may be locked in a job that pushes us to a corner. Irrespective of whether others forced us to take those options or we willingly took them, they needn't be totally negative or useless experiences. In fact, some high-pressure environments teach us lessons that happy paths can't. We need to look at each situation and see what we can get from them. These learnings will come in handy when the tough road ends and our smooth journey begins.

☑ **The Warren Lesson:** ***Even tough situations have takeaways; learn from them.***

❑

67

I Don't Know!

When attending a job interview, one of the biggest fears in the minds of the job candidate is not knowing the answer to a question. They are hesitant to use the words "I don't know" because they can be seen as a direct reflection of their knowledge or talent. Hence, they conclude that the interviewers may reject them for not knowing an answer and wish for only those questions which they can answer comfortably.

Answering every question asked in an interview might be a great indication of someone's skills and knowledge. But, except for some rare, clearly defined topics, it is difficult, impractical and even impossible for someone to know all the answers. Even if someone manages to remember all the answers, it only proves that they have a great memory.

Practically speaking, even experts don't know all the answers. So, it is a wrong expectation in an interview setting. You should prepare well and try to get all the answers right, but having it as the mandatory expectation is unreasonable.

Hence, experts recommend that interviewees should remove the fear of 'not knowing an answer' and they should be willing to admit that they don't know the answer to some of the questions. Trying to avoid this and giving some fake answers to those questions may be more dangerous than simply saying, "Sorry, I don't know." As long as you don't repeat this for every question, this won't be seen as a personal weakness and in most cases, the interviewer will simply smile understandingly and move on to the next question.

This fear of saying "I don't know" extends beyond interview settings. When we work in a company or face media interviews or answer audience questions in a public forum or even when a neighbour's kid asks us a question, we are hesitant to admit that we don't know the answer. We believe it will make us lose face in front of all those people.

Contrary to popular belief, saying "I don't know" to a question for which you don't know the answer actually enhances your reputation as you are being transparent and honest. If it is an important detail that you should've known, gently apologise, promise that you will get back to them with the answer and genuinely research, find out the answer and close the loop by conveying it to the person who asked the question. This is a much better approach that will benefit you and the other person.

"Tough questions are fine", says Warren Buffett. "If we [Warren and his partner Charlie Munger] know the answer, we will try and respond. If we don't know the answer, we will say we don't know it."

If Warren and Charlie, seen as great experts in their domain, face tough questions now and then and say "I don't know", we all should take it as a licence and use it in genuine cases. As long as it is followed up with a quest for learning, admitting that we don't know an answer is not a weakness, but a strength.

☑ ***The Warren Lesson: If you don't know the answer to a question, admit it.***

❑

68

The Right Story

Bob Woodward, a famous journalist and author, became rich at a relatively young age. He once met Warren Buffett and asked for his advice on how to handle his money.

Warren used the terminologies from Bob's own field (journalism) to answer this question, "Assign yourself the right story, research, write and deliver it as per the timeline."

In a world full of stories, journalists can't write every story even if they want to. They need to look at the possible story leads, decide what makes them excited, assign it to themselves (or take assignments from senior journalists or editors) and start researching. Then they should read the right sources, speak to the right experts to get details about this story and perform fieldwork until they have all the required raw materials to write. Finally, they should write it and deliver it before the given time. This is a standard process in any newspaper or magazine.

Warren feels investing is just about assigning yourself the right story. If you want to invest in a particular asset class or in a particular company, you need to assign that story to yourself, do the required research, arrive at a decision and move on with the investment if it makes sense. Just like stories, there are too many investment possibilities and we need to pick the right story so that we make best use of our time.

Also, we need to understand that we are not capable of writing all the stories. There may be some topics for which Warren is not the right person to write. This is perfectly acceptable as long as there are other areas and topics which he can write about.

Warren's advice makes sense even in fields other than investing. Every task, every project, every program we take up, can be visualised as a story and we can go through to assign it to ourselves, research, write and deliver methodology. If the right stories are picked, we will be motivated to follow the remaining steps and over time, our repository of work will grow, resulting in our progress.

☑ **The Warren Lesson:** ***Assign yourself the right story and work on it.***

❑

69

Financial Support from Customers

One of the many things you need to start a business is capital. Some people use their personal savings to start their business; a few others borrow money for this purpose; it is also a common practice to get financial support from friends, family and coworkers and give them a share of the business.

Warren Buffett points out that Insurance companies typically get financial support from their customers. That is, customers prepay an amount (premium) for their coverage and the Insurance company has the advantage of using this money for its business development. Of course, they have a commitment to pay the customer or their dependents if and when the covered risk occurs. But, in general, the money is available for immediate use.

Not all businesses can enjoy such advance payments or financial support from their customers. But, there are industries where such practices exist which can be a great idea for newbies willing to enter the world of business.

For example, Joe Mansueto, founder of MorningStar Inc., started a publishing business precisely because of this advice from Warren.

As publishing companies collect subscription amounts from people in advance to provide their publications over a period of time, it acts as financial support coming directly from their customers. Joe mentions that this seemed a perfect option as he didn't have much capital when he started.

Another recent example is the advent of SaaS (Software as a Service) companies. These are built by passionate programmers who create a basic version, demonstrate it to the world, collect subscriptions from the customers and use it to build more features and grow. In fact, many of these companies provide a good discount for upfront annual payments instead of monthly payments so that they can have a better cash flow supported by loyal customers.

Getting financial support from the customers has the dual benefit of taking care of your capital needs to grow the business and giving you a longer commitment of business from them. When you know hundreds or thousands of people have agreed to use your product or service over a long period, there is no question of "who will use my creation?". We can be assured that people will use it and they have confirmed this by opening their wallets. This acts as a motivation to keep the bar high and build some wonderful solutions for them, which in turn can get us more financial support from the new customers they bring in. A perfect upward spiral! Hence, even if your business or industry doesn't seem to have a customer-funded innovation model, you can go out of your way to find creative ways to make it happen.

☑ **The Warren Lesson:** ***Can you get the financial support of your customers to grow your business?***

❑

70

Great Author, But...

An author is invited to a conference to talk about the art of writing. He is thrilled and accepts the invite. He prepares well and delivers a speech rich with data and insights.

But, when the feedback came, his session scored the least. The audience didn't like it even though most of them are big fans of his writing. How is this possible?

When you are great in one field, that brings fame and following. Hence, even if you do something else in a related or unrelated field, people tend to notice. For example, if a famous actor sings a song, people want to listen to it because of the popularity he has already gained in another field. But, there is no guarantee that they will love the song or buy his future albums. It happens only when the actor is talented in both acting and singing.

Similarly, this author is great at expressing himself in words. But, when it comes to presenting them on stage, his public speaking skills are not as great as his writing skills and hence he is not able to make an impression. This is not a thing to be ashamed of because everyone can't be an expert in everything. As long as we understand where we are good and where we are average or below average, we will be able to set up our careers accordingly.

"We are all duds at one thing or another. For most of us, the list is long", says Warren Buffett. "The important point to recognise is that if you are Bobby Fischer, you must play only chess for money."

This learning extends beyond individual skills. When you want your organisation to diversify and enter a new product line or geography, you should do a careful analysis to understand whether we are as good as our current product line or geography in the new one too. If we realise that we are going to be duds there, either don't enter or enter with lower expectations and slowly build your skills to become better in the new area. Having this mindset avoids disappointments and helps us focus on the right things for success.

☑ **The Warren Lesson:** ***Understand what we are good at and do only that for money.***

❑

71

Doing after Understanding

A friend of mine regularly invests in stocks. He doesn't understand the basics of the share market or does his own research. He doesn't even know much about most of the companies he invests in or the domains in which they operate. Instead, he follows some great experts who are good at analysing trends and giving recommendations and he simply goes by their advice. "My returns are great", he declares. "Much better than what I expected."

I feel happy for my friend and want him to be successful. Yet, I also remind him that his formula has a weakness: he does things without understanding them. He might have the backing of experts and trust them fully. But, if any of them makes a wrong judgement or purposefully gives a wrong recommendation that is favourable to them, my friend is going to suffer because he hasn't invested time in understanding what he is doing.

"When you start doing things that you don't understand or because they worked last week for somebody else, [it] doesn't work", warns Warren Buffett. He is a big advocate of individual research and taking investment decisions with full understanding.

However, what Warren says also applies in fields other than investment. If a company welcomes its new employees with, 'simply do what your seniors are doing' instruction, they are not setting up those young people for long term success. Instead, if seniors explain each task very well, with clear inputs on why they are done in a certain way, juniors understand what they are doing and are likely to become better at them. If they don't understand, they should be encouraged to ask questions until things are clear and they are not simply following someone's instructions. Even questions like "why are we not doing things some other way?" should be welcome because a new pair of eyes can spot some missed opportunities.

Similarly, whenever we are set to do anything new, we shouldn't narrow our focus to the usual questions of "What needs to be done?" and "How it needs to be done?" We should extend it by another important question, "Why is it done this way?" If the answer to this question is "I don't know" or "This is how we always did it", or "This worked for someone else", we should push back and analyse further until we understand why we are doing things in a certain way. Something that worked for someone else in another situation may not work for us because our conditions or even goals/targets may not be the same. Hence, a detailed analysis will give us clarity on whether it is likely to work or not and will guide us in the right direction, reducing the risk of failure. That's how we arrive at the unique solution which will work for our unique requirements.

☑ ***The Warren Lesson: Don't do things you don't understand just because they worked for others in some other situations.***

❑

72

Fair or Wonderful?

Let us say you have a small amount of money in hand. You can use it and buy one of the following drinks:

1. A great drink which you love, which makes you feel happy and gives you energy for hours. It is normally worth $15 but is now available for $10.
2. A decent drink that is not bad, but not something you adore. It is normally worth $5 but is now available for $1.

When you go by pure calculations, the first drink is available at a 33.33% discount, while the second drink is a great bargain as it is available at an 80% discount. As the second drink's current price is much smaller than that of the first drink, you might be able to buy a higher quantity as well.

However, when we pick the drink, mathematical calculations are not the only things in our minds. We also look at the quality of the drink and what benefit it can bring to our body and mind. With this context, you may give a higher weightage to the first drink which is not deeply discounted, but still, you feel it is a better choice.

When Warren Buffett started investing in companies, his strategy was to look for Cigar Butt Stocks, which means fair businesses available at wonderful prices. You pay a small amount to get a decent business and wait for it to grow a bit so that you can make some profit. This is exactly like picking a cigar butt thrown on the floor. It looks dirty, but it still has one puff left in it and you get it for free!

However, a cigar butt from the floor will only give you one puff. After that, you need to look for another cigar butt elsewhere.

Warren's partner Charlie Munger had a different idea: buy wonderful businesses at fair prices instead of fair businesses at wonderful prices. This means, paying a bit more (a fair price) but investing in a great business that is likely to grow big. This way even though the initial investment is (comparatively) high, the returns are expected to be much bigger and bring wealth. Warren adapted this strategy which helped both of them and their company.

We can use this lesson when we invest our money or time in any project: instead of focusing on things that have a low entry cost and light benefits, we can focus on things with a fair entry cost, but higher benefits. For example, if there is a business or technical skill that is easy to learn (less time investment), and the returns are small, is it really worth the effort? Instead, we can look beyond and find another skill which demands a higher time investment but is likely to get us much better returns.

☑ **The Warren Lesson:** ***Look for wonderful results at a fair cost, instead of fair results at a wonderful cost.***

❑

73

Same Question, Fifth Time!

Recently, I attended a webinar as one of its speakers. As the audience doesn't know me personally, I prepared a short introduction (sort of a 2-minute elevator pitch) and presented it before presenting my topic. It went well and I felt the audience would've got a fair idea about me.

But, technology was not on my side on this occasion. The organisers of the webinar told me that they couldn't hear me properly and asked me to repeat the introduction for the benefit of everyone. I sighed and repeated the introduction.

While doing so, I noticed an interesting difference between my first and second introductions. Both were almost the same, I used the same words and similar sentences, facts didn't change. But, the second introduction didn't have the passion and energy of the first introduction. When I had to repeat my introduction, I suddenly lost interest and just did an average job.

The reason for this difference lies in human psychology which prefers to do new things. If we have already seen something or done something, seeing it or doing it again rarely brings us the same level of excitement and energy. We would prefer to do something else which is new and innovative.

However, our personal and professional life demands that we do certain things again and again, whether we like it or not. For example, when you are speaking to a new business associate for the first time, you need to talk about yourself and your program which you might have done 100 times earlier. Sometimes different people ask us the same question and we are forced to repeat the same answer. It is also possible that the same person asks the same question to us after a few days because he/she didn't pay attention to the answer the first time or simply forgot all about it. These instances make us frustrated and do a less than perfect job.

Journalist Anthony Bianco observes that Warren Buffett answers even the lamest questions with the same expansiveness and wit, even if he is hearing them for the fifth time. We can observe this if we watch four or five interviews with Warren where most of the questions (and his answers) tend to repeat. But, we won't spot any tiredness or irritation or lack of interest in Warren's voice or expressions. He will try to present the same answer with the same enthusiasm because he believes the answer truly.

There is another important reason too: it may be the fifth time he is hearing this question. But, for the person who is asking that question, it is new and they want to hear his answer in the best possible manner. They deserve it!

☑ **The Warren Lesson:** ***Even if you have to repeat yourself, be enthusiastic and do a good job every time.***

❑

74

Compatible Partners

Having partners is a great way to get ahead with a complex task such as starting and running a business. This is because one person can't be an expert in every skill that is required to perform that complex task. Hence, if multiple people collaborate and bring different skills to the table, they can complement each other and run a successful show with each contributing in a different way.

For example, a few friends may become partners and start a magazine each contributing differently: writing, field research, interviewing, editing, proofreading, designing the pages, collecting advertisements, distribution, collecting subscriptions, handling foreign publishing rights and so on. Together they are able to bring the magazine successfully and share the returns.

However, such a partnership works only when those partners are compatible with each other. For example, if one of those partners joins this magazine expecting quick money, while the other partners have a long term business plan, he/she is likely to face disappointment and exit. Or, worst, he/she may try to influence others to change the business strategy which can result in the magazine losing its original vision.

Warren Buffett's suggestion to handle this problem is to find compatible partners by setting the ground rules and expectations clearly. This acts as a filter that keeps others (who are not compatible with the company's vision) away.

For example, Warren has clearly explained the ground rules based on which Berkshire Hathaway will be run. Now, when someone wants to invest there, they can look at these ground rules to decide whether they will be happy there or not. A few people may read these rules and decide not to invest, which is fine. No Hard Feelings. They will be happy elsewhere and Berkshire Hathaway will get other compatible partners (shareholders). This is good for everyone.

When we want to start or join a partnership of any size, any kind, we need to set or look for these ground rules. They are the real guidelines that help us decide whether a partner relationship is going to work or not. Those guidelines can be changed rarely with the full consent of all partners, but, once they are defined and published, everyone should respect them and follow them so that the environment is smooth and conducive to progress.

☑ **The Warren Lesson:** ***When looking for partners, find compatible ones, using a set of ground rules and expectations; keep all others out.***

❑

75

Environment Makes Us

Today's newspaper has a story about a 14-year-old boy creating a mobile app to help war-torn countries and their citizens. This app connects people who want to donate money to such Nobel causes and people who actually need them.

This is a fantastic idea and the fact that a schoolboy has created it, gives us so much hope for the future. But, one interesting question remains: what made this boy build such an app when other students of his age are having fun or building fun things?

"Both my parents are software engineers who constantly discussed how technology can make a difference in people's lives", the boy says. "Similarly, my grandfather is a Gandhian who keeps talking about giving back to the society and serving others. As I grew up hearing their words, I started thinking in this direction."

With due respect to the boy's interest and efforts, he should be thankful that he was in the right place (house) and heard the right conversations which shaped his thoughts and actions. Many times, what we hear frequently has a deep impact on our thinking and guides us in the right (or wrong) direction.

"When I was a kid, I had the advantage of a home where people talked about interesting things", says Warren Buffett. He feels these conversations gave him new perspectives and made him visualise a world in which he wanted to live in and how he can contribute to the same.

Every child may not be as lucky as Warren or the boy who created the app described above to have parents who discuss interesting things. But, there are many other environments that can shape them in a good way. For example, school friends, teachers, college campus, societies he/she belongs to, office setting and so on. If we purposefully look for such intellectual environments and become part of them, we can learn a lot and get support and guidance for our early thoughts and activities. In addition, we can also contribute to others in the same environment as the support is mutual. This gives us the satisfaction of giving back to the society which helped us grow.

☑ **The Warren Lesson:** ***Seek environments where interesting conversations happen.***

❑

76

Be Kind, Oh, Stranger

Life is full of surprises. They may come at a different pace at different times. But, no one can predict the exact path life is going to take. That's where it becomes important to plan for a situation where our plan doesn't go as per the plan.

For example, a common man can set aside a certain amount of money in a special account which takes care of 'x' months' expenses for his family. He won't touch this money under any circumstances. Even if he is forced to take it out, he will fill it as soon as possible so that this money always remains accessible for him and takes care of situations where he doesn't have an income for an extended time period.

Similarly, different people and companies set up different strategies to take care of unknowns that might happen. They may not be able to predict all the unknowns, but whatever they are able to think of, they will have a strategy to mitigate it.

However, Warren Buffett reminds us that when thinking of such strategies, we shouldn't be dependent on the kindness of strangers. If we do, then we are leaving too many things to others whom we don't even know. This results in a fake sense of security where we think the risk is taken care of, but in reality, it is not.

For example, if the common man in the example above keeps his "safety money" in the share market instead of his personal bank account, technically the money is still with him and it has the potential to grow in a better way year on year. But, if an unexpected event occurs and he needs to take out the money urgently, he is dependent on the strangers who are transacting on the share market to give him a kind price on that day. If they are not kind and the market moves down, he may not get the full amount and will suffer as a result.

Of course, this argument is not against investing in the share market. After all, we are learning from one of the greatest investors of all time and he would never say investing in shares is bad. However, in this particular example, the common man should've kept the money in his personal account instead of depending on the strangers' kindness. The main idea here is that depending on the kindness of strangers can backfire and give us a less than perfect situation. That's why Warren takes an approach of intentionally keeping his personal life and the companies he runs have a comfortable plan to withstand economic discontinuities on their own without depending on others, especially strangers.

☑ **The Warren Lesson:** ***Depending on the kindness of strangers is not a sound strategy; be independent, be on your own.***

❑

77

The Cream-Skimming Approach

Dairies have a machine called a cream separator which draws off the cream from fresh milk. It does this easily by just picking the cream which is lighter and hence floats. This process is known as cream-skimming.

Warren Buffett recommends a similar approach when looking for companies to invest in or when finding managers to run those companies. He explains this process using the example of a basketball coach. When this coach is facing a crowd of students, he/she speaks to seven-footers, which are people above the average height. As height is one of the key factors in determining basketball success, one of those candidates the coach is speaking to is likely to be a suitable one for his/her team's needs.

Of course, there is no guarantee that someone taller will be a great basketball player. They may still need many other skills for them to be successful. But, when we think about the reverse scenario (someone having the skills, but not being tall enough to succeed), the benefits of this approach become clear.

Hence, if Warren wants to invest in a company and has a few options, he looks for seven-footers among them (those who satisfy his must have expectations). Once he finds one or two such options, he acts as a separator machine and does further research on those companies to decide whether to invest in them or not. All the other companies which didn't pass his seven-footer test are simply ignored. This gives Warren maximum time and energy to focus on deserving candidates. A similar approach is used when he is looking for the right people to fill roles in his companies.

There are arguments against the cream-skimming approach. Sometimes the criteria we use to skim may make us ignore a great candidate. In those cases, we should listen to the feedback and continuously improve the original criteria. Over time, we will become better at this which results in better shortlisting, focussed analysis of the shortlisted candidates and a faster, better decision.

☑ **The Warren Lesson:** ***When you have many options, follow the cream-skimming approach to pick a smaller set and focus on those options deeply.***

❑

78

The Other Guy is Doing It

This may sound illogical. But, sometimes walking away from an opportunity is the most intelligent thing to do.

For example, a prospect is requesting quotes for a particular job and they have set the ground rules in terms of their expectations, budget, etc. Your organisation reads the requirements and arrives at a proposal that doesn't match these ground rules. You try to analyse it further to spot areas that can be improved so that you save costs and arrive at a workable budget. Even after this exercise, the proposal stands outside the limits set by the prospect.

In this case, you have two options: either talk to the prospect and explain to them that meeting all their needs with the given constraints is improbable, back up your argument with data and request for a change in the ground rules, or, walk away from the deal. There is no third option as you couldn't find a way to solve this problem with these constraints without losing money on your side.

While you are doing this analysis, you come to know that your competitor has already submitted a proposal to the same prospect agreeing to meet all demands within the given cost. What will you do?

Warren Buffett says that in this situation most companies will go ahead and submit a proposal from their side too even though they know it can't be done. They are doing this because they can't turn their back on business that is being accepted by their competitor. Hence, they decide to win this business to ensure the competitor doesn't get this.

But, if this game is played in the long run, it is our company that will be on the losing side. That's why Warren's advice is to walk away if the appropriate business can't be done. If the other guy is doing it, there is no condition that we should also do it.

Hence, when considering whether to pitch for an opportunity or not, our main and only decision criteria should be "can I meet these expectations in the given budget and still make the profit I desire?" If the answer is no, we shouldn't hesitate to walk away even if others are willing to do this business. Finding another suitable opportunity and spending our time there will be an intelligent investment of our resources.

☑ **The Warren Lesson:** ***If a business opportunity doesn't make sense to you, don't hesitate to walk away from it.***

❑

79

Super Skill that Increases your Value by at Least 50%

Schools and colleges teach many lessons and skills to students. Depending on the stream chosen by those students they may not learn the same set of subjects, but some basic subjects are taught to almost all the students because they are essential for everyone.

Warren Buffett feels communication is one such skill that everyone should learn. He tells students that if they learn to communicate well in person (spoken communication) and in writing (for example, letters, e-mails, articles, proposals and other documents), they increase their value by at least 50%.

For example, if a student has a fantastic idea that he/she wants to research and get further help for implementing it, it is essential that the student speaks about it to a few people such as other students, teachers, potential sponsors, investors, government and private officials, etc, to convey what is in his/her mind clearly. During these discussions, he/she may have to explain the original problem, pain points, proposed solution, expected benefits, returns (profit) and answer questions such as who is suffering, how many people are suffering, how is this solution different from other similar solutions, how it will be implemented, how much the implementation would cost, why it needs to be implemented now, why you are the right person to implement it etc. Sometimes he/she may only get a few minutes of time to explain all these and still make an impressive pitch and win the audience to their side.

The same example can be imagined as a written exercise as well. The student may be asked to submit a 4-page proposal explaining their idea and the quality of the document that determine how likely they are to get the required support.

While these examples focus on students, communication is an essential skill for everyone to succeed. Warren explains its importance by quoting a funny negative example: if you can't communicate well, it is like winking at a girl in the dark; not much will happen because of that.

☑ **The Warren Lesson:** ***Learn to communicate well.***

❑

80

Finding Our Strength(s)

The history of the business world is ripe with examples of great people who changed the world, built big empires and made tons of money. New entrants to this world look up to them, get motivated and plan their journey with the hopes of reaching the top someday.

However, a careful analysis of these great people will give us two puzzling inputs: not all of them succeeded in their first business; not all of them succeeded with a unique solution that no one in the world has created before. If this is the case, what differentiates great business people from others who might fail or attempt something others have already done?

"The test is not whether you get the greatest business idea in the world for the first time", says Warren Buffett. "The test is whether you keep learning as you go to understand what your strengths are, what you can do to your customers, what you can bring to the party."

For example, let us say you are starting a restaurant in an area where a few other food options already exist. This by itself is not a bad idea just because others are also doing it. If you can differentiate yourself from others and focus on what you can do to win the customers' business, that can provide you with the winning edge. But, getting there is a continuous process where you may have to experiment with different options depending on your skills, market needs and other factors.

During this journey, great business people don't lose steam and they continue to wonder what their real strengths are. They continuously monitor the situation, listen to customers, understand their pain points, look at their personal resource set to see how they can solve them well and focus on their learning to fill the gaps if any. This entire process can extend beyond one business too. This means, their first or second entrepreneurial attempt may not be a great success as they didn't figure out their strength(s) then. Once they find their strength(s), their next attempt will be aligned to it and will bring them success.

☑ **The Warren Lesson:** ***Keep learning; Keep looking for your strengths.***

❑

81

The Brain Work

The word "work" has evolved from humankind's early days to give different meanings in different centuries. For a caveman, work may mean actively going out and seeking food. A few centuries later, work meant preparing the land, growing food and collecting it. When the industrial revolution happened, work meant going to a factory and operating a machine. Around the same time, a white-collar work category emerged where people worked with pens, papers, files, typewriters and cabinets. Later the same people worked on their computers to achieve similar results.

While the meaning of the word "work" has changed a lot, it essentially means doing something with our hands. That's how humans earned their bread and got the comfort they needed. As this memory is very strong in our brains (and possibly in our genes too), we consider someone not doing anything with his/her hands as a lazy person. If someone sits in a corner and thinks about something, we ask him/her to get up and do some work.

In reality, someone can just sit alone and work too. They don't need to write down anything on a paper or a whiteboard and can simply think about various facts they collected by reading, listening to others, watching etc, connect the dots and make decisions for the future. This silent, invisible work can also bring good results in the right circumstances.

For example, if a company is continuously losing money on their production processes, an expert can observe the factory operations, its layout, various machines and workers and then think about possible improvements in these areas. Based on this, he/she can come up with a proposal that can help the company improve. This work happening in the expert's brain is as important as the work that happens in those hundreds of workers' hands.

'I insist on a lot of time being spent, almost every day, to just sit and think', says Warren Buffett. He understands that this is uncommon in American business as leaders are expected to 'get up and do something', not 'sit alone and think about what to do'. But, he doesn't believe in this general theory and spends a good amount of time every day reading and thinking. As a result, he believes he makes fewer impulse decisions than most people in business.

Moving continuously brings us progress. But, sometimes, the movement and the associated pressure can overwhelm us and cloud our thinking and decision-making process. This problem can only be resolved when we give ourselves time to stop and think. Today's knowledge workers and leaders need this time to digest all the information they are getting from various sources and to have clarity on the next steps. This investment will help them move beyond people who simply follow others' instructions and make them original thinkers who can come up with creative solutions to any problem.

☑ **The Warren Lesson:** ***Every day, spend some time sitting and thinking.***

❑

82

The Narrow Vision

A company announces its forecasts every quarter. Later, they meet those numbers or exceed them or they may perform below their own forecasts.

This process looks harmless to an outsider: someone says they will hit some score; they are able to do it or not. That's it.

But, this seemingly simple process can introduce some serious issues in the organisation if those forecasts are considered as end games by themselves. That is, if everyone is only focusing on the forecasts of the current quarter and miss the big picture, it can result in some short term benefits, but in the long run, the company will suffer.

For example, let us say a company has announced $500 million as their quarterly forecast. But, when doing the actual calculations, they realise that they will be missing this forecast by $15 million. This company has met its forecasts for the past many quarters and they don't want to set a bad example by missing this. Hence, they find an R&D investment and move it to the next quarter. This adjusts the overall numbers, making them meet their original forecasts. This may be legally correct. But, the decision to postpone the R&D investment happened only because forecasts narrowed their focus to the current quarter, resulting in a possible long term loss by slow innovation.

"I tell my managers to pretend that this is the only business they and their family will own for the next 50 years and they can't sell it", says Warren Buffett. When leaders think from this perspective, missing a quarterly forecast doesn't look like a major issue and they will make the right decisions for the long term benefit of the organization.

Just like the quarterly forecasts for business leaders, we also may have short term goals and activities which cloud our vision and make us lose focus on the long-term goals and activities. We need to learn to spot them and adjust the perspective in the right manner to ensure we are not compromising long term success for some quick wins.

☑ **The Warren Lesson:** ***When making decisions, look at things from the long-term perspective, not from the short term perspective.***

❑

83

An Unusual Race

You are participating in a race along with ten other people. The rules are simple: you all need to run a distance of 200 metres and the one who reaches the finish line first will be declared a winner.

So, all of you reach the starting line and get ready to run. The organiser says, "Ready on your mark, get, set, go."

When the organiser utters the word "Go", you suddenly find yourself 20 metres ahead of all other race participants. You don't know how; but, it has happened. For a moment don't worry about this being unfair to others. Just assume that you somehow got 20 metres ahead of all your competitors and it is not challenged by anyone. Will this give you a better chance of winning that race?

Of course, it would. As you are starting from 20 metres and all others are starting from 0 metres, you will only be covering a distance of 180 metres instead of 200 metres and you are likely to reach the finish line before others.

But, what if you are 20 metres behind all other competitors? What will it do to your winning chances?

It might affect you badly because you now need to cover a distance of 220 metres instead of 200 metres and all others would have an advantage over you. You may still win, but you need to put tremendous effort for that to happen.

Warren Buffett uses this beautiful example to explain how important it is for young people to be financially independent when they start their careers. When the career race starts, that is, when they come out of college, if they have some savings, skills, experience and network, they are equivalent to starting 20 metres ahead of all others. If they have a big debt to pay back and bad habits, it is the equivalent of starting 20 metres behind all others. Warren advises students to start thinking about it early and plan a better start to their active work life.

While this example suits perfectly for students, anyone of any age will find it to be true because being financially independent sets us free and gives us less anxiety about the future. Similarly, not being financially independent adds heavy pressure like swimming against the tide. When faced with such a situation, we should carefully analyse our commitments and see how we can make the race normal (instead of being behind others). Once this is achieved, the next step is finding ways to stay ahead of others so that we can definitely win.

☑ **The Warren Lesson:** ***Be financially independent, it sets you up for success.***

84

The Ideal Job

What is the ideal job for someone?

People accept a job for many reasons: money, power, fame, opportunity to do something good for the world, mental satisfaction of good work done, happiness in solving complex problems, helping others, leading others and so on. Each job may provide one or more of these benefits and people make the right selection based on their needs and expectations at that time. Hence, it is difficult to define 'the ideal job' and expect it to suit everyone in the world.

However, Warren Buffett suggests one general rule which fits in most scenarios for most people: look for a job that you would take if you don't need a job. Assume that you have everything you need and there is no need for you to work. At that time, what work will you take? That's the one that is likely to give you mental satisfaction even now.

For example, Warren does his work at Berkshire Hathaway not because it gives him a lot of money. The huge income he earns is only a byproduct and he does his work because he gets to work with fascinating people every day. That's his ideal job and something he would do (that is, he does) when he doesn't need a job.

Similarly, everyone has something which they absolutely love and would do it even if there are no other benefits. They may not get that opportunity in their very first job, or the second job, or the third job… but, Warren advises people not to give up and keep looking for it. When you find it, you know you have arrived.

However, when you are on this journey, those intermediate responsibilities and the benefits which come with them may try to deviate you from your search for your true love. That's when you need enormous control and understanding that the journey is still on and anything on the way is just a temporary arrangement. Only very few people find that ideal job and when they do, the satisfaction they get is priceless.

☑ **The Warren Lesson:** ***The ideal job for you is the job you would do if you don't need a job. Look for it and grab it when it appears.***

❑

85

The Real Boss

The word "boss" is defined as "a person whose job is to give orders to others at work" in the dictionary. This person may be your manager or owner of the firm where you are working. These days they are usually not called "bosses", but there is no denying that he/she gets to boss you around.

When we look at the corporate hierarchy charts, another interesting fact emerges: most employees don't have a single boss. The boss has a boss, who in turn has another boss and depending on the level of an employee, he/she may have multiple bosses. Those higher level bosses may not talk to this employee on a regular basis, but they remain his/her bosses anyway.

However, there is one ultimate boss whom those employees can miss to notice amid all this hierarchical analysis: the customer. Irrespective of whether someone manages others or works in a desk or a machine, they all work for the customers' benefit and their paychecks are ultimately paid from the wallets of those customers.

For example, an employee may simply fix car parts in a factory and a supervisor can be his/her boss. But, both of them work for the customer who will drive that car someday and should always remember that in their mind, have fun and enjoy working for that customer. That's when true great work gets done because our best comes out when we keep our customers in the centre of our thinking and activities. With this, we understand the purpose of our work and it motivates us.

"Working for you [Berkshire Hathaway shareholders] turns our [Warren Buffett's and Charlie Munger's] jobs into fun and satisfaction", says Warren. "There is nothing more rewarding to Charlie and me than enjoying the trust of individual long-term shareholders who have joined us with the expectation that we would be the reliable custodian of their funds."

Similarly, customers of each one of us have placed their trust in us expecting us to take care of certain things well. Understanding them and addressing those needs gives ultimate happiness and satisfaction, making work meaningful.

☑ **The Warren Lesson: *Understand your true customers and take care of their needs.***

86

The 'No Games' Approach to Negotiation

Search for the word "negotiation techniques" in Google or Amazon. You will get hundreds, if not thousands of articles, videos, training courses and books promising to teach you many tricks for negotiating a better deal from anyone. They make you feel negotiation is a dirty art and those who don't know it will not be able to get the best value in their everyday transactions.

But, this common belief assumes that only one party (that is us) should win the negotiation and the other party should lose. The more they lose, the more we win because it is a zero-sum game. When you approach negotiation with this attitude, you need to learn many tricks so that you can squeeze every bit of value from the other party.

Warren Buffett, one of the most successful business negotiators of all time, says he doesn't do any tricks at a negotiation table. "I don't play games. I just say what I'll do and nothing else. People know, what I mean and what I am saying."

This means that when someone is negotiating with Warren, they hear the best deal early in the game, not later. Warren says what he can do clearly and doesn't keep his best cards for a future moment. This transparency makes the discussion go smoothly instead of wasting time on back and forth discussions and both parties guessing what is in the other's mind.

Also, this technique respects the other party. There is a genuine interest that the other party should win too and there should be a fair value exchange. As Warren has got such a reputation, people from all over the globe reach out to him when they want to sell their businesses. They know he will have the best interest of both parties in mind. Warren respects that and responds with a quote that he feels is workable. After that, some minor discussions can happen, but Warren's offer is already on the table, not hidden somewhere else to trick the other party.

Being transparent during negotiations may look dangerous. But, in a world where everyone seems to play games, there is huge value for being open-minded. If you make it clear and explicit, the other party will respect that and meet you on level ground.

☑ **The Warren Lesson:** ***Don't play games during negotiation; say what is there in your mind openly and take it forward from there.***

❑

87

Cross-learning

Is Warren Buffett a great investor or a great businessperson?

Warren started his career as an investor. He helped himself and others by picking the right stocks to invest in so that their wealth can be grown. Later he started doing the same under his company where he invested in some businesses as a whole (outright purchases) or part (common stock purchases). As his company now owns many companies in multiple domains and actively looks for other such investments, he is considered a great businessperson too.

The interesting aspect is that Warren doesn't see them as two distinct things. While his thought process as an investor or as a business leader might be slightly different, he feels he applies learnings from one to the other. "My experience in business helps me as an investor and my investment experience has made me a better businessman", he says, "Each pursuit teaches lessons that are applicable to the other."

For example, a college professor writes a book in his field. His/her experience as an author gives him/her various skills such as researching, articulating thoughts and editing/rewriting them. These skills may be used by him/her while preparing for the next class or when teaching students. Similarly, he/she may use his experience as a professor when approaching the next book project.

Hence, lessons from a particular field or pursuit are not limited to that environment alone. In fact, cross-learning and applying thoughts from elsewhere refreshes us and does wonders by opening our minds to new possibilities.

But, what if we don't have another pursuit? What if we only have one role in one domain?

Even in that case, we play other personal roles such as husband/wife, father/mother, son/daughter, volunteer etc. which provides a wide range of experiences that can be used for our business pursuit. Similarly, we can apply what we learn as businesspeople in our personal roles. Idea is to keep our minds open and not apply learnings narrowly. If we move away from the thought that only boardroom thinking can solve business problems, suddenly the world will be full of interesting learnings that we can use.

☑ **The Warren Lesson:** ***Use lessons from one pursuit in another.***

❑

88

Good Information and Quick Information

Do you have a reading feed?

We all do. They are the list of newspapers we read every day, television channels we watch, websites we browse, notifications we pay attention to and so on. These things combine and create a feed that we refer to very often and it acts as our information pool. This is where we observe the world and understand it better.

Technology has made news and information travel faster. Earlier, something happening in one corner of the world used to reach the other corner after a few days, sometimes after a few weeks, sometimes never. But now, everyone gets to know about everything immediately. As a result, we get information at such a pace that it becomes very difficult for us to digest and understand everything. Many times we feel like drinking from the fire hose.

However, Warren Buffett says his primary information source hasn't changed in the previous 40 years: annual reports.

This is surprising. When so much information about each and every company is coming into our reading feeds every day, every hour, how can we ignore all that and wait for the annual reports to come many months later?

Warren reminds us that judging a company needs good information, not quick information. Hence, he is okay to wait for a few weeks or a few months before the good information becomes available, ignoring anything which is quick and dirty.

This attitude can be applied to information about companies, countries, people and everything else. We don't have to feel anxious just because some quick information is continuously available. Instead of trying to chase all the breaking news, waiting for the good information to arrive is a better strategy as we would avoid the natural inaccuracies, ups and downs of such quick news items and can focus on the long term information which matters.

☑ **The Warren Lesson:** ***Good information is needed, not quick information.***

❑

89

When your Hypothesis is Wrong...

You have a wonderful hypothesis that has the potential to become something big for yourself and your organisation. You discuss this with your boss and she is thrilled too. "Go ahead and get to the next level of details, write a proposal, we will make it happen", she says and gives you her full support.

For the next few weeks, you ignore other unimportant tasks so that you can focus on this matter entirely. You read books, speak to people and do experiments to get more details.

However, when doing this due diligence, you come to know that your original hypothesis may not be true. You understand its loopholes and weaknesses and suddenly it doesn't look like a great idea anymore.

In this situation, what will you do? Will you go to your boss and say, "Sorry, my original hypothesis is wrong. We better discontinue this line of thinking." Or will you continue your research hoping to get more material that can prove you right?

Warren Buffett uses the example of journalism to explain this and says many journalists would usually go for the second option. He calls it their 'greatest sin' because in this situation the best thing to do will be to give up that wrong hypothesis instead of going in the opposite direction trying to find proof for it. As a result, "there is a lot of momentum towards a lousy story. [Instead] you have to be able to say, "My hypothesis is no longer correct'. It is hard to do."

We all face such conflicts in our life even though we are not journalists. We continue to spend more time on a project just because we assumed something to be true and invested a lot of time in it. Instead of exiting that wrong thought process, we struggle to find evidence for our original assumptions. This leads to dual loss by creating anxiety in our minds (about not being able to prove our hypothesis and about being criticised by others) and by denying the opportunity for us to work on something else more meaningful. We need to swallow our pride and accept our mistakes so that we can move on to the next hypothesis. There is no shame in being wrong, as long as you accept it the moment you realise it.

☑ **The Warren Lesson:** ***Don't work on a wrong hypothesis just because you once thought it to be right. Declare it as wrong and move on to the next one.***

❑

90

Looking for 1-foot Bars

A banker was passionate about dancing. She wanted to have her own dance school, perform on stages across the globe, appear on television and so on.

However, all these looked like distant dreams because at that time she only had skills and passion. No one knew her outside her small circle of friends. Hence, getting students or program opportunities was not easy. As a result, she was focusing on her banking job and kept postponing the steps that are necessary to make her dream a reality.

Warren Buffett has a piece of simple, practical advice to people like this banker-dancer, "I don't try to jump over 7-foot bars. I look around for 1-foot bars that I can step over."

If you are new to the art of jumping, it will be near impossible for you to jump over a 7-foot bar on the very first day. Hence, you would look for 1-foot bars that anybody can step over. Then, you will use that success and build on top of it. You will move slowly, but steadily and will conquer that 7-foot bar too.

For example, this banker-dancer can easily start her dance school with one student who could be a friend's child or a relative. Or, she can start a dance YouTube channel and showcase her talents to the world. These are 1-foot bars that she can manage even with her current newbie state. Once these are achieved, she will have the confidence to use them as a stepping stone and move to bigger and better things.

When we look at an enormous task, it looks impossible because the gap between where we are today and where we should be, is huge. However, we can identify and conquer smaller intermediate steps (1-foot bars and 2-foot bars) that can help us get there. These early wins will immediately give us confidence. They may look insignificant when compared to the ultimate goal that we want to achieve. But, they provide important motivation (for us) and social proof (for others) which prepare us mentally and physically for the next steps. Every success story across the world will have this pattern even though it is not visible to everyone.

☑ **The Warren Lesson:** ***Want to jump over a 7-foot bar someday? Start with 1-foot bars that you can easily jump over today.***

❑

91

Loving What We Do

There is a small snack shop near our home where they sell a famous Indian delicacy called "Pani Puri". The young person who manages (and probably owns) that shop always has a smile in his eyes, handles any number of customers without issues and delivers tasty food fast. Even when the crowd is too much, his smile is intact and everyone can see that he enjoys what he is doing and not just doing it for the money.

One day I asked the gentleman how he learnt these skills. He explained that he got this interest during his college days, decided to intern with an expert and learnt it by practice. "I made many mistakes and the food I made was horrible. But, it was a good start and I improved from there. The main reason for my success was that I loved doing this."

Warren Buffett agrees with this young person when he says, "If you love something, you will get really good at it." As a teenager, Warren started loving investing/capital allocation and taught himself, learnt from others and improved, reaching the pinnacle of success. All these were possible because he loved it. When such love for a task or skill exists, you will find ways to become better at it because you enjoy the process.

For example, there are many executives who are experts in what they do. But, if we carefully notice, two patterns will be observable: they got better at it because of the love they had for the job and they didn't stop after becoming really good at it. They continue to invest time and learn new things because it is fun and enjoyable.

Hence, anyone who wants to become better at something should first find ways to love it. If you don't love teaching and want to become a top-class teacher, it is not going to work. Either start loving teaching or find another work that you love. This is because loving what we do is an important and must-have ingredient for success.

☑ **The Warren Lesson:** ***Love what you do; you will get really good at it.***

❑

92

The Power of Habits

Many years back, Warren Buffett was addressing more than a hundred students in a Columbia University investing class. One of the students asked, "What can I do now so that I can prepare for a career in investing?"

Warren thought for a moment and then pointed to a pile of documents (reports, publications, papers etc.) he had brought with him. "Read 500 pages like this every day. All of you can do it, but I guarantee that not many of you will do it."

Reading relevant material every day might look like an oversimplified technique. But, Warren believes that knowledge can only be built up like that, like compound interest. As we read more, we know more, we understand better, we are able to connect the dots between various things we read/understood/thought about at various times and the structure grows massively over many years.

As Warren explains, this can be done by anyone, but only a few will do it. This is because simple techniques look incapable of creating magic. But, even a great masterpiece is nothing but a collection of strokes. Each stroke created by the artist may look like simple lines, but the combined effect produces something wonderful. Similarly, daily habits such as reading or writing code or drawing or exercising or listening to experts add up and build our knowledge and skills. Practice makes us perfect and working on something every day gives us enough of that practice.

One of the common tools used by people to form a habit is marking a certain time in the calendar for the same. Warren reserves time every day for his reading and thinking. Similarly, we can also reserve time, even if it is 30 minutes per day, and dutifully start the habit we want to form. Recording the everyday progress and doing a weekly/monthly analysis also helps in moving in the right direction. But a bigger and better motivation will come when you see the compound effect which comes after a certain period. Till that magic happens, we can depend on the systems to keep us motivated. After we experience the magic, we wouldn't need any external reminders.

☑ **The Warren Lesson:** ***Find out what helps you win in your field, start doing it every day.***

❑

93

Finding a Good Partner

Relationships are two-way streets. Both partners may not contribute in the same way, with the same role, but they both bring something to the table and benefit from each other. This is an implicit expectation whether it is a business relationship or personal.

For companies, finding the right partner can be a big enabler and something which helps them scale up, enter new territories, business lines, etc. However, finding the right partner is not easy and the cost of a wrong partnership is very high. Hence, companies tend to do long due diligence before signing the dotted line. They speak to potential organisations to understand their skills, experience and connections and ensure that their culture will be a good match too. Even after such elaborate filtering, some partnerships don't work and the companies part as friends (or foes) after a few failed attempts at working together.

Warren Buffett gives a simple solution to this problem, 'if you want to get a good partner, the way to do it is to be a good partner.' In other words, when looking for a potential partner, instead of focusing entirely on what the other person can bring to the table, also look at what you can do to them. How can you make them feel welcome in this relationship? How can you help them succeed? How can you enhance their strengths and help them address their weaknesses? How can you give them the best relationship experience? When focusing on questions like this, the default assumption that "I am perfect and I want nothing but a perfect partner" gives way to "I am looking for someone to grow with."

The same mindset is useful even after the partner is selected. When two companies or teams are working together, instead of one party playing the commanding role and always looking at the other party to follow instructions, both of them can try to be a good partner by collaborating together, co-creating solutions and building on each others' thoughts. When such a relationship is established where both partners respect each other and genuinely want to work together, even average companies can combine and create a masterpiece partnership. If this doesn't exist, even great companies can fail to work together.

☑ **The Warren Lesson:** ***If you need a good partner, be one.***

❑

94

Only Twenty Punches

A few large beaches across the globe have a famous game called "Balloon Shooting" which people enjoy a lot. As the name suggests, there will be many inflated balloons fixed on a board and the players should try to shoot at them from a distance. Depending on the number of balloons they successfully hit, they might win a prize or just go back with fun memories.

One of the key rules of this game is that you are only given a certain number of bullets for each game. If you are not able to hit any balloon in those many attempts, you should accept defeat and give way to other players.

As people generally play this game for fun, they don't care much about this number of bullets rule or the possible defeat. They just try to shoot every bullet with as much precision as possible and that's it. Even if they don't hit any of the balloons, they wouldn't worry too much about it.

Imagine that a player playing this game is in desperate need of money. He has 6 bullets and can win a big jackpot if he hits 4 balloons. So, he takes a careful aim and shoots his first bullet.

Oops. Tough luck. It doesn't hit any of the balloons. His second bullet also gets the same result.

This means, this player has 4 bullets and has to hit 4 balloons with them. He can't make a mistake and every shooting has to result in a hit. In such a case, do you think he will be extra careful in his aiming and shooting when compared to all other players?

Of course, he would be. As he can't make any mistakes now, he will try everything possible to ensure success before pulling the trigger.

Warren Buffett recommends a similar attitude when taking investment decisions. He uses a punch card example which is similar to the balloon shooting game: assume that every time you make an investment pick, a single punch will be made in a punch card you carry. Once you reach 20 punches in that card, your investment game ends. You can't invest anymore anywhere.

In reality, such a card doesn't exist and no one can stop us from investing anywhere we want. But, Warren feels this freedom makes us not think enough before making a decision. It is like a balloon shooting game with an unlimited number of bullets. We will just randomly shoot and take the next bullet. Won't we?

Instead, if we assume that only 20 punches are allowed in the card, every investment decision we make will be well thought of. Even though such a restriction doesn't exist, having this mindset will help us avoid impulsive decisions and pick only the right stocks.

Even outside the investment world, deep analysis of available information before making a decision is recommended wherever feasible. Instead of assuming that we can do endless trials before hitting on the right solution, we can assume that the number of punches is restricted and we need to be thorough in our analysis.

☑ **The Warren Lesson:** ***Assume that you are allowed to make only a certain number of picks in life. That will make you analyse data thoroughly and carefully before every decision.***

❑

95

The Light Calendar

Bill Gates, Founder of Microsoft and one of Warren Buffett's close friends, likes to fill every minute of his calendar with different tasks. He then goes ahead and finishes those tasks one after the other and feels good about it. According to him, that's the only way to work, that's the only way to do things.

One day, Warren showed his calendar to Bill. It was not empty, but there were only a few tasks here and there and compared to Bill's calendar, it was very light. When Bill expressed his surprise, Warren gave a simple answer, "A full calendar is not a proxy for your seriousness."

When you are good at something, it is natural that people around you, especially your coworkers, subordinates and partners, want your guidance. They want a slice of your calendar and you gladly create those slices day after day, week after week. Slowly, these requests from other people pile up and at some point, your calendar is controlled by them. You feel busy and important, but the reality is that you won't have enough slices left to do things that are important to you. This is why people with busy calendars are tired towards the end of the happy but rarely satisfied.

"You can't buy time", Warren declares. "Time is the only thing you can't buy. You better be careful about it."

Warren's way of keeping a light calendar is an indication of how careful he is about his own time. As he doesn't consider "filling the calendar with tasks" as the most important value addition from him, he is able to have a clear picture of what is important and which task deserves his time and how much time he should allocate to it. This is why he is able to spend more thinking time than many other contemporary business leaders.

With the introduction of digital calendars, we were supposed to have better control of our time and have a firm say in what we wanted to do at which time. But, ironically, they have become the primary reason for others to block our time which means we have very little left to us. There is no harm in helping others. But, we should first block our own calendar with the tasks which are essential and important for our immediate and long term commitments. The remaining time can be (carefully) shared with others to support their initiatives. This way we add value as individual contributors and as collaborators.

☑ **The Warren Lesson:** ***Be careful with your time.***

❑

96

Intentional Confusion

You are reading the latest report from a company. But, even after a careful study, you are not able to understand it fully. Something feels wrong and the entire text is giving you confusion.

At this time, it is natural to imagine that we don't have the right skills to understand this text. After all, there are so many subjects in this world and one can't be an expert in all of them. Some information will go above our heads and we need to accept it.

While humility is an essential quality that everyone needs, Warren Buffett reminds us that in this case, our intelligence (or lack of it) may not be the real reason for the confusion. What if the author intentionally made it confusing?

But, why would someone do that?

When Warren reads accounting reports of a firm, he is looking for simple, clear facts presented in a way anyone can understand. This helps investors and the general public to get a good picture of what is happening in that company, where the money comes from, where it goes, how good is the organisation's financial health, etc.

However, some companies purposefully write these reports in a confusing way so that the answer to such important questions is ambiguous. This may be a trick they use to hide some bad news or internal wrongdoings. That's why even someone like Warren with decades of experience reading such reports gets confused when reading them.

Warren advises us to avoid a company if their accounting appears confusing because the confusion may be intentional and reveal the character of the management. If you are not in a position to avoid the company altogether, minimally you should ask the right questions and ask for better answers which clear the confusion.

There is another important angle to Warren's message. When we are writing something, we need to ensure that the reader gets clear answers to the typical questions with which they are coming to our text. If he/she gets confused when reading our text, our intention/integrity itself may come under the scanner. Hence, we need to be extremely careful to ensure all our communication is clear and transparent.

☑ **The Warren Lesson:** ***Clarity in communication is essential.***

❑

97

Sitting on the Sidelines

One of my relatives is a regular investor in the stock market. Every month, he reserves a certain amount for his investments, researches a few companies of his interest, picks the right ones and spends his money on the right stocks.

My relative's employer pays him a performance bonus every six months. Depending on how well he performed during that half-year period, he gets a small, medium or large amount on top of his regular salary.

"Those are my toughest months", my relative says. "Having extra money is cool. But, when I have extra money, suddenly I want to spend it on stocks. I still do my research, but they are not as detailed as I normally do. As there is excess money in my account, I want to buy some stocks immediately and that pressure affects my judgement."

If this is the case with a small retail investor like my relative, imagine how companies with large piles of cash will be thinking about their investments. Will they make similar judgement errors and buy some shares at a very high price?

"Sit on the sidelines if you can't find investments of value based on your criteria", says Warren Buffett. "Many emotional investors make the mistake of buying at a very high price relative to value [just because they have excessive cash]."

When resources (such as cash) are in short supply or available in the exact amount required, using them effectively comes naturally to anyone because there are no other options. They need to think creatively to make the best use of the available resources and many great decisions are made due to this necessity. Bringing the same discipline when your resources are overflowing is tough. That's what differentiates normal people from experts. They don't act emotionally and look at the available resources as something that needs to be used as soon as possible. Every opportunity needs to be analysed based on the standard criteria that we use and the decision should only be dependent on this analysis. If no opportunity seems to pass those criteria, instead of throwing away the resources for the wrong cause, we should be patient and wait for the right opportunity to come.

☑ **The Warren Lesson:** ***Even if you have an abundance of resources, use them only on the right opportunities based on your criteria.***

❑

98

Feeling Good About You!

How to extract the best from people?

This is a constant question faced by every manager, every boss and every entrepreneur. They have wonderful hiring processes; they analyse each profile carefully, picking the very best; they give them an amazing interview experience and ensure all skills are tested well before finalising the right candidate; they give the candidate an apt responsibility, a welcoming, yet challenging program, wonderful employee benefits along with constant encouragement. Yet, only a small percentage of those experts do well. Others either simply hang around or exit for better opportunities.

An organisation can grow only if it can rapidly get the right candidates in the right roles giving their best. This can't be random and we need a dependable, repeatable process that ensures this. Warren Buffett gives one such process: make them feel good about you.

Yes. Warren feels this is not about the other person's skills, experiences, or anything else. It is about your (the employer's) ability to make them feel good about you and your company. When they feel part of the organisation and like the people they work for, they naturally give their best because they want to. This intrinsic motivation is better than any extrinsic motivation the company can offer them.

When we review success stories of large companies with a specific focus on their early days, we find that many people joined those companies even before they became giants in their field. They may not have gotten a great salary or benefits, but they felt good about the company and decided to give their most productive years to it. As a result of many such contributions, the company grew and gave back to them. Later, the company has much better resources and is able to attract wonderful talent from the market. But, suddenly their ability to retain these talented individuals drops because of the same factor: are they feeling good about the company?

Making people feel good about us goes beyond the occasional praise or pat on the back. They should see meaning, passion in our work. They should find genuine care for them in us. They should see ability, interest from us to support them in their functions in whatever way we could. Instead of seeing them as yet another resource that any company needs to operate, their contribution should be respected and appreciated truly and openly. Actions should be consistent with words when decisions are made. When they know we always have their backs, they feel good about working for us as it is no more a simple business transaction. When everyone in a team feels this way, the effect becomes multifold and real great work gets done.

☑ **The Warren Lesson:** ***People will give their best if they feel good about you.***

❑

99 The Confidence

Do you ever think about Oxygen?

Yes. Everyone knows that it is essential for our life and we all breathe in oxygen continuously. But, we think about all this only when someone asks a question. Otherwise, we take it for granted because it is always there and we get plenty of it.

However, if you are underwater for a few minutes or if the oxygen level goes down in your flight, suddenly you want oxygen. At that time, that's the only thing you think about and nothing else matters.

Warren Buffett uses this example to explain how important confidence is for a person's or a company's success. When they get plenty of it from everywhere, they don't even think about it. But, if they lose it for some reason, they immediately feel its absence and can't do anything else until it is restored.

For example, a famous chocolate brand enjoys the confidence of millions of customers as they buy it in large numbers every day. They use this as the vehicle for their growth and expand their company, enter new territories, introduce new product lines and so on. While doing all these, they don't realise that the confidence their customers have in their brand is the prime reason for their continued success because it is available in plenty.

Suddenly, a newspaper article declares that this brand's chocolate has a chemical that causes some serious health issues. The company denies this report with their test results and threatens to sue the newspaper. But, the public has lost confidence in the brand and that's when the company starts to notice it. Now their every step becomes slow and shaky because they have lost the business equivalent of oxygen and it would take time to get it back.

This applies to individuals too. When others keep their trust in us (due to our earlier accomplishments or other reasons), we don't take it seriously even though we enjoy and make the best use of that trust. If that trust breaks because of some reason, we immediately become aware of its absence and want it back. This happens because we don't realise its importance when it is available in abundance. Only after it goes away, we realise how essential it is for our survival. Pretty late response!

A better way of handling this will be recognising such oxygen-like aspects that we normally take for granted and making sure that we don't lose them carelessly. This ensures that our Oxygen supply is uninterrupted and we can enjoy a higher quality of life.

☑ **The Warren Lesson:** ***Confidence is like oxygen; when you have it, you don't think about it; when you lose it, that's the only thing you think about.***

❑

100

Important Things

There is a gun with 100 chambers in it. One of those chambers has a bullet and all others are empty. This means that if someone places the gun on their own head and pulls the trigger, there is a 99% chance that they will survive. Very high odds. But, will anybody do that?

What if there is a one million dollar reward for doing this? Will this make some people try their luck? What about five million? Twenty million? One billion? We can keep on increasing the prize money, but an intelligent person won't play this game even though his/her chance of losing is only 1%. This is because that 1% worst-case scenario doesn't balance out the 99% best-case scenario. It is not a game worth playing.

"Don't risk something that is important to you for something that is not important to you, whatever be the odds", says Warren Buffett. In this case, if someone values their life and considers it more important than money, they won't play this game irrespective of the prize value or odds of success.

However, such situations in life are not as explicit as facing a gun with 99 empty chambers and 1 bullet. Hence, people might risk something that is important to them for something that is not important to them just because the odds seem to be in their favour. For example, rash driving mostly helps a person reach his/her destination faster; but, there is a chance of failure and the loss is much bigger when compared to the gain from the success. Here he/she is risking something that is important to them (their life) for something that is not important to them (saving a few minutes of driving time or the thrill of driving fast or winning a bet) and doesn't even realise it.

This is not an argument against risk-taking itself. Life will have some risks at any given point in time and we all should learn to analyse them, understand their probability, severity, possible impact, mitigations to avoid them, strategies to handle the worst-case scenario etc. and take calculated risks to progress. But, there are some risks that one should never take and some things one should never give away: doing things we love, with the people we love, helping others, keeping ourselves fit, spending time with our loved ones, giving back to society and enjoying life. When we realise these as must-haves and use them as the general rule in every decision-making, we will live a happy and contented life.

☑ **The Warren Lesson:** ***Don't risk things that are important to you, irrespective of the odds.***

❑

Money Making
Skills

Author's Note

Warren Buffett is commonly known as a longterm investor. But, if you have a look at the list of companies where Berkshire Hathaway, the company owned by Warren Buffett, has stakes, you would be surprised to find that it has 90% to 100% holdings in 67 other companies. These subsidiary companies are in major or controlling positions in different consumer markets and together they earn revenue of USD 109 billion (2017). Besides this, Berkshire Hathaway also has stakes ranging from 0.01% to 27.25% in 42 other companies. With all this, Berkshire Hathaway was making a net profit of USD 24.07 billion (2016) out of the total revenue of USD 223.60 billion. This also is a testimony to Warren Buffett's great management acumen.

And in both of these forms, the core mantra of Warren Buffett's success has been—picking the right business. Yes, long before starting his professional life as an investor, Buffett had already uncovered the mystery that all the businesses did not have the same economics, and there were some specific kinds of businesses whose economics by nature worked profusely in their favour. He had deciphered that the companies that got support from their inherent economics required minimal capital investment as compared to their earnings. These kind of companies mostly manufactured brand products that never needed to be replaced. Or else, they provided such vital services that did not have any competitive substitute. Thus, they are in a way 'monopoly businesses' only. Hence, these companies had the freedom to charge more for their products and services, thus providing them much better profit margins.

That is the reason that, during his entire professional life, Warren Buffett has always been looking for such specific businesses that enjoyed support from their inherent economics and he has been considering them only the 'right businesses'. Evidently, picking the 'right business' has been the most important aspect of Warren Buffett's investment strategy. However, Warren Buffett's main objective has not been only to make a regular income by picking the 'right business' and investing in the same; instead, he wants to even acquire ownership of the 'right business'. Not only that, he also wants to work for the 'right business' in order to help the same in attaining its optimum potentials. But he is not interested in only making maximum profits by exploiting the optimum potentials of the 'right business'; rather he wants to maintain his holding in that company as long as possible, as he believes that a 'right business' also provides greatest career opportunities.

Thus, Warren Buffett is of the opinion that only those companies that are in a position to provide career advancement, job security and greatest opportunities for sustainable earnings can be the most suitable for ownership, investment and to work with. Warren Buffett considers such companies only as the 'right businesses' capable of providing 'durable competitive advantage', as their inherent economics work in their favour. But, the matter does not end here. Warren Buffett further subjects these 'right businesses' to serious financial analysis, techniques of which would be presented to you in detail in the second chapter.

However, for Warren Buffett, it is not enough to just pick the 'right business' and perform its 'financial analysis'; he pays equal attention to choose the 'right manager' for running that business. Just think, Warren Buffett had taken over control of Berkshire Hathaway almost 53 years back in May 1965. During that period, the market value of its shares kept growing at the rate of 21% pa whereas the average annual return of Dow Jones Industrial Average (DJAI) was only 2.075%. Now, the question comes up naturally - how was it possible for Warren Buffett to achieve such an amazing performance? Most of the people would just say that he is the greatest investor of the world. Of course, there is not an iota of doubt in the fact that Warren Buffett has been the greatest and the most successful investor of our time. But, this is not a full answer to the question. In fact, the most important point to understand in respect of Warren Buffett is that he has been an exceptionally successful 'manager' also.

Yes, Warren Buffett is that single particular individual who has been in control of the huge multinational conglomerate like Berkshire Hathaway continuously for the last 53 years. However, even most of the followers of Warren Buffett's investment strategy have not made serious attempts to understand and absorb his 'management sutras'. Had that happened, multinational corporates would have definitely undergone transformation in their work culture. You are going to read in the third chapter, how Warren Buffett had gone ahead with his selection of the 'right managers' for his different businesses and how he had developed for himself the art of delegation of authority to those 'right managers'. But, Warren Buffett had gone ahead still further and had also developed the unique art of motivating the managers; you will read about the same in fourth chapter. This was the reason that Warren Buffett had transformed various businesses of Berkshire Hathaway into a powerful business empire. You would be surprised to know how much Warren Buffett had learnt from other people, including the pioneer of self-development Dale Carnegie and how he had incorporated those lessons into his management style. Be it the skill of making impression in the very first meeting or the magic of showing appreciation or dangers of making criticism or precise use of counselling - Warren Buffett is ranked at the top among the most efficient leaders of the modern age in respect of encouraging, motivating and influencing their managers.

However, as a business expands, its growth providing opportunities for better earnings is also accompanied with problems and challenges. In Warren Buffett's opinion, business pathways are replete with pitfalls and disaster planning is required to safeguard against them. He counts risks associated with excessive credits, violations of rules by employees, straying away from good thoughts, making unintentional mistakes, inability to manage sycophants and missing right opportunities as the pitfalls of business pathways and lays emphasis on using specific management techniques to confront all those problems and challenges. Buffett believes that only when we are capable of managing them, we would be able to notice the opportunities of concerned businesses. However, Buffett had, on the basis on his experiences, gradually developed his disaster planning for safeguarding against those pitfalls. In the fifth and the last chapter, we are going to discuss Buffett's those very invaluable experiences that would help every leader in keeping himself away from those management pitfalls and extricating himself out of them.

I am sure, 'Money Making Skills' would not only provide an opportunity to the sensible readers to understand the 'money skills' of the greatest investor of the world but also help them in ensuring success in their personal and professional life by applying these management sutras.

– Pradeep Thakur

❑

1

Picking the Right Business

Warren Buffett has not only been a long-term investor but also an exceptional business manager. And in both of these 'avatars', the core mantra of Warren Buffett's success has been - picking the right business.

Yes, long before starting his professional life as an investor, Buffett had already uncovered the mystery that all the businesses did not have the same economics, and there were some specific kinds of businesses whose economics by nature worked profusely in their favour. The companies with such inherent business economics required minimal capital investment as compared to their earnings. This kind of companies mostly manufactured brand products that never needed to be replaced. Or else, they provided such vital services that did not have any competitive substitute. Thus, they are in a way 'monopoly businesses' only. That is the reason these companies had the freedom to charge more for their products and services, thus providing them much better profit margins.

During his entire professional life, Warren Buffett has always been looking for such specific businesses only that enjoyed favourable inherent business economics, as he considers them only the 'right businesses'. Buffett always believed discovering or picking the 'right business' to be the most important aspect of his investment strategy. However, his main objective has been not only to make a regular income by picking a 'right business' and investing in the same; Warren wants to even acquire ownership of the 'right business'. Not only that, he also wants to work for the 'right business' in order to help the same in attaining its optimum potentials. But, he is not interested in only making maximum profits by exploiting the optimum potentials of the 'right business'; rather he wants to maintain his holding in that company as long as possible, as he believes that a 'right business' also provides greatest career opportunities.

Companies Having Durable Competitive Advantage

Warren Buffett is of the opinion that only those companies that are in a position to provide career advancement, job security and greatest opportunities for sustainable earnings can be the most suitable for ownership, investment and to work with. Warren Buffett considers such companies only as the 'right businesses' capable of providing 'durable competitive advantage', as their inherent business economics work in their favour.

In fact, these companies have basic products and services that are certainly always in demand but they never require too much of modification or alteration. Hence, such companies do not have to make huge investments in upgradation of plant and machinery either for research and development or on account of modifications in product design. These companies continue to run their old plant and machinery for years with minimal maintenance expenses, until they wear away completely. Thus, the companies use such huge saved funds for expansion of their business, and they neither have to go for bank borrowings at high interest rates nor have to raise funds from market by issuing fresh shares of equity. Not only that, it is also generally easy to sell such basic products and services and they are able to keep their brand image set in consumers' minds without incurring too much of advertisement expenses. For these very reasons, such products and services are always in heavy demand that helps concerned companies attain high levels of profit margin associated with high sales volume. In such a case, these companies generate cash internally to the extent that they are able to continuously expand their business out of their own funds.

For example, companies like Coca-Cola do not need to invest billions of dollars on continuous improvement in design or quality of their products and upgradation of their plant and machinery for the same to maintain their competitive edge. Thus, such companies accumulate enough cash to make them capable of taking over other companies to expand their market without resorting to borrowings or selling their shares of equity. On the other hand, take a look at the companies like General Motors. The designs of their products - automobiles, keep changing almost every year and they have to spend billions of dollars every year on upgradation of their plant and machinery. If General Motors does not do that, it would not be able to compete with companies like Ford Motors and Toyota. This is the reason that, for meeting their capital expenditure requirements, all the companies in automobile industry have to resort to sale of bonds and shares of equity along with bank borrowings over and above their sales revenue.

Since, in this case, the 'inherent business economics' of the soft drink industry works in favour of companies like Coca-Cola, they are able to provide durable competitive advantage. On the other hand, the 'inherent business economics' of the automobile industry does not work in favour of companies like General Motors and they are not capable of providing durable competitive advantage. Now the question arises as to which of the two kinds of companies can provide career development, job security and the best opportunities for long-term earnings - one that is capable of generating huge amount of cash internally, or the other that is burning huge amounts of cash? We all would have the same answer - the companies that are generating huge amounts of cash, as extra cash holdings reflect well on the management of those companies and also provide them generous bonus at the end of every year. It is obvious that such companies only can provide job security to their employees and also opportunities to their shareholders for better earnings.

It is clear that Warren considers only such companies the 'right companies' that are capable of providing durable and competitive advantage. Such companies have three basic business models - those who sell unique products, those who provide unique services and those who trade in low-cost products and services that are part of common people's needs and are always in heavy demand.

Companies Selling Unique Products

We may include Coca-Cola Company, PepsiCo Inc., Philip Morris Marlboro, Budweiser (Anheuser-Busch InBev Group), Gillette (Proctor & Gamble/ P & G), Hershey Company, Wrigley (Mars, Inc.), Kraft Foods Group, Marc & Co. and Johnson& Johnson etc. among the companies selling unique products. Here, we are providing brief details for unique products of some companies and their brand image.

Coca-Cola Company: Coca-Cola is considered to be the most successful brand of its kind. Everybody has heard the name 'Coca-Cola' and it would be difficult to find a person who would not recognise its red trademark. 'Forbes' magazine had estimated the brand value of 'Coca-Cola' at USD 58.5 billion with 4% annual growth and had placed it at the fourth position among the top 100 most valuable brands of the world in 2016. During that period, 'Coca-Cola' brand alone had earned revenue of USD 21.9 billion whereas Coca-Cola Company had spent only USD 4 billion to promote its brands including 'Coca-Cola'.

Coca-Cola Company is the most significant player among those operating in the non-alcoholic industry across the world. Coca-Cola has its headquarters located at Atlanta, the capital of the state of Georgia in southeast America. This controls and operates the vast network of around 300 bottling plant operators spread across the world through its regional sub-headquarters. During the year 2014, the Company had achieved operating revenue of USD 46 billion which included 46.7% share of North America and that was the biggest market for Coca-Cola. Coca-Cola has a share of around 30% in the world market.

You may be surprised to know that Coca-Cola was not the first to launch a coca-based drink. Coca plants have been grown as a cash crop especially in Argentina, Bolivia, Colombia, Ecuador and Peru in western South America. Coca leaves are known around the world as a source of psychoactive alkaloid 'cocaine', though cocaine content in the same ranges from 0.25% to 0.77% only. Hence, chewing coca leaves or drinking coca tea does not induce feeling of excitement or depression like that caused by cocaine. The juice of coca leaves is being used as medicine for ages; however, it was in 1863 when French chemist Mariani discovered the chemical formula of coca wine. This wine launched in the market with brand name 'Vin Mariani' had become quite popular among the nobility. Nevertheless, the maximum cocaine content in this wine was just 10 mg per ounce and hence, this was very tasty but this induced addiction to drinking.

Twenty-three years after that incident, when 'Vin Mariani' was at the top of its sales in Europe, pharmacist John Pemberton, a retired Lieutenant Colonel of American Army from Georgia, was busy with his experiments to find an alternative for the same. He had created a new wine named 'Pemberton's French Wine Coca' by mixing Coca fruit (a tree native to tropical rainforests of Africa) and damiana leaves (a shrub native to western Texas) with Coca leaves. However, around the same time, the local administration had banned all kinds of alcoholic beverages because of the temperance movement. John Pemberton had then, in 1896, developed a sweet cold drink by modifying the chemical formula of that wine and using seven natural tasty syrups including carbon-based sugar drink, coca leaves and kola fruits. This chemical formula is even today preserved as a secret. Though this was a non-alcoholic drink, it basically had content of cocaine and was launched in the market as a brain tonic. It was not Pemberton but his bookkeeper Frank Robinson who had inspired him to give it the name 'Coca-Cola'. Robinson had used his cursive writing to create the trademark for 'Coca-Cola' that is the most recognised handwriting in the world. Though the credit for suggesting the name goes to Robinson, the honour of Coca-Cola's initial success and popularity is given to Pemberton only.

As such, Pemberton had found it difficult to recover even the production cost for Coca-Cola for the first year. He had started selling Coca-Cola from a medicine shop in Atlanta as a soda fountain drink for five cents a glass. Though the original Coca-Cola also had addiction-inducing properties, it did not prove to be as popular as 'Vin Mariani' and its average daily sale during initial days was limited to just six glasses. However, John Pemberton had proved to be more prudent with respect topromoting and publicising his brand much faster as compared to Angelo Mariani. He had very quickly recognised the power of advertising and had published the first advertisement for Coca-Cola in the local newspaper 'The Atlanta Journal' just three weeks after the drink was invented. This was the reason that while the once popular wine 'Vin Mariani' disappeared from the market due to lack of promotion and publicity, sales of Coca-Cola saw huge jump on the back of advertisements. John Pemberton himself managed advertisements for two years. However, just a week before his death, he sold his interest in Coca-Cola to a local pharmacist and his business friend Asa Griggs Candler.

Candler founded the Coca-Cola Company in 1892 and registered its trademark a year later. However, much before that, in 1885 itself, Candler had executed his expansion plans in all the states of the United Statesand sale of bottled Coca-Cola had started in all major markets. Bottling plants had taken shape during initial years of the 20th century and in the next 100 years, Coca-Cola had established itself as the most recognised brand in the world. It may be noted that the name of 'cocaine' had been already removed from Coca-Cola much earlier and in 1893 itself, its competitor cold drink company the Pepsi-Cola Company had been launched in New Bern (Craven County), North Carolina, an American state close to Georgia; this was constantly trying to compete with Coca-Cola.

Still, Coca-Cola had gone ahead expanding its market as the most successful brand. Why? Because 'Coca-Cola' had made all possible efforts to sustain the market's trust and belief in itself. Now, just have a look at the catch-phrases used by Coca-Cola in its advertisement campaigns - 'The Great National Temperance Drink' (1906), 'Six Million a Day' (1925), 'The Real Thing' (1942), 'What You Want is Coke' (1952), 'Coke is it!' (1982), 'Always Coca-Cola' (1993), etc.

And, don't you remember the historical tag line 'Thanda Matlab Coca-Cola' of the advertisement campaign of Coca-Cola in 2002 in India, which the company had used to enter the rural markets? This tag line in rural language was written by Prasoon Joshi and delivered in the ad film by cine star Amir Khan. At that time, Prasoon was working as a simple copywriter with multinational advertising company Ogilvy & Mather (Delhi). However, this advertisement went on to become so popular that it had won Prasoon Joshi the opportunity to join competing multinational advertising concern McCann Erickson as Executive Vice President and National Creative Director, leaving his almost 10-year old job. Many ad films were created on this tag line and Coca-Cola was able to make its entry into the rural market across India on the back of this campaign.

Of course, the fact that it has always been able to linger in the mind and brain of customers through its incessant ad campaigns based on convincing tag lines has been the greatest strength of the Coca-Cola brand. In 2014 alone, Coca-Cola had spent a total amount of USD 3.50 billion for only this very brand on different ad campaigns and mass-contact activities across the world. The Company had also spent the same USD 3.50 billion on its second biggest brand 'Sprite'. Thus, the Coca-Cola Company was the one spending the most on advertisements during 2015 among all the 100 most valuable brands.

PepsiCo Inc. - PepsiCo is considered to be a differentiation brand. This is not as successful as Coca-Cola. As such, there is no brand on this earth as successful as Coca-Cola, but this also is a fact that it is the majestic position of 'Coca-Cola' that makes 'Pepsi' special, as Pepsi is the only non-alcoholic drink brand that has been able to retain its identity parallel to 'Coca-Cola' for such a long time. You may clearly differentiate between 'Coca-Cola' and 'Pepsi' and that is the reason it is called a differentiation brand. Definitely, this is the best non-alcoholic beverage brand of the world to remain at the second position so close to its main competitor. Although the brand 'Burger King' is also at the position next to McDonald, the gap between the two is quite significant. Such fiercely and closely competing brands like Pepsi and Coca-Cola are not found in this world.

'Forbes' magazine had estimated the brand value of 'Pepsi' at USD 19.3 billion with annual growth of 3% and had placed the same at the 29th position among the 'World's Most Valuable Brands' of 2016. During that period, the Pepsi brand alone had attained a revenue of USD 11.8 billion (USD 39.10 billion less than that of Coca-Cola) whereas PepsiCo had spent USD 2.4 billion on promotion and publicity of all its brands including 'Pepsi'. Thus, by spending just USD 16 million more on advertisement as compared to PepsiCo, the Coca-Cola Company had managed to earn extra revenue of USD 39.10 billion on its primary brand. The Coca-Cola Company had spent 6.8% of its brand revenue on advertisements whereas, PepsiCo had to spend 12.6%. Of course, there is no non-alcoholic beverage brand in between Coca-Cola and Pepsi.

It was in 1893 when University of Maryland School of Medicine educated pharmacist Caleb Davis Bradham had started selling the cold drink named as 'Brad's Drink' from a soda fountain located at his pharmacy Bradham Drug Company in the city of New Bern situated at the confluence of Trent and Neuse rivers close to the sea beach of the south-east American state of North Carolina. Some 489 miles away from this place, 'Coca-Cola' had already taken birth seven years back in Atlanta (Georgia). Though both the drinks had contents of cola fruit, the two were different. While 'Pepsin enzyme' was used in Brad's Drink, 'Coca-Cola' had contents of 'coca leaves'. Coca leaves in Coca-Cola provided it a little bit of cocaine that triggered in the drinker a sense of energy boost associated with a feeling of exhilaration. On the other hand, pepsin enzyme in 'Brad's Drink' improved digestion as well as provided a sense of energy boost. There was a clear difference between the two drinks but by that time, Coca-Cola had established its identity in the market by promoting itself as the original/real beverage. That is why, when Bradham, in 1898, renamed his Brad's Drink to 'Pepsi-Cola' on the lines of Coca-Cola and started to promote the same also with the tagline 'The Original Food Drink', consumers had not taken it seriously. The majority of people considered Coca-Cola only as the original food drink and hence, they started treating 'Pepsi-Cola' as an imitation of Coca-Cola.

Not only that, until 1950, Pepsi-Cola had used 'price' only as the basis of its competition with Coca-Cola, as its managers considered that alone to be the best marketing strategy. This had badly damaged Pepsi-Cola's brand image and it got coined as 'kitchen cola', a cheap and the best alternative of the 'real cola'. However, starting from 1958, Pepsi focused on refining its brand image with its tagline 'Be Sociable, Have Pepsi', targeted at the younger generation. Again, starting 1961, Pepsi made attempts to make its brand image still more widespread with new ad slogan 'Now It Is Pepsi, For Those Who Think Young'. The two words 'Now' and 'Young' in the tagline had worked towards defining the features of Pepsi. The most interesting aspect of this tagline was that it had connected 'concept of youth' to the 'state of mind' instead of the 'real age'. This was also a correct brand strategy, as the brand Pepsi itself had already crossed the age of 60.

In fact, 1963 proved to be the real year to define the Pepsi brand when the company launched its 'Pepsi Generation' ad campaign.

This campaign was also effective because the advertisements were based on mental attitude instead of price, quality, taste etc. of the product. However, it was the 'Pepsi Challenge' ad campaign of 1975 that had played the pivotal role in establishing the Pepsi brand. This campaign had not only challenged the customers by running a 'taste test' programme, but had also dared Coca-Cola openly to declare that Pepsi had a better taste. In the coming years, the 'Pepsi Challenge' campaign had created so much excitement and its communication had proved to be so effective that the same scared Coca-Cola and it had to modify its 'chemical formula' and launch 'New Coke' in the market. As Coca-Cola had always been a leading brand, its defensive strategy of being a 'follower' proved to be unsuccessful and 'New Coke' was badly beaten. As if Pepsi was just waiting for Coca-Cola to falter, it immediately launched its 'New Generation' ad campaign in an extremely aggressive manner. In this historical ad campaign, Pepsi had presented Michael Jackson when he was at the pinnacle of his popularity across the world.

Later, Pepsi had continued its campaign by securing appearance of other famous personalities. However, Pepsi's ad campaign in coordination with the 'Like a Prayer' album (1989) of Madonna had run into some controversies and it had to withdraw its campaign on account of boycott by its customers and criticism by the Vatican. However, the support from those personalities had overall helped Pepsi brand achieve huge success and it had established itself as the favourite brand of the youth in comparison to classic image of Coca-Cola. In recent years also, Pepsi has continued with its attempts to improve its brand image through innovative ad campaigns and it appears to be ready, with its differential identity, for every challenge from Coca-Cola.

Philip Morris/Marlboro: Marlboro is the world's largest selling cigarette brand. This is produced and distributed in the United States by Philip Morris USA (A company of Altria Group) and in other parts of the world by Philip Morris International (an independent company separate from Altria Group). At present, Marlboro is at the top position in the United States for the last 35 years, currently having 44% market share and its total sales being even more than combined sales of the rest of 10 American cigarette brands put together. 'Forbes' magazine had estimated its brand value as USD 21.90 billion with annual growth of

11% and had placed it at 26th position, one position up over previous year, among the 'World's Most Valuable Brands' of 2016. During that period, Marlboro had earned a revenue of USD 23.10 billion. As advertisements for tobacco products are largely banned across the world, Philip Morris had to spend USD 473 million only in 2015 to indirectly promote its 'Marlboro' brand.

Philip Morris, belonging to a German family living in England, had established his tobacco shop at Brand St. (road connecting Oxford St. in the north and Piccadilly in the south) in London in the year 1847. He had started producing cigarettes in his name in 1854; later in 1870, he had launched his cigarettes in the market with brand names 'Philip Morris Cambridge Blues' and 'Philip Morris Oxford Blues'. After his death in 1873, his widow Margaret Morris and nephew Leopold Morris carried on the trade and made the company public; the company was given the name 'Philip Morris & Company' in 1885. In 1894, the Morris family relinquished its control over the company and William Curtis Thomson and his family took over the same.

Again, in 1924, Philip Morris launched a new brand 'Marlboro', different from its own name; this was a high-quality brand targeted towards women. This name was picked up from the Great Marlborough St. (Soho, London) where the company had its factory earlier. Marlboro was promoted and marketed with the tagline 'Mild as May'. When scientists confirmed lung cancer to be a result of smoking during 1950s, Philip Morris had started to establish Marlboro as a cigarette for men. Till that time, filtered cigarettes were being marketed only for women, but now Marlboro was launched in the market with filter. In order to launch Marlboro in the market in its new form, the advertising agency in Chicago, Leo Burnett had launched a widespread ad campaign under which, captains of ships, weight-lifters, war journalists, construction workers etc. were presented as 'Marlboro Man' in a series of advertisements. The company management was initially hesitating to launch this campaign, but within a year of running this campaign, Marlboro brand hitherto having a market share of just 1%, jumped straight to the fourth position.

TV commercials were created in 1963 based on theme music of the film 'The Magnificent Seven',composed by American musician and music event organiser Almer Bernstein; however, after the ban was imposed on tobacco advertisements in 2006, the company started to promote 'Marlboro' brand by organising motor sports. If the sales of 'Marlboro' have gone up throughout the world despite limited advertisement options, it is only because of the legacy of the brand and exceptional quality of the product that attracts its fans.

Budweiser (Anheuser-Busch InBev Group): Budweiser, known as the 'King of Beers', is the largest selling (over 50%) pale lager brand of the United States. This is one of the 16 brands having sales of over USD 1 billion out of more than 200 alcohol brands produced and distributed by the world's largest alcohol-producing company (having over 25% share of the world market) Anheuser-Busch InBev (Leuven, Flemish Brabant, Belgium). This company was formed in 2007 through the amalgamation of three international alcohol-producing groups - Interbrew (Belgium), AmBev (Brazil) and Anheuser-Busch (USA). However, Anheuser-Busch (USA) had already introduced 'Budweiser' in American markets in 1876.

'Forbes' magazine had estimated the brand value of 'Budweiser' at USD 23.40 billion with an annual growth of 5%and had placed it at the 25th position among the 'World's Most Valuable Brands' of 2016. During the period, Budweiser had earned a revenue of USD 10.90 billion, but 'Forbes' has not provided any information on advertisement expenses incurred by the company.

Produced using barley and hops plants along with 30% rice, 'Budweiser' is a traditionally filtered beer that is served through fountain or offered in bottles or cans. Due to trademark controversies, this is sold in 80 countries of the world in different names. Though 'Budweiser' has been recording fall in its sales in the United States during the last few years, its total sales had gone up by 6.4% in 2014 on account of continuous growth in China, Russia and Brazil. The company pays a lot of attention to promotion of its brand, though no clear estimate is available on advertisement expenses for this specific brand.

Gillette (Proctor & Gamble/ P & G Group): Gillette is the leading brand in shaving and is world famous specifically for its safety razors. In January 2005, Proctor &Gamble (P&G) had acquired the Gillette Company established in 1901, along with its personal care products and various other brands through a share deal amounting to USD 57 billion. 'Forbes' magazine had estimated the brand value of Gillette at USD 20.20 billion with 1% annual decline and had placed the same down by 2 positions at 28th position among the 'World's Most Valuable Brands' of 2016. During that period, Gillette had earnedxc brand revenue of USD 7 billion, though for that, Proctor & Gamble (P&G) hadas\ to spend USD 8.30 billion, USD 1300 million more than the revenue, on advertisements for 'Gillette'. (Previous year also, to attain brand revenue of USD 7.90 billion for Gillette during 2014, P&G had to spend a total of USD 9.20 billion i.e. 1300 million extra.)

During the same period, P&G had spent a total of USD 8.30 billion on promotion and publicity of its baby care brand 'Pampers' and 'Pampers' was able to earn revenue (more compared to Gillette) of USD 10.40 billion. However, 'Forbes' magazine had estimated the value of 'Pampers' brand a USD 11.50 billion only (i.e. USD 8.70 billion less than that of Gillette) and placed the same at 50th position (22 places below Gillette) among the 'World's Most Valuable Brands' of 2016. However, the above figures present some interesting facts about Proctor & Gamble (P&G). P&G is the only company in the world that had spent USD 16.60 billion in a year to promote its two product brands.

In fact, it was during the summer of 1895 when the idea of developing a safety razor and a special kind of double-edged steel blade came up in the mind of the Boston (Massachusetts, USA) resident roving salesman King Camp Gillette, then working for Crown Cork & Seal Company, as he had got fed up with his straight razor. Camp Gillette had taken six years to perfect his ideal safety razor, as the machine tool makers that he had contacted had turned to be pessimistic and had termed his design to be impracticable. However, in 1901, Gillette finally teamed up with William Nickerson, an Massachusetts Institute of Technology (MIT)educated machine tools specialist, to turn his idea into a reality and founded 'The American Safety Razor Company'. In the beginning of 1903, it had started producing razors and blades, which were launched in the market in October through an advertisement published in 'Systems Magazine'. In the first year, a total of 51 razors and 168 blades were sold at the rates of USD 5 per razor and USD 1 per blade.

However, Camp Gillette was successful in getting patents registered in 1904 for his razor, blade and razor-blade set and sales had jumped to 90,884 razors and 1,23,648 blades during that year. Next year, the company had bought a six-storey building in south Boston area and had made payment of cash dividends to its investors for the first time in 1906. In the meantime, Gillette had started to expand his business in European countries by opening his first foreign sales centre in London in 1905. On the back of advertisements for his revolutionary razor and blade in various newspapers, Gillette was able to multiply his sales to such an extent that, by 1909, he had to install manufacturing plants in Paris (France), Montreal (Canada), Berlin (Germany) and Leicester (England) and expand his sales network. The American Army had placed an order for 3.50 million razors and 36 million blades during the First World War (1914 to 1918). Gillette had to engage 500 new employees to execute the order. In 1921, when the term of his patents had expired, Gillette had applied for a patent for an advanced version of the razor and had started selling the same at old prices.

Later, the Gillette Company had acquired other companies and expanded its presence in writing instruments (Paper Mate, Parker and Waterman brands), correction products (Liquid Paper brand), toothbrush and other oral hygiene products (Oral-B) and alkaline batteries (Duracell) also and had started selling its products in 200 countries after setting up 64 manufacturing facilities in 27 countries across the world. Thus, 60% of its sales were coming from outside the United States. However, only its razors and blades were the primary drivers of its business. In recent times, despite changes in customer behaviour with regard to shaving, Gillette has been successful in maintaining its business level on the strength of its innovative products and widespread promotion campaigns. As Gillette is now a part of P&G, clear figures relating to the business of this specific brand are not being made public.

Hershey Company: When there is a talk of chocolates, the first name that comes to mind of consumers is 'Hershey'. With a market share of 44.3%, the Hershey Company was the largest producer and seller of high-quality chocolates in the United States at the end of 2016, whereas its nearest competitor brand Marsh was lagging far behind with market share of just 29.3%. Of course, Marsh was at the top position in the American market of chocolate-free confectionery products with a market share of 18.2%, whereas Hershey was at the 2nd position with a market share of 13.5%. Hershey manages distribution and sale of its products with over 80 brand names in 70 countries. In the world market, Hershey is considered to be the 4th largest producer of chocolates after Mondelez (Cadbury), Marsh and Nestle. 'Forbes' magazine had estimated the brand value of Hershey at USD 6.7 billion with 7% annual growth and had placed the same at 99th position in the list of the 'World's Most Valuable Brands' of 2016. During that period, Hershey's revenue was USD 4.7 billion whereas the Hershey Company had spent USD 562 million on advertisements for its brands including 'Hershey'.

When Hershey's founder Milton Snavely Hershey dropped out of school at the age of 14, his mother had arranged for his apprenticeship with a local confectioner at Lancaster (Pennsylvania). During the next four years, Hershey learnt the art of making confectionery and started his first confectionery business in Philadelphia. Six years later, when his business had failed, Hershey apprenticed with a confectioner in Denver (now capital of Colorado state) and learnt to make caramel with fresh milk. After that, Hershey tried to establish his business in New York, but that attempt also failed. He then returned to Lancaster (Pennsylvania) and founded Lancaster Caramel Company in 1886. The use of fresh milk in caramels proved to be successful. Hershey expanded his business quickly. Soon, 1400 employees started working for Lancaster Caramel Company and Hershey started exporting caramel to entire America as well as Europe.

In the meantime, an international exhibition, the World's Columbian Exposition was organised in Chicago in 1993. It was with this very exposition that the Chicago Parliament of Religions was convened where Swami Vivekananda had delivered his historic speech. Milton Snavely Hershey was so impressed after seeing German chocolate-making machines in the exhibition that he immediately bought two machines and sent them to Lancaster. Using some other equipment, Hershey started to create chocolate coating for his caramels. The ever growing demand for chocolates prompted Hershey to upgrade his entire production system to make the same capable of producing a unique concoction of milk chocolate. In 1894, when Hershey formally incorporated Lancaster Caramel Company, he also established Hershey Chocolate Company on 9 February 1994 as a subsidiary to the same.

During the next six years, Hershey found his milk chocolate business to be so promising that he sold his Lancaster Caramel Company in 1900 to American Caramel Company for USD 1 million (equivalent to approximately USD 287.88 million as on today). Hershey invested the entire amount in 'Hershey Chocolate Company' and started producing 'Hershey's Milk Chocolate Bar' brand. In 1903, Hershey started construction of a chocolate plant in his hometown Derry Church (Pennsylvania), which later came to be known as Hershey (Pennsylvania). This town was an inexpensive place for the workers and their families to live. The milk chocolate bars manufactured at this plant proved to be popular and the company grew rapidly.

Wrigley (Mars, Inc.): Whenever we talk of chewing gums, the first brand that comes to our mind is 'Wrigley'. William Wrigley Jr. had founded the 'Wm. Wrigley Jr. Company' on 1 April 1891 in the industrial city Chicago (Illinois) of the United States of America. The American multinational confectionery group Mars Inc. had announced its acquisition on 28 April 2008 for USD 23 billion. It sells its products in more than 180 countries through its operational network in over 50 countries. It has 21 production facilities in 14 countries including the United States of America, Mexico, Spain, United Kingdom, France, Czech Republic, Poland, Russia, China, India, Japan, Kenya, Taiwan and Australia.

Wrigley's story is quite interesting. It was in 1891 when 29-year-old William Wrigley Jr. moved from Philadelphia to Chicago with just USD 32 with him and started a business to sell soaps. Wrigley started to offer his customers baking powder as free gift to improve sales of his soap. Wrigley was then aware that baking powder was more popular among people. He then started selling baking powder and to boost its sale, started offering chewing gum strips as free gifts. Very soon, Wrigley found out that the chewing gum was getting more popular. He thus concentrated on the manufacture of different kinds of chewing gums.

At that time, chewing gum was popular among women only. Soon, Wrigley offered two kinds of chewing gums in the brand names of 'Sweet Sixteen Orange' and 'Lotta Gum' targeted towards the youth market; this brought about a revolution in the entire chewing gum market. However, Wrigley tasted real success only when, during the economic slump in 1893, he brought out two other products with brand names 'Wrigley's Spearmint' and 'Juicy Fruit' that were going to become identities for the company. And when the economic downturn became still severe, William Wrigley Jr. took an unimaginable risky step. Wrigley pledged everything he owned and launched advertisement campaign on a large scale and very soon, Wrigley emerged as a national level company. Wrigley now understood the strategy of market expansion on the back of ad campaigns and he never had to look back after that.

Warren Buffett has always maintained that when an investor buys shares of stocks of these companies, he actually acquires ownership of a piece of the consumer's mind. The essence of Warren's observation is that when a company acquires ownership of the 'piece of consumers' minds', it never requires changing its products. In such a case, the company gets opportunities to realise better prices for its products as well as sell more products. Clearly, the company enjoys much better profit margin in that case and it achieves better inventory turnover; this is just like a big bottom line on income statement of the company. It is easy to identify such companies, as figures of their annual income are consistent and remain strong and debts are quite low or nil.

Warren asserts that these special kinds of companies providing durable competitive advantage present their managers the greatest opportunities for the best and the easiest growth in their professional lives. As such companies have fast cash flow, they are capable of making generous payments to their managers and employees towards their salary and various allowances as well as annual bonus. Not only that, these companies have plenty of funds to start new business and to acquire other companies to expand their business. Hence, young managers working for these companies also get great opportunities to excel in their professional lives.

Companies Selling Unique Services

Warren Buffett counts companies selling unique services also among the companies providing durable competitive advantage. Among such companies, he includes Moody's Corporation (business and financial services company), H & R Block (tax preparation company), American Express (financial services company), Service Master Global Holdings (residential and commercial services company) and Wells Fargo & Company (banking and financial services company).

Moody's Corporation: The name 'Moody' has been a synonym for securities for more than a century. This name has always been moulding itself to match the changing requirements of the American capital market Wall St. and financial markets across the world. Even this is interesting to note that while majority of the people in the world know about 'Moody's Investor Services' and its ratings and research reports, there are very few people who are aware of Moody's Corporation, a public company listed on the New York Stock Exchange. Yes, during 2016, Moody's Corporation was performing rating and analysis for 120 sovereign nations, around 11,000 corporations, 21,000 public financial services companies and 72,000 structured finance obligations through its offices and 11,700 employees in 36 countries. Moody's Corporation had reported revenue of USD 3.60 billion for the year 2016.

John Moody founded John Moody & Company in 1900 in New York, the financial capital of the United States, and published the first edition of 'Moody's Manual' that was full of statistics related to financial institutions, government establishments and companies listed on New York Stock Exchange. Within next few years, 'Moody's Manual' became a must-have for every investor and the company attained national reputation. John Moody then decided to publish books based on other financial matters through Moody Publishing Company. The first book 'The Truth About Trusts' was published in 1904; this contained details and analysis for public trusts in the United States. However, after the steep stock market crash of 1907, Moody and many of his loyal readers had to face suffering and he was compelled to sell his business along with his 'Moody's Manual'.

However, Moody returned with a new outlook within next two years. Moody's new approach was not just to provide information about companies to the investors worried about impending dangers but going a step further, to provide estimation of their assets and their performances also. Moody decided to address the fast-growing rail industries at that time and published a book titled 'Moody's Analysis of Railroad Investments' in 1909. In the book, Moody utilised the rating method followed by the then 'credit rating agencies', for in-depth analysis of rail industry. In 1912, Moody authored the book titled 'How to Analyse Railroad Reports' and in 1913, he widened his speciality beyond railroad industry to general financial ratings. Like his initial success, Moody's professional expertise once again took him to a leading position in securities business. His ratings started getting popular among investors and in July 1914, he founded a new company named 'Moody's Investor Services'. During the next decade, Moody started to rates tocks as well as entire debt securities/bond market. Moody authored many books for Yale University Press; two of those books published in 1919 - 'The Masters of Capital: A Chronicle of Wall Street' and 'Railroad Builders: A Chronicle of Welding of States' had been quite popular.

When in 1929, the share markets had crashed and the period of world recession had started, John Moody did not have to sell his business like before. Both he and his ever-growing 'rating services' survived. Despite collapse of many in the financial sector, Moody continued to write and publish his ratings and analysis results. He also wrote a memoir tilted 'The Long Road Home: An Autobiography' (McMillan, 1933), the next part of which was published with title 'Fast to The Road' (McMillan, 1942). John Moody breathed his last in February 1958 at the age of 89 years. Four years later, in 1962, Dun and Bradstreet, a major firm engaged in credit reporting and data collection, bought Moody's. During 1970s, Moody's started collecting fees from the companies getting rated. The time-taking in-depth research reports prepared by Moody's proved to be invaluable for both investors and the companies being analysed. Companies soon realised that getting a good rating from Moody's was just like having a good bank balance. Eventually, Dun and Bradstreet Corporation, having decided to take out Moody's services out of its private ownership spun off the same into a public traded company 'Moody's Corporation', listed on the New York Stock Exchange.

H&R Block: When an individual or a small businessman thinks of filing tax return, especially in the United States, the first name that flashes in his mind is that of H&R Block, the company providing specialised services in tax preparation; this company is however expanding its business to other countries of the world also. Yes, H&R Block also provides the same tax return filing services that your accredited chartered accountant does. However, it has been successful in developing this simple service as a specialised international brand and today, it is the largest tax services company in the world. In 2016, H&R Block was operating a total of 11,933 offices across the world; this included 10,223 offices (6,614 under company ownership and 3,599 as franchisees) in the United States, 1,282 in Canada, 438 in Australia and 5 in India. According to 'Forbes' magazine (May 2015), around 88,000 employees were working in these offices. During 2016, H&R Block had prepared a total of 2,31,68,000 tax returns (1,96,95,000 in the United States and 34,73,000 in other countries) and earned revenue of around USD 3 billion (with net profit of USD 374.20 million).

Henry Wollman Bloch, second son of a famous lawyer of Kansas City (the largest city of Missouri, a mid-west state of the United States), had joined Army Air Force services after completing his graduation from Michigan University; there, he was deputed to Harvard Business School for graduate training in statistical control. After returning from army services in 1946, Henry, along with his elder brother Leon, founded 'United Business Company' to offer tax return and book keeping services for common people and small professionals. However, as the business did not pick up in the first year, Leon left for seeking a law degree. Later, when the business picked up, Henry placed an advertisement to hire an employee. In response to the advertisement, his mother suggested him to hire his younger brother Richard who had just completed his graduation in economics from the Wharton School of Finance (Pennsylvania University). Both the brothers then started running the business; their business picked up slowly.

Henry and Richard placed an advertisement in local newspaper for their services and number of their clients started growing. When, in 1955, the Internal Revenue Service announced closure of their free service for tax return preparation, Henry placed an ad in a local newspaper and after that, there was sudden jump in the number of clients seeking tax preparation services. Finding the demand for their services growing, Henry Bloch renamed his company to 'H&R Block' that was easy to pronounce. The company business grew so rapidly that Henry went ahead to open seven offices in 1956; the company's revenue went up three times over previous year. In 1962, when the number of offices of the company had gone up to 206 and 'H&R Block' had become a national tax service brand, Henry made the company public and listed the same on the New York Stock Exchange.

American Express: American Express is known as an 'Integrity Brand'. 'Forbes' magazine had in May 2017 estimated the brand value of American Express at USD 24.50 billion with 1% growth and had placed the same at 23rd position in the list of the 'World's Most Valued Brands' of 2017. During that period, American Express had earned a revenue of USD 33.80 billion.However, the company had to also spend USD 3.7 billion on advertisements for brand promotion.

'American Express' has had a remarkable history. In 1850, it was founded as an express freight company and it earned its reputation and credibility by carrying out supplies to the eventual winners Union Army during the American Civil War (1861 to 1865). While continuing with its freight operations, American Express expanded its activities to financial service industry in 1980. Streams of European immigrants were at that time entering the United States and American Express offered them the service of making remittances to their home countries. In that course only, American Express in 1891 invented 'Travellers Cheque' that brought about revolution in travel as well as the finance industry.

However, another primary innovation emerged much later in 1958 in the form of 'American Express Card', a green coloured plastic charge card. Just like travellers' cheques, charge card also provided people an opportunity to get free from both eration of keeping cash in their pockets. As charge card could not be issued to all, very soon the 'American Express Card' became a status symbol among the American nobility. For the rest of the 20th century, American Express continued to run its ad campaign with tagline 'Membership Has Its Privileges' to promote this card. This tagline became quite famous and the elites across the world were clamouring for owning this card.

Though American Express has now grown to be a multinational company offering travel, financial and network services and promotes itself as a 'Financial Super Market', most of the people still consider it as a 'charge card' company only. As such, both 'American Express' brand and the card have changed their connotations during recent decades. This has continued to transform from an exclusive brand to an inclusive brand. In order to expand its customer base, the company started issuing 'credit card' also in addition to the charge card. Customers were buying this for practical convenience instead of as a status symbol. Though it was a very risky business strategy to transform from an 'Integrity Brand' to a 'Popular Brand', American Express has attained grand success in establishing itself as the 'World's Most Respected Service Brand' on the strength of its long experience and its unblemished and distinguished reputation for financial integrity and security. This is the reason that the company keeps on running widespread ad and mass-contact campaigns.

Service Master Global Holdings: Especially in the United States, 'Service Master' is regarded as the most popular brand for residential and commercial services. Service Master operates more than 7,000 company-owned and franchisee branches around the world. It has 13,000 corporate employees whereas the franchisee network independently employs around 33,000 additional people. The core services of the company include termite and pest control, home warranty, disaster response and restoration, janitorial service, home cleaning, furniture repair and home inspection. During 2016, Service Master Global Holdings earned a net profit of USD 155 million on total revenue of USD 2.746 billion.

The founder of Service Master, Marion E. Wade had to drop out of his 8th standard and take up the job of a peon to help his family. Along with that, he continued to play baseball and even joined the semi-professional team of 'Chicago Braves' in 1915. After the death of his brother during the First World War, Wade joined the US Navy in 1918 and even underwent combat training. However, the War was soon over. A few days after returning from the services, Wade married in 1920 and leaving baseball, he started his professional life as a sales person. Nine years later, when the period of great recession had begun in 1929, Wade started providing moth proofing services for residences and offices. Some 18 years later, in 1947, Wade incorporated 'Wade, Wagner & Associates' and started offering carpet-cleaning services also in addition to moth proofing. The business picked up rapidly and in 1954, Wade renamed his company to 'Service Master'.

After the death of Wade in 1973, his successors took the business forward. In July 2007, a group of private equity investment firms led by Clayton, Dubilier and Rice (CD&R) acquired Service Master. In June 2014, the company with name 'Service Master Global Holdings' was incorporated as a publicly traded company and listed on the New York Stock Exchange.

Wells Fargo & Company: 'Wells Fargo' is a major financial services brand of the world. In May 2017, 'Forbes' magazine had estimated its brand value at USD 13.2 billion with 4% growth and had placed the same at 43rd position in the list of the 'World's Most Valuable Brands' of 2017. During that period, Wells Fargo had earned a revenue of USD 94.2 billion and the company had spent USD 595 million on brand promotion.

In the list of the 'World's 2000 Largest Public Companies' of 2017, 'Forbes' magazine had placed Wells Fargo at fifth position after Industrial and Commercial Bank of China (ICBC), China Construction bank, Berkshire Hathaway and JP Morgan Chase; at that time, its total sales amounted to USD 97.60 billion, profit USD 21.90 billion, assets USD 1,943.40 billion and market capitalisation USD 274.40 billion. It may be noted that on 22 July 2015, Wells Fargo & Company attained the status of the world's largest financial institution by surpassing Industrial and Commercial Bank of China (ICBC) with a market capitalisation of USD 301.60 billion, and then, its market price was USD 40 billion above that of JP Morgan and USD 120 billion above that of Citi Group. Not only that, Wells Fargo had beaten ICBC even in 2013.

In the beginning of 1848, when gold was found at Sutter's Mill near Coloma (California), entrepreneurs and financiers from all over North America and the world had flocked to California, drawn by the promise of huge profits. Vermont native Henry Wells and New Yorker William G. Fargo had also then watched the California economy boom with keen interest; but, as they were so busy with their profitable businesses at that time,they did not show any hurry to rush there. However, they founded Wells Fargo & Company on 18 March 1852 with an initial capital of USD 0.30 million, to provide banking services in California. After going through all the ups and downs, the present Wells Fargo & Company took birth in 1998 by merger with Norwest Corporation. As Wells Fargo enjoyed a historical brand image, that very name was carried forward.

For the above companies, the economics of selling unique services may be extraordinary. Such companies have to neither modify or replace the design of their products nor spend money on installation of production units. They have to spend a major part of their fortune on constant upgradation of plant and machinery and on godowns to store their products. Not only that, these companies that provide unique services and possess ownership of a part of the mind of the consumers, are able to generate better profit margin as compared to the companies selling products. Obviously, the managers who work for these companies enjoy much higher remunerations. Their professional lives are more productive and stable, as such companies do not have to face the financial ups and downs that impact other businesses badly.

Now, if we examine the operating histories of companies like H&R Block and General Motors, we may notice that, irrespective of severity of economic slump, the business of tax return preparation never faces any slowdown, as people, in any case, are required to file their tax returns. On the contrary, even an economic slump for a short period may damage the financial condition of companies like General Motors, as people stop buying motor vehicles. Not only that, the managers and directors of companies like H&R Block do not have to burn midnight oil as those in companies like General Motors do, worrying either for the demands of the workers unions or increasing debts or sudden changes in consumers' behaviour.

Companies Trading At Low Costs

According to Warren Buffett, the third kind of companies that provide durable competitive advantage are those who buy things at very low costs and sell them to consumers at the lowest prices. Among Warren's such favourite companies are Walmart, Costco, Nebraska Furniture Mart, Borsheims Fine Jewelry and Burlington Northern Santa Fe. These companies are successful in keeping their profit margins high due to high volumes of sales. As these companies make purchases at large scale, their costs are low and hence, they are able to achieve high sale volumes and good profit margins at the lowest prices as compared to their competitors. The lowest prices become goodwill for these companies and keep attracting consumers to their stores.

Walmart Stores: Walmart is a 'scale business' brand. During the period between 1980s and 90s, Walmart, besides expanding in regional markets of the United States, had established its dominance on national level also. By 1988, Walmart had become the highest profit earning and by October 1989, the highest revenue earning retail stores chain of the United States. In 2002, Walmart had become the largest company of the United States by earning a net profit of USD 6.70 billion on total revenue amounting to USD 219.80 billion. By earning a net profit of USD 15.40 billion on total revenue of USD 422 billion (that included contribution of 109.20 billion from international operations) for the year ending 31 January 2011, Walmart had secured the position of the world's largest company (in terms of revenue).

In May 2017, 'Forbes' magazine estimated Walmart's brand value at USD 24.10 billion and placed the same at 24th position in the list of the 'World's Most Valuable Brands' of 2017. During that period, Walmart had earned a revenue of USD 326.30 billion, the highest among all in the list, and had spent USD 2.90 billion on its advertisements. For the year ending 31 January 2017, Walmart Stores had earned net profit of USD 14.293 billion on total revenue of USD 485.873 derived through a huge network of 11,500 stores operating under 65 trade names in 28 countries of the world. In the list of the 'World's Largest Public Companies' of 2017, 'Forbes' magazine placed Walmart Stores at the 9th position in the overall category, first position in sales revenue, 11th position in net profit, 35th position in assets and 15th position in market capitalisation category.

The interesting fact is that it was in 1945 when 27 years old Sam Walton started Walmart as a simple retail business. Then, how did this grow into the world's largest retail brand and the world's largest revenue earning company? Sam Walton has mentioned in his biography 'Made in America - My Story' that his strong resolve to connect with the customers was at the core of his business philosophy. In his list of 'Business Building Rules', Walton has written in his 8th rule –'Let them (your customers) know you appreciate them.' Yes, Walmart implements this in its business in many ways. Despite being huge in size, Walmart has always tried to provide its customers a homely atmosphere, treat them as neigh bours and develop personal rapport with them. For measuring customers' spending pattern, Walmart has been utilising specialised high-grade software right from its initial phase, and on the basis of the information coming out of the same, the suppliers of Walmart were able to find out the items, their quantities and the stores where the same were required to be supplied.

However, the key to Walmart's success is the scale of its business. Walmart, on account of huge size of its stores, makes all possible efforts through its 'store receptionists' to turn the buying experience of every customer personal. It is because of its size only that Walmart is able to buy any product in large quantity at minimum cost and sell the same at minimum price. It is Walmart's size only that enables it to offer its customers 'Every Day Low Prices' i.e., items offered at the minimum sale price in comparison to any other store. Walmart has always kept on growing in size and moving ahead. This is the reason that Walmart has not been able to get permission for direct retail business in many countries, including India. The Government of India is concerned that Walmart's entry into retail business might sound the death knell for small and medium retailers. However, Walmart cannot abandon its customer-centric business philosophy just for that.

Nebraska Furniture Mart: Nebraska Furniture Mart (NFM) is the largest home furnishing store of North America. Located at South 72nd St. in Warren Buffett's hometown Omaha (Nebraska), its main store has retail space extending to 4,20,000 square feet (39,000 sq. m) within a 77-acre (3,10,000 sq. m) single collective campus. Nebraska Furniture Mart was founded by Rose Blumkin, popularly known as Mrs. B., in 1937. Though, at the age of 89 years, Mrs. B. sold 80% stake in Nebraska Furniture Mart, amounting to USD 60 million, to Warren Buffett in 1983, she continued, at Buffett's request, to manage the store almost for her entire life.

Rose Blumkin was born on 3 December 1893 in Schedrin, a village near Minsk (capital of Belarus). She was one among eight children of Solomon and Chasya Gorelick. His father was religious teacher in Judaism (rabbi) and her mother ran a grocery store to support her struggling family. All the siblings had to sleep on straw in a single room. Rose used to feel pity for his father's prayers who was not capable of even providing a mattress to his family. When her mother had to bake breads in oven in the night like slaves, she used to get awake at midnight. She would feel quite distressed to see her mother toiling and hence, right from the age of 6, she had started assisting her mother in running her retail store. The Gorelick couple did not have enough money to send their children for school education. In the circumstances, Rose did not get a chance to attend any class in a school, but she learnt reading, writing and counting in an affluent family. The greatest lesson she learnt from her mother was that begging was the most despicable job. This was the reason that, right at the age of 13 years, Rose took up a job at a dry goods store in Minsk. Three years later, when she was 16 years old, Rose became manager of the store with six male employees reporting to her.

When Rose was twenty, she married shoe salesman Isador Blumkin, who soon thereafter immigrated to the United States in order to avoid conscription in Russian Army. Rose also had then thought that she would soon join her husband in the United States. But, the War started before she could leave. Later, during the unbearable cold of 1917, when Europe was burning and Russia was trembling, Rose boarded the Trans-Siberian Railway (the world's largest railway network from Moscow to Vladivostok - connecting Lake Baikal and the far-east region of Russia in East Siberia and touching the borders of Mongolia, China and North Korea). The Russian security forces detained Rose at the border region of China, as she did not possess a passport. Rose told the Russian security forces that she was going to buy leather for army and she would bring bottles of vodka for them while returning. Thus, she reached Japan after crossing Manchuria in northeast China; there, she secured a place on a ship and some six weeks later, she somehow managed to get down at Seattle port (United States). Though Rose could not speak English, she was successful in locating her husband Isador Blumkin in Fort Dodge, Iowa.

Later, the Blumkin couple relocated to Omaha (Nebraska) in 1919. Isador opened a used clothing store and Rose started selling furniture from its basement. Though they themselves were quite poor, Rose asked her parents and siblings to join them and they all were living together under the same roof. As Rose could not speak English, her children taught her English after they started going to school. In 1937, when she was 44, Rose managed to save USD 500 and she took a store on rent on Furnam St. Rose had big dreams and hence, she named her store as 'Nebraska Furniture Mart'. Her way of selling and her motto - both were the same - 'Sell cheap and tell the truth'. Branded furniture houses found Rose Blumkin's way of selling detrimental to their businesses and hence, they stopped supplies to her; however, Rose was expert in selling illegitimate goods. She would go to Chicago or Kansas where retailers like Marshal Field would sell their extra items at prices just a little over their cost. This way, Rose Blumkin continued to sell furniture at the lowest prices.

Rose had applied for a loan for expansion of her business, but bank officials ridiculed her and rejected her request. This experience developed an everlasting sense of hatred in her mind towards so-called 'big people'; however, she, on the strength of her unwavering resolve, carried forward her business ideal. She continued working for 7-days a week, 52-weeks a year without taking leave even for a day. Yes, Rose Blumkin had affection with her work and her middle-class consumers. These loyal customers would come to this very store for their entire home furnishing needs and gradually, Rose Blumkin became popular among them as 'Mrs. B'.

In 1949, Mohawk Carpet Mills dragged her to court alleging violation of 'fair trade law' by her. As a manufacturer, Mohawk had fixed the minimum retail price for its carpet at USD 7.25 per yard, but 'Mrs. B' was selling the same at the rate of USD 4.95. The judge in fact asked the lawyer of Mohawk, "Then, what's wrong in that?" and rejected their charge. Not only that, that judge himself visited Nebraska Furniture Mart next day and bought carpets for USD 1,400.

Next year, when 'Mrs. B' was unable to make payments to her suppliers, one of her friends, a bank officer, extended a loan of USD 50,000 for 90 days. Mrs. B had then taken a big risk to keep her business afloat on any condition. She rented a big conference hall and sold furniture amounting to USD 2.50 in the next three days and took a pledge never to borrow again. Thus, at the age of 57, 'Mrs. B' had started running her business entirely in her own way.

'Mrs. B' also used to treat her workers and her family members quite mercilessly. However, Mrs. B's eldest son, Louis also was a hardworking businessman like his mother. Contrary to his mother, he was a very gentle and soft-natured person. Thus, whenever Mrs. B fired a worker, he would employ him again. This way, Louis used to save his mother from her mistakes. But, Mrs. B's business principle was so attractive and tempting that customers were not able to stop themselves from coming to Nebraska Furniture Mart. She would make purchases in large quantities, keep her costs to the minimum and try to pass on all her saving to the customers. Normally, she used to sell her items at prices just 10% more than her costs; however, she was famous for creating exceptions. She would instantly reduce prices depending on customers' needs and their pockets and sell items at just their wholesale prices.

As such, Warren Buffett was desirous of acquiring Nebraska Furniture Mart for a long time; but it was a privately owned company. However, when Buffett put forward his proposal for acquisition in 1983, Louis and his three sons were managing the store and 'Mrs. B' was the chairperson of the company and fulltime administrator of its carpet section. When Buffett learnt that she was willing to sell the store, he went through the tax return of the store. The store's pre-tax income at that time was USD 15 million. Warren did not make any enquiry about the assets of the store and offered Mrs. B the proposal for 80% ownership for a value of USD 60 million, that was five times its income, and Mrs. B immediately accepted the same. It may be noted that Nebraska Furniture Mart was having annual sales of USD 100 million at that time and it had two-thirds share in total furniture sales in Omaha. Even the furniture store chain like D Lords that was grossing annual sales of USD 4 billion had not opened its store in Omaha only for the reason that it was not in a position to compete with the prices offered by 'Mrs. B'. This was the reason that, even after acquisition, Warren Buffett left the management of the store with Mrs. B and her family only. However, in 1989, when her family members forced 'Mrs. B' into retirement at the age of 95, she was quite upset with their decision and just after three months, she opened "Mrs. B's Clearance & Factory Outlet" just in front of the store. Mrs. B's new store came into profit within next two years and it grew to be the third largest furniture store of Omaha. The following year, Warren Buffett bought this store also and got it merged with the old store.

In 1994, Nebraska Furniture Mart added an electronic and home appliance store also. In 1998, when 'Mrs. B' died at the age of 104, she had left behind the largest furniture store of the United States. In 2001, the Mart acquired 'Homemakers Furniture' and opened its second store in Iowa; in 2003, the Mart opened its third store in Kansas. By 2011, the business attitude had changed and in 2013, Nebraska Furniture Mart opened its fourth and the largest store in The Colony (Texas).

Borsheims Jewelry Company: Warren Buffett was so impressed by the business style of Mrs. B that just six years after acquisition of Nebraska Furniture Mart, he had acquired Borsheims Jewelry located in Omaha . Louis Borsheims had founded this jewellery store in 1870; but, when Mrs. B's sister Rebecca and brother-in-law Louis Friedman purchased that small jewellery store in 1948, they also adopted her motto 'Sell cheap and tell the truth' and the store started gaining popularity rapidly.

In 1986, when they found the 116-years old 8000 sq. ft. Borsheims store, located in Omaha city centre, to be too small, it was relocated to a 23,000 sq. ft. facility at Regency Court, the most expensive shopping centre in Omaha. Very soon, Borsheims had grown to be the largest selling jewellery store, after Tiffany & Company, of the United States. Later, Borsheims further expanded its retail space to 62,500 sq. ft., adding large watch section, gift gallery and jewellery repairs and design facility to the same. More than 100,000 jewellery items, watches and gifts were displayed in the store. Borsheims Jewelry Company meets demands of its international customers spread across 50 countries through this sole facility.

Burlington Northern Santa Fe Corporation: This is the parent company of the BNSF Railway (formerly the Burlington Northern Santa Fe Railway). This corporation was incorporated in 1993 to facilitate the merger of Burlington Northern and Santa Fe Pacific Corporation. The BNSF Railway is one of the largest freight railroad networks in North America. It has 44,000 employees, 32,500 miles (52,300 km) of track in 28 states and more than 8000 locomotives. It has three transcontinental routes that provide rail connections between the western and the eastern Unites States.

On 3 November 2009, Berkshire Hathaway had offered its proposal to buy the remaining 77.4% share in Burlington Northern Santa Fe Corporation for a value of USD 26 billion. Considering the earlier investment of Berkshire and USD 10 billion of loans and other liabilities of Burlington Northern, this deal was finalised for USD 44 billion. Concluded on 12 February 2010, this was the largest acquisition in the history of Berkshire Hathaway.

In this chapter, we have till now discussed three kinds of business models that provide durable business advantage. Out of them, the low-cost trading companies provide minimum opportunities for career advancement. As the managements of these companies are always under pressure to keep the costs to the minimum, they try to maintain their employees' emoluments also at a low level. Still, compared to other average grade businesses, these companies offer better opportunities for jobs and management. Warren Buffett considers the companies working in all these three business models to be 'right businesses'. However, he also performs economic tests of the concerned companies to pick the best out of them.

❑

2

Economic Test of a Business

As we have read in the previous chapter, in Warren Buffett's point of view, only those companies can be the best for ownership, investment and working that are capable of providing the greatest opportunities for career advancement, job security and long-term earnings. Warren considers such a company only the 'right business' able to provide 'durable competitive advantage', as the inherent business economics of the company works in its favour. In the previous chapter, we have learnt about three business models of the companies providing 'durable competitive advantage' and we will now discuss the methods that Warren Buffett uses to perform the economic test for those companies.

It may be noted that Warren Buffett had always considered investing as a pure business. This concept or philosophy of investing is called 'business perspective investing' in professional language. In Buffett's view, the real investment is the one that follows the fundamental principles of business and there is no place for conjecture or speculation in the same. The primary aim of a business is to earn profit that operates on the basic formula of economics of demand and supply. The mystery of the historical investment Buffet's success is implied in this very 'business perspective investing'. This phrase may appear to be simple but it is a very challenging concept. It is not because investing with business approach requires superlative financial and accounting knowledge, but because this is entirely different from the prevalent wisdom of the capital market.

Warren Buffett's concept of 'business perspective investing' is a special kind of professional skill that is based more on business discipline that on 'business philosophy' and once you are able to understand this concept, you would know that this skill also demands absolute devotion. This absolute devotion helps you to maintain your existence in financial landscape. Even a minor deviation would force you to dance to the tune of senseless concepts of 'fear' and 'greed' and, you would never be a prudent investor and would turn into an imprudent speculator forever.

Please keep in mind that all the capital markets in the world have large numbers of imprudent speculators who help create atmosphere of fear and greed by fanning silly business behaviour based on conjecture. People having dreams of getting rich quick get caught in their net, as they find this route of speculation easy. Such people are never able to enjoy the strenuous practice of prudent investors and become a part of the large team of speculators or withdraw from the market itself after losing everything. On the contrary, if you invest with the perspective of business, others' stupidity becomes a fertile land for you to harvest the crop of profit; that means imprudent speculators in capital markets indulge in silly business behaviour because of the widely popular mentality of fear and greed whereas prudent investors, who only make disciplined and prudent investments with business perspective, get opportunities to make profits out of their mistakes. Hold on! Prudent investors making investments with business perspective do not get profit-making opportunities only from others' silliness. In fact, they are able to enjoy these profit-making opportunities created by others' mistakes just because of their disciplined business behaviour.

In order to adopt Warren Buffett's fundamental investment philosophy based on business perspective, we will have to definitely learn the art of evaluating a business or else, our investment decisions would not be prudent and we also would join the team of the gamblers of the capital markets and get entangled in speculations. And, in order to determine the condition of any business entity, its business balance sheet will have to be analysed and the meaning behind its figures will have to be understood thoroughly.

Warren Buffett's 'Pinball' Business

Keep in mind that,before starting his business, young Warren Buffett had never thought that he would grow to be the richest person of the United States or the world. He did not have any such dreams also. Yes, he was definitely eager right from his childhood to earn a lot of money and for that, he had decided to start a business. As he wanted to reap the amazing benefits of compound interest fully, he was also fully aware that the sooner he started his business the better would be its results. He was also aware that it would not be possible to earn compound interest after death; instead, the tax department would be at the door for recoveries.

In fact, Warren had started displaying his inborn interest in business and investing at a young age. In his childhood itself, he had started making money by selling chewing gums and Coca-Cola bottles and delivering weekly magazines door-to-door. He had also worked in his grandfather's grocery store. While still in high school, he had already made good money by selling golf balls and stamps, cleaning cars and delivering newspapers. In 1944, when he filed his first income tax return, he had reported his income after claiming deduction for use of his bicycle and watch for newspaper delivery.

In 1945, as a high school sophomore, he had made a lot of research on high-income businesses. And finally, he bought a used pinball machine (special kind of coin-operated amusing game machine) in good working condition for US$ 35. Thus, he had created the first asset for his business and now, to install the machine, he was looking for a site where maximum people could use the same. He first of all contacted the local billiard hall operator who told him that he already had four pinball machines. In fact, he did not want Warren also to install his machine there and break his customers. Hence, he turned Warren away. Warren was then able to figure out that the billiard hall operator had created his monopoly over indoor games in the local market and he did not want anybody else to enter that field.

Naturally, for Warren Buffett who was already impatient to start his business, this was his first encounter with the market reality. And, he did get highly frustrated with this shock depriving him the opportunity to make money. But he was not ready to accept defeat. As he had already made a complete analysis of the profitability of the business even before buying the pinball machine, there was no question of going back. He was determined to use this business to make money. He had also understood well that the most important factor affecting the success of a retail business was - its location. Access to the location that had the maximum movement of customers was in any case denied to Warren. Hence, Warren started looking for other options. Very soon, a great idea clicked in his mind. He observed that most of the youth playing pinball sported 'crew cut' hair. He then found out that alocal barber named 'Searge' was offering that style of haircut.

When Warren inspected Searge's barber shop, he found out two things - firstly, there was no pinball machine there and secondly, the shop had a large space where the youth willing to play pinball could wait for their turn. Then itself, the idea of the first joint venture of his life clicked in Warren's mind and he offered Searge the proposal to share 20% of total revenue if he permitted him to set up his pinball machine in the shop. As if Searge was waiting for such an offer, he immediately said 'yes' to Warren. Very next day, Warren installed the pinball machine there. Next day, when Warren went to the shop, he found US$ 10 in the machine. He gave 20% share (USD 2) to Searge and pocketed 80% of revenue (USD 8). While coming out of the shop, Warren realised that this business was going to be quite lucrative.

But it is complicated to answer what would be the valuation of Buffett's pinball business. We will have to study the economics of the business.

Study of Balance Sheet: To study the economics of a business, we need to first of all look at its balance sheet i.e., its financial condition. (See table)

One-day Balance Sheet of Pinball Business

Assets	
Cash (from a day's operation)	$ 8.00
Property	$ 35.00
Total Assets	$ 43.00

Liabilities	
Debts	$ 0.00
Paid-up Capital (Money used to start business)	$ 35.00
Retained Income (Money retained out of business operations)	$ 8.00
Shareholders Equity / Book Value	
Paid-up Capital + Retained Income	$ 43.00
Total Shareholders Equity & Liabilities	
	$ 43.00

In fact, a balance sheet is the report of financial position of a company. The one-day balance sheet of Warren Buffett's pinball business reveals that his total assets amount to USD 43 and he does not have any liabilities. We can see under assets category a figure of USD 8 that represents amount collected from a day's operation and property of USD 35 that represents the value of the pinball machine. As Warren has not taken any loan for his business, he does not even have any liabilities. Paid-up capital is the amount that was used to start the business, and here, that amount is USD 35. Retained income is the amount kept out of income from business operations and in this case, USD 8 is the amount generated after a day's operation. The total of paid-up capital and retained income is shareholders equity that is also called book value or net worth and here, that amount is USD 43 (35 + 8).

It may be noted that we may create balance sheet for our business as on any date, but incorporated units/companies prepare the same at the end of fiscal/financial quarters and financial year.

Study of 'Income Statement: Another important document for evaluation of any business is – the income statement. Income statement for one-day operation of Warren's pinball business would be prepared as below.

One-day Income Statement for Pinball Business

Revenue	$ 10.00
Expenses	$ 2.00
Income	$ 8.00

Revenue is the amount generated by business operations or other sources. Here, one day's operation has generated USD 10.00 that represents its one-day revenue. As there is no income from any other sources, hence the same is not reflected above. 'Expenses' represents the amount that is spent to operate the business and in the above case, Warren made a payment of USD 2 to Searge and the same is categorised under expenses. Thus, business income amounts to USD 8 that Warren could pocket.

Evaluation of Pinball Business: Till now, we have studied his one-day balance sheet and income statement to evaluate Warren Buffett's pinball business. Then, what would be the value of this business? The balance sheet shows the book value or networth as USD 43. Does this mean the value of the company is just USD 43? Or, is it possible that Warren Buffett would have sold his business at this price? Clearly, Warren would have never done this and if the business belonged to you, you also would not have done this, as it had the potential to make an average net income or profit of USD 8.

As Searge's barber shop remained open on all seven days of the week, even on holidays, the business was to run on all 365 days of a year. Also, as Searge's customers were not going to go anywhere else for haircut and they would have waited for their turn in that hall where Warren had installed the pinball machine, at least that many people would have definitely used the machine to result in average daily revenue of USD 10. Further, as Searge was also receiving his 20% share in income, he was going to take proper care of the machine and also encourage his customers to use the same. Hence, the possibility of profit was definite. Thus, at the rate of USD 8 per day, this business was going to earn profit of USD 2,920 per year ($8 x 365 days). Had somebody bought the business at USD 43 of shareholders equity or book value or net worth, he would have made a profit of USD 2,920 before corporate income tax, at the end of first year. This way, the investors would have got an opportunity to achieve a great return on investment.

Was Warren a fool then that he would have sold his business with such a potential to an investor for just USD 43 of shareholders equity or book value or net worth? Definitely not! Warren would have affirmed that his pinball business was going to make annual profit of

USD 2,920; he expected the business to run at the same level for next ten years and hence, the buyer would have got an opportunity to make a total profit of USD 29,200 in next ten years. Does this mean Warren would have indicated the present value of his business to that buyer as USD 29,200? Absolutely not! Because, the buyer of the business could have enjoyed opportunities to make USD 44,516 out of the profits from this business. But how? This was possible if the business profits were invested regularly in a bank's recurring deposit or money market fund earning average 8% interest.

Then, how would have the buyer evaluated Warren's business? It is clear that Warren had estimated the future value of his business as USD 44,516, assuming the buyer regularly invested daily income of USD 2,920 ina deposit account or any other financial product earning 8% interest. Thus, had the buyer decided to buy Warren's business assuming 8% annual return on his investment, he would have estimated its present value as USD 20,619.52 approximately.

It would be better if you use a financial calculator for this computation, as manual computation of compound interest may take a lot of time. You may even use financial calculator for this, but it is costly. Hence, you better use financial calculators available on the Internet. There are separate calculators for future value and present value. For now, in the present value calculator, write $ 44,516 in the space for FV (future value), 10 in the space for N (number of years) and 8% in the space for I/Y (interest per year) and click on 'Calculate' button. The result you get would be - 20,619.52.

Had the buyer paid the present value USD 20,619.52 for Warren's pinball business, it would have meant that he expected a return of 8% compound interest on his investment and he found it appropriate to receive a future value of USD 44,516 at the end of 10th year. This would have also meant that the buyer did not have any other investment option that could have generated a better return. Would he have accepted Warren's sale offer if he had another investment option giving 10% compound interest? Definitely not! Then, what would have he estimated as the present value of Warren's pinball business? In the present value calculator, leave all the values as entered earlier and change the value for I/Y (Interest per year) from 8% to 10% and click 'Calculate' button. You will get the answer as - $17,165.85.

This means that the buyer would have got an opportunity to earn a total interest amount of USD 27,353.15 on his purchase price of USD 17,162.85 at @10% pa.

Then, what should be the real value of Warren's pinball business? According to Warren, at least USD 20,619.52. However, the final value depends on the fact whether the buyer is ready to buy at that price. If the buyer has a risk-free option to earn better return on his investment, he would not buy the same at that price. He would try to look for another option at USD 17,162.85 to earn compound interest @10% pa. Clearly, if you evaluate any investment proposal this way, you can find out its appropriate present value. And, from the point of view of Warren, remember the first lesson of investment - the price one pays eventually determines the return of investment. The lower the purchase price, the higher will be the profit. Only the investors who take their investment decision this way are considered to be 'prudent investors' by Warren Buffett; those indulging in guesswork are called speculators.

Earn Compound Interest, Get Rich

Since, Warren Buffett was very, amazed by compound interest, he would always explain its amazing beneficial results to his initial partners. The history of the phenomenal success of the Berkley Hathaway, company that manages Warren Buffett's investment empire, presents an exceptional example of the 'miracle of compound interest'.

Berkley Hathaway was established in 1839 as the Valley Falls Company in Cumberland (Rhode Island, the United States of America). In 1962, Warren had started buying shares of Berkley Hathaway through his partnership investment company. During the initial months of 1965, he had amassed 49% shares and on 10 May 1965, he had even acquired the company. Though Warren had started buying the shares @ USD 7.60 per share, the average buying cost for all the shares ultimately came out to be USD 14.86 per share. At that time, the value of each share on the basis of book value of Berkley Hathaway was estimated to be around USD 19.

As Warren, from the start itself, wanted to earn compound interest, he had persuaded all his partners for a long-term investment. That was the reason that he neither allowed his original shares (Class-A) to get split nor issued any dividends. Thus, in the initial 25 years, Berkley Hathaway, listed on New York Stock Exchange, saw its share price jump more than 373 times to a level of USD 7,100 (1 June 1990). Five years later, in 1995, the average market price of Berkley Hathaway's share had gone over USD 22,000, much beyond the reach of most of the investors. Considering market demand for higher accessibility and liquidity, Berkshire Hathaway issued shares under class-B category on 9 May 1996; average investors then got the privilege to include this reputed company in their portfolios. However, the stock right of a class-B share was just 1/1,500 and voting right 1/10,000 as compared to a class-A share.

It may be kept in mind that the company never issued dividends except in 1967, as Warren Buffett had invested shareholders' money in more profitable enterprises. This resulted in steady increase in the price of Berkshire Hathaway's share, rising to USD 2,66,013 as on 1 March 2017. Thus, during 52 years from 1965 to 2017, Berkley Hathaway's share price has gone up 14,000 times.

Warren Buffett had been always telling his partners that the perfect way to get rich in real sense was to earn maximum compound interest on their investments. Warren's investment strategy based on compound return can be understood easily with the help of the following table.

Compound Return on Investment of USD 1,00,000

Period/ Interest Rate	5%	10%	15%	20%
10 years	$ 1,62,889	$ 2,59,374	$ 4,04,555	$6,19,173
20 years	$ 2,65,329	$ 6,72,749	$ 16,36,653	$ 38,33,759
30 years	$ 4,32,194	$ 17,44,940	$ 66,21,177	$ 2,37,37,631

Thus, if USD 1,00,000 is invested for 10 years with compound interest rate of 5% pa, we can get a return of USD 162,889. If the rate of compound interest is increased by 5% (i.e. 10%), the return goes up to USD 2,59,374. And if the rate of compound interest is 20%, we may get an opportunity to receive a return of USD 6,19,173 on investment of USD 1,00,000. And, if we continue our investment at compound interest rate of 20% for 30 years, it is possible to even get the maximum return of USD 2,37,37,631. Yes, it was because of this very strategy of Warren Buffett that it was possible for Berkshire Hathaway's per share book value or net worth to grow at an average rate of 20.3% during the period of 45 years from 1965 to 2009.

However, another aspect of Warren Buffett's mystery of the magic of compound interest is that, by not issuing dividends, he saved a lot of personal taxes for the investors. To understand this, let's have a look at the table below showing 'Compound Return on Earned & Retained Profits (8%)'.

Compound Return on Earned & Retained Profits (8%)

Year	Invested Amount	Earned & Retained Interest
1	$ 1,000.00	$ 80.00
2	$ 1,080.00	$ 80.40
3	$ 1,166.40	$ 93.31
4	$ 1,259.71	$ 100.77
5	$ 1,360.48	$ 100.83
Total		**$ 469.31**

Assuming that a person puts USD 1,000 intoan investment offer of a company providing 8% annual return, he may get an opportunity to earn a compound return of USD 469.31 at the end of the 5th year if the company, instead of paying dividend at the end of each year, keeps retaining the earned interest and reinvesting the same. After paying a minimum 33% (2017) i.e., USD 154.87 towards personal income tax on this dividend income of USD 469.31, the investor will be left with the real return of USD 314.43 (469.31 - 154.87) on his investment of USD 1,000.

However, an investor can achieve the same only if he invests in shares of a company that, instead of paying him annual dividend, retains the same and invests it in investment options providing better returns. Warren had done the same. He had retained annual dividends of Berkshire Hathaway's investors and invested the same in more profitable options. As Warren did not make dividend payments to his investors, they did not have to pay income tax on the same every year. Berkshire Hathaway had reinvested those dividend amounts in more profitable options; the price of the company's share was hence constantly going up and the investors kept on enjoying the opportunity to earn compound return on their original investments.

On the contrary, had Berkshire Hathaway kept on paying dividends every year, the investors would have had to pay personal income tax and the effective rate of return on their investments would have gone down considerably. And, Warren had done this also because the investors did not have better options to reinvest their dividends. Had they invested their dividends in government or corporate bonds earning average 8% returns, they would have had to pay income tax on their income and effective return on their investments would have gone down every year by the rate of income tax.

Beware! Most of the investment analysts do advise investors to invest in shares of companies doing excellent business and hold on to the same for long periods, but they do not tell them at what rate they should buy the shares. However, if we follow Warren Buffett's investment strategy, we would not allow ourselves to be taken for a ride by such investment analysts, as Warren says - rate of return depends on the price paid.

For example, in 1987, shares of the food products and tobacco group Philip Morris were trading at prices between USD 6.07 and USD 10.36 (share split adjusted price) per share. Ten years later, in 1997, the average price of those shares had gone up to USD 44. Had you bought Philip Morris's shares in 1987 at the rate of USD 6.07 and sold the same in 1997, after holding the same for ten years, at the rate of USD 44, your pre-tax compounding rate of return would have been 21.9% approximately. But, had you bought the same shares at the rate of USD 10.36 and sold them at the rate of USD 44, your pre-tax compounding rate of return would have been 15.56% approximately. Thus, your investment of USD 1,00,000 in shares @6.07 per share would have grown in ten years to USD 7,24,497.77 with the annual compounding rate of return of 21.9%. But the same investment of USD 1,00,000 in shares @10.36 per share would have grown to just USD 4,24,693.22 with annual compounding rate of return of 15.56%, i.e., the difference in compound returns for the two purchase prices would have been USD 2,99,804.55. You may easily calculate all this using the free online financial calculator we discussed earlier.

Nine Financial Questions to Pick a Business

It is clear by now that if we want to earn the maximum compound return on our investment, we will have to identify incorporated companies doing excellent business before we determine the right prices for the investment options. To develop the philosophy for identification of an outstanding company, Warren incorporated the philosophies of much-acclaimed American investor Philip Arthur and his partner Charles Thomas Munger (Vice Chairman, Berkshire Hathaway) in the philosophy of his guru Benjamin Graham. And finally, he decided that he would invest only in the companies that had strong economics and whose future income could be estimated properly. For this, Warren uses following questions for evaluation:

Question No. 1: Does the business have an identifiable consumer monopoly?

As we have seen in previous chapter, Warren Buffett had been able to pick many such companies that offered unique products or services and enjoyed monopoly-like status in their segment of the consumer market. Warren has been referring to such companies as 'consumer monopolies', like companies maintaining and operating toll bridges.

In Warren's view, this is a classic form of 'consumer monopoly'. If a consumer wants to cross a river without swimming or using a boat, he may have to pay toll-tax to use a bridge, as toll bridge enjoys near monopoly on crossing the bridge at a specific location. It is the same when a big city is served by a single newspaper. If you have to advertise your product or service in that specific city, you would have to place your advertisement in that very newspaper. Clearly, whether it is a toll bridge at a specific location or an exclusive newspaper in a specific city, consumer monopoly provides them the freedom to fix higher prices for their services.

In fact, Warren Buffett had identified some conceptual tests to confirm presence of 'consumer monopoly' in companies engaged in any specific business. For this, the first question he would ask himself

- Had he possessed billions of dollars and had he been capable of employing 50 top managers, could he start the same business and run the same successfully like the concerned company? If the answer was 'No', Warren would assume that the company was protected with some specific kind of consumer monopoly. In Warren's view, the real test for a 'consumer monopoly' company is whether any competitor can, without bothering for its income, harm that company in any way.

For instance, Warren had tried to find out whether it was possible for anybody to compete with 'Wall Street Journal'. And he had figured out that no newspaper, even if it invested billions of dollars, would be able to dent Wall Street Journal's readership. Similarly, he had examined whether he could compete with 'Wrigley' (the world's largest chewing gum manufacturing and marketing company; now a wholly owned subsidiary to Mars Inc.) by launching a company to manufacture tasty chewing gums. Warren had found out that many companies had attempted to compete with 'Wrigley', but most of them had badly failed. And those who could protect their identity also had to be content with their negligible market shares as compared to that of 'Wrigley'. Warren had also made similar assessments for chocolate bar producing company Hershey (now one of the largest chocolate marketing companies in the United States), soft drink company Coca-Cola etc.

For a moment, let's think about Coca-Cola. Just try to imagine all the places where it is sold. You will find Coca-Cola at all street corners, shops of all sizes, restaurants, buildings and public facilities. The popularity of this cold drink compels every shop or restaurant to stock it. Why? Because, non-availability of Coca-Cola might impact their business. Now, try to compete with Coca-Cola. You would need capital base equivalent to two companies of the size of General Motors. You may still not be able to claim that you can compete with Coca-Cola. Only one of its competing companies in the world could grow- that is none other than PepsiCo; because, Coca-Cola has a secret formula to make the cold drink.

Yes, Warren had found out after research that consumer monopoly companies, benefiting from their huge cash flow, are usually almost debt-free. That is the reason such companies are able to launch new enterprises or increase their stakes by buying back their own shares.

Not only that, such companies generally manufacture products that require low level of technology and hence, they do not need to set up high-technology plants. As their products face almost negligible competition in the market, they are able to use their manufacturing plants for longer periods. Being free from competition, these companies do not have to incur regular expenses on upgrading their plants. On the other side, let's consider the case of automobile manufacturing companies. They are also price sensitive like commodity products. That is the reason that even to launch just a new car with a fresh design in the market they have to spend billions of dollars on upgrading old machinery and setting up new production facility. And, cars or other motor vehicles are the products that need constant modifications to keep themselves relevant in the cut-throat competition of the market. To do that, motor vehicle companies have to keep making heavy investments in their production facilities on regular basis.

Question No. 2: Are the earnings of the company strong and showing an upward trend?

A company may be enjoying consumer monopoly status but is its top management capable of constantly taking its earnings to higher levels? Yes, just like Warren, we also would have to attentively go through balance sheets of such companies and examine their figures for per share income. For this, Warren used to study at least ten years' balance sheets of the concerned company and make a table of its per share income figures. If the earnings were strong and showed an upward trend, Warren would infer that the top management was able to convert the favourable consumer monopoly status of the company into real shareholders' value.

Question No. 3: What is the long-term debt position of the company? Is it conservatively financed?

Warren likes the companies that hesitate to avail heavy long-term loans. If the company enjoys consumer monopoly, it is definite that its cash flow would be quite good and it would not even need to impose the burden of a long-term loan upon itself. Wrigley and International Flavors & Fragrances are counted among Warren's favourite companies because their books generally do not show any long-term debt and if at all such debts are there, they are negligible.

Warren's highly profitable companies like Coca-Cola and Gillette do not allow the load of long-term loans in their books to go beyond their 'current net income'.

However, even excellent companies enjoying consumer monopoly sometimes incur long-term debt to acquire another company; for instance, Capital Cities had availed a long-term loan amounting to more than double of its current net income for acquiring American television and radio network American Broadcasting Corporation (ABC) Group. In such a case, Warren would just check whether the company acquired was a consumer monopoly.

If 'Yes', it was ok else, something was wrong.

In this regard, Warren has clear opinion that if a consumer monopoly company avails a loan to acquire another consumer monopoly company, heavy cash flows of the two together negate the impact of the debt. On the contrary, if a consumer monopoly company incurs debt for acquiring a commodity company, it would definitely impact its profitability even if its cash flow is able to withstand the burden of debt. The third situation is the most dangerous where a commodity company incurs debt to acquire a similar company just for the expansion of its market, as it does not have a definite cash flow for the same.

Question No 4: Does the business consistently earn a high rate of return on shareholders' equity?

Warren Buffett has been investing in only those companies that are capable of consistently earning a high rate of return on equity, as such companies could generate wealth for their shareholders.

Here, equity refers to shareholders' equity. In fact, the shareholders' equity represents the amount left after adjusting total liabilities against total assets. In other words, total of the capital investments made by the shareholders in a business is the shareholders' equity in total assets.

For example, to buy a house for ₹ 60 lakh, you invest ₹ 15 lakh out of your savings and avail a mortgage loan of ₹ 45 lakh from a bank, your i.e., shareholder's equity would be ₹ 15 lakh (₹ 60 lakh - ₹ 45 lakh) in the total asset of ₹ 1 crore. Now, if you rent out this house, the amount left after making payments towards maintenance expenses, equated monthly instalments and house tax would be shareholders' equity. Suppose you rent out the house at ₹ 25000 per month, i.e. ₹ 3 lakh per year and your total expenses amounts to ₹ 2.50 lakh (maintenance expenses of ₹ 6000, EMI payments ₹ 2.40 lakh and house tax ₹ 4000), you are left with ₹ 50000 only. Thus, your (the shareholder's)net earningsare ₹ 50000 per year (approximately 3.33%) on your capital investment or equity of ₹ 15 lakh. In other words, your house (business) earned return on equity at the rate of 3.33% for you (its shareholders).

Similarly, if you own a corporate/company having total assets of ₹ 1 crore and the company has a total liability of ₹ 40 lakh, it means that you have made a capital investment of ₹ 60 lakh in the company and the same represents shareholders' equity in the company. If the company makes a net profit of ₹ 19.80 lakh after tax, it means it has earned return on equity at the rate of 33% for you (its shareholders).

In this situation, if Indian companies were collectively earning 12% return on equity, your company would be referred to as 'above average'. And the companies earning less than 12% return on equity would be called 'below average'. Clearly, you would like to invest in companies earning above average return on equity, as they only are able to grow your investment faster i.e., make you rich quicker.

However, Warren Buffett has been treating only those companies as the best, which were able to earn average 15 per cent return on equity at least for the last 10 years; in other words, Warren had invested his precious capital only in the companies that were capable of definitely earning above average return on equity. Yes, when Warren started buying shares in General Food Corporation, its average return on equity was 16 per cent. Similarly, when he started buying shares in Coca-Cola, it was earning 33 per cent return on equity and its average earning was around 25 per cent for the last 5 years. 'Hershey' (chocolate) was one of Warren's favourite companies as its average return on equity for the last ten years was 16.7 per cent. Similarly, when Warren started buying shares in Philip Morris, it was earning 30.5 per cent average return on equity for the last ten years. Also, when Warren acquired a major shareholding in Capital Cities, it was earning 18 per cent return on equity. And, Service Master Global Holdings and Gannett Corporation were earning 40 per cent and 25 per cent returns on equity respectively when Warren had acquired their shares.

Question No 5: Does the business get to retain its earnings?

Warren Buffett believes that the companies that, instead of paying dividends at high rates, are able to retain their net profits to invest the same in more profitable ventures provide their shareholders opportunities to earn compound return through value addition to their original shares. Warren has done the same in his controlling company Berkshire Hathaway. However, he also agrees that all companies that retain their profits are not able to do the same. Hence, we should look into the history of such companies thoroughly.

Question No 6: How much does the business spend on maintaining current operations?

Earning profit, retaining the profit and not spending the retained profit on maintenance of current operations are three different matters. Warren Buffett makes a thorough analysis of these three figures before investing in a company because, if the company is reinvesting surplus retained income into maintaining current operations, there is little money left over to invest in other profitable ventures and to increase the shareholders' fortune.

Suppose a company is making net profit of ₹ 1 crore every year. Instead of making dividend payment to its shareholders, it retains the profit; however, it has to spend ₹ 2 crore every alternate year on replacing its plant and equipment to maintain its operations. It is hence clear that the net profit of the company is in fact zero. Yes, Warren considers only those business operations to be excellent that have to incur no expenses out of their profits towards replacement of their plant or machinery.

In fact, when Warren Buffett managed night classes at College of Business Administration of Nebraska Omaha University in his hometown Omaha on the subject of investments, he would deliver lectures on capital requirements of companies and their impacts. He would quote examples of AT&T and Thomson Publishing in this regard. Warren would demonstrate that AT&T was a bad investment for its shareholders before its disintegration. Though it was earning good income, it had to arrange funds even more than its income to meet its capital requirements like research & development and infrastructure. AT&T used to issue fresh shares or bonds to finance its expansion. On the contrary, companies like Thomson Publishing were publishing many newspapers in cities having single newspaper and making good money for their shareholders. This was possible for such a company as once its basic infrastructure related to printing press was ready, its capital requirements were minimal and it did not need to use shareholders' money for the same. Hence, such companies used to have a lot of cash to acquire new newspapers and increase shareholders' fortune.

This way, Warren would try to impress upon that while one business was able to achieve its value enhancement without much of capital requirements, the other was not able to grow as it required additional capital investments.

American motor vehicle company General Motors may also be quoted as a reference for the same. Between the start of 1985 and the end of 1995, General Motors had earned an average of USD 17.92 per share and had paid an average dividend of USD 20.60 per share. However, during the same period, the company had to spend total of USD 102.34 per share towards capital requirements involving maintenance, upgradation and expansion of the business. Thus, during those ten years, General Motors had to arrange USD 2.68 per share (20.60 - 17.92) towards payment of dividend more than its income and USD 102.34 per share towards its capital requirements.

Thus, the question naturally arises that how could General Motors arrange such a huge amount? Of course, records reveal that during that period, the company had added around USD 33 billion to its debts i.e., the company had taken an additional debt load of USD 43.70 per share. It is clear that the company had not serviced its requirements out of loans only. During that period, the company had issued 132 million fresh shares out of its common stock. This had resulted in a decline of USD 34.29 in the book value/net worth of each share of General Motors during the period. Its book value per share had gradually declined from USD 45.99 in 1985 to just USD 11.70 in 1995.

But surprisingly, the market value of shares of General Motors did not go down. This was trading at USD 40 per share in the beginning of 1985 and it was floating at the same level even after ten years. This meant that even after ten years of business activities, General Motors did not add any value to shareholders' capital as it had gobbled up primary shareholders' capital by adding debt burden of USD 33 billion and issuing 132 million fresh shares to meet its capital requirements; what did the primary shareholders get on their investments? Just a dividend of USD 20.60 per share! If we calculate its pre-tax compound return, it would be around 5.8 per cent. Now, if we adjust tax and inflation against the same, we may find that the invested capital actually lost its real value during those ten years.

And all this happened because the capital requirements of motor vehicle companies are actually so massive. As designs of cars and trucks kept changing, General Motors had to constantly keep its manufacturing plants upgraded as per new requirements. And as its capital requirements were more than its income, it had to take in extra load of debts and also issue fresh shares to collect additional funds. Thus, General Motors had badly failed in adding any value to the shareholders capital just to keep itself in business.

This was the reason that Warren Buffett never invested in companies like General Motors i.e., motor vehicles businesses that required spending shareholders money to keep themselves operational. Clearly, we should also keep away from investing in businesses that constantly require capital investments in their basic infrastructure and research and development; companies involved in such businesses, irrespective of the expertise of their management, are never able to provide their shareholders opportunities for compound return on their capital investments.

Question No 7: Is the company in a position to reinvest retained earnings in profitable options?

In the course of picking excellent businesses, Warren Buffett has always been probing whether the related company is in a position to reinvest retained earnings in profitable options. Keep in mind that Warren's fundamental investment philosophy is - investment with the perspective of business i.e., investment that provides an opportunity to earn more than average return on capital. Earning more than average refers to options that provide opportunities to earn more than bank or government bonds without any risk.

Suppose you save ₹ 10000 every year and keep the same in your cupboard. After ten years, you would have a total of ₹ 100,000. Had you deposited the same amount in a recurring deposit account of a bank earning interest at the rate of 5 per cent, the amount would have grown to ₹ 1,32,067 at the end of tenth year. Had you invested the same amount, like Warren, in investment options earning compound return of 23 per cent, the amount would have grown to ₹ 370,388 at the end of 10th year. And, had you saved the same amount for 20 years with the same rate of return, your savings of ₹ 200,000 could have grown to ₹ 3,306,059. That means, investment made with Warren's skill could turn ₹ 100,000 to ₹ 370,388 in ten years, thus earning an extra amount of ₹ 270,388 on your actual investment; and in the next ten years, your additional investment of ₹ 100,000 could provide you a great opportunity to earn ₹ 2,835,671 in the next ten years. This only is Warren's magic of compound interest, and only a company that is able to reinvest its earnings in more profitable ventures to make such magical returns on your long-term investment is an 'excellent business' in Warren's view.

Of course, Warren has done just the same thing in his controlling company Berkshire Hathaway. He did not make dividend payments every year to his investors; instead, he invested the earnings in more profitable ventures and provided an opportunity to his investors to earn compound return much above an average of 23 per cent on their shareholdings. It may be noted that Warren had applied his magical investment philosophy even in the companies where he has acquired minority stakes. Take for example Capital Cities. What did it do before its merger with Disney? Capital Cities had retained the earnings from its high-cash-flow cable TV business and utilised the same to acquire ABC Group's TV network that itself was a high-cash-flow business. In other words, Capital Cities had reinvested its shareholders retained earnings in more profitable options. ABC Group was a kind of consumer monopoly company as federal laws at that time protected markets of companies involved in TV business and there was no market competition as is prevalent today. As setting up a TV centre required only an initial capital investment and the same could exist for next 40 years, ABC Group was in a position to reinvest retained earnings of its shareholders in more profitable ventures instead of utilising the same for its own capital requirements.

Though TV network business, on account of competition, did not continue to be a very profitable business later, Warren had continued to count the same among 'excellent businesses' for a long time, as the number of main competing companies in any market sector of the United States of America continued to be only three (ABC, CBS and NBC) and they all were able to get their share of advertisements. More or less, the situation in media business continues to be the same even today and this business is more profitable in terms of long-term investment. As the capital requirements of this business is limited, it can fund its market expansion needs with retain earnings of its shareholders and provide them opportunities to earn compound return for a long period.

Question No 8: Is the company free to adjust prices to inflation?
We all know that inflation is a major cause for increase in prices of products and services; however, all businesses are not able to adjust market prices of their products and services to inflation. Now, if we consider a commodity business, we can find that, despite increase in the cost of labour and raw materials, the companies in this sector when faced with higher production, are compelled to lower prices of their products instead of adjusting the same to inflation. It is clear that, in an attempt to sell their products at prices lower than their production costs just to keep themselves in business, they cover their loss with their shareholders' retained earnings. And, when even that is not sufficient to meet their requirements, they increase their debt burden or collect funds by issuing fresh shares. This results in gradual decline in book value/ net worth of the company; it hence finds itself unable to increase value of shareholders' capital investments.

Aviation business also faces similar situations from time to time. All kinds of fixed costs of aviation companies keep growing with inflation. And when they are faced with competition, they are compelled to sell tickets at prices even below their actual costs just to keep themselves in business. It is obvious that they also have to indulge in utilising their shareholders' retained earnings, worsening their debt burden and collecting funds by issuing fresh shares to meet their capital requircments. Thus, they are left with no capital to reinvest in profitable ventures and are not able to add value to their shareholders' capital investments.

Yes, Warren keeps himself away from such businesses that are not in a position to reinvest their shareholders' retained earnings in more profitable ventures, as they are not free to adjust prices of their products to inflation.

Question No 9: Will the value added by retained earnings increase the market value of the company?

Warren's guru Benjamin Graham also, during the last years of his professional life, had said that the capital market consisted of two components. The first was long-term investment centred such that over the long-term, the market price of a company's share would reflect its intrinsic value. The other component was like a gambling house where people would bet on short term fluctuations in market prices.

Graham believed that the gambling house component of the market was dominated by the organisations or people who speculated on the impact of daily news on share prices. At the same time, Graham also maintained that this very gambling house aspect of the market provided the patient investors focused on long-term investments the opportunities to test their skills. For some time, when groups having speculative mentality are dominated by people's fear and greed, market prices also crash in anillogical manner thus providing patient investors to acquire shares of companies at prices even lower than their intrinsic values.

Definitely, Warren also had embraced his guru's this very philosophy in his professional life; he had even made an addition to the same. Warren has always maintained that if a company allocates its capital properly and keeps on improving its book value / net worth consistently, the long-term investment tendency of the market would constantly reflect the same in the market price of its share. The same thing had happened with Warren's own company Berkshire Hathaway. The company had kept on improving its book value by investing shareholders earnings in profitable ventures and the same had been reflected in the market price of its shares. This was the reason that while looking for excellent companies, Warren would definitely investigate whether the value addition by a company through retain earnings was actually getting reflected in its market value.

And, these very nine questions had made Warren Buffett successful in picking excellent companies and finding the opportunities for earning magical compound returns through long-term investments in them.

❑

3

Picking the Right Manager

Sometime in the middle of December 2016, around a month after Donald Trump getting elected as the 45th President of the United States of America on 8 November, when the major stock market index Dow Jones Industrial Average (DJIA) was approaching the figure of 20000, not only the USA but the entire world was immersed in discussions on impending changes in international politics. Very few people at that time would have thought about Warren Buffett as one of the top beneficiaries of the bull run in stock markets. The price of a share of his company Berkshire Hathaway had touched the level of USD 249,711 for the first time on 13 December and after some fluctuations, had reached the level of USD 266,013 on 1 March 2017.

It was some 52 years back, in May 1965, when Warren Buffett had taken over control of Berkshire Hathaway. During that period, the price of a share of Berkshire Hathaway had gone up at the rate of 21 per cent per annum against the average annual return of just 2.075 per cent for Dow Jones Industrial Average (DJIA). Obviously, this performance of Buffett's company had gone beyond even the flight of a mind. Thus, had somebody invested USD 1000 in shares of Berkshire Hathaway in 1964, that investment would have grown to USD 45 million after 52 years. Now the biggest question is - how could Warren Buffettdeliver such an amazing performance? Most of the people would just say that he is the world's greatest investor. There is no doubt in the fact that Warren Buffett has been the greatest and the most successful investor of our time, but this is not a complete answer to the question. The most overlooked point of view in respect of Buffett is that he has been an extraordinarily successful manager also. And, this is also the most useful and inspiring point of view for the leaders of business world.

Yes, Warren Buffett is the only particular individual who has been in command of a large multinational conglomerate like Berkshire Hathaway for the last 52 years. This needs to be given special attention. Perhaps the most talked about chief executive officer in the commercial history of the United States was the one who had run General Motors for 23 years. John D. Rockefeller had managed Standard Oil for 27 years and in recent times, Bill Gates had been chief executive officer of Microsoft for 25 years. However, it is surprising that even though investors around the world try to follow Buffett's investment approach, it may be right to say that his management model has not made any impact on corporate work culture. In this connection, Buffett's old friend and Vice Chairman of Berkley Hathaway Charlie Munger has said in his letter written to shareholders in 2016, "Berkshire system is essential for its success. I am not aware if any other corporate has even half of these elements".

Development of the Skill of Delegating Authority

When Berkshire Hathaway got bigger and bigger and took over control of multiple businesses, Warren Buffett felt the essentiality of 'delegation of authority'. This was required not only for his sanity i.e., his ability to think and behave in a normal and rational manner but also to ensure that the companies were managed competently and managers were happy running them. If there is a single management skill that is uniquely Warren's, it would be his willingness and promptness to 'delegate authority'. In fact, the boldness that Warren has exhibited in delegating unlimited authority to his managers may be a cause of worry for most of the chief executive officers. And this is the biggest reason that made Warren Buffett successful in transforming a regional textile company like Berkshire Hathaway into a giant multinational conglomerate.

Yes, Berkshire Hathaway is a public holding company owning more than 88 companies engaged in different kinds of businesses. Managers vested with complete authority run all these companies. A total of 367,700 employees work in those companies and Warren Buffett, sitting in headquarters located in his hometown Omaha, guides them from the top. In the annual report of Berkshire Hathaway for the year 1999, Warren Buffett had himself given an account of his managerial skills that you may not find anywhere else.

"Berkshire's collection of managers is unusual in several important ways. As one example, a very high percentage of these men and women are independently wealthy, having made fortunes in the businesses that they run. They work neither because they need the money nor because they are contractually obligated to — we have no contracts at Berkshire. Rather, they work long and hard because they love their businesses. And I use the word "their" advisedly, since these managers are truly in charge — there are no show-and-tell presentations in Omaha, no budgets to be approved by headquarters, no dictums issued about capital expenditures. We simply ask our managers to run their companies as if these are the sole asset of their families and will remain so for the next century."

"Charlie (Munger) and I try to behave with our managers just as we attempt to behave with Berkshire's shareholders, treating both groups as we would wish to be treated if our positions were reversed. Though "working" means nothing to me financially, I love doing it at Berkshire for some simple reasons: It gives me a sense of achievement, a freedom to act as I see fit and an opportunity to interact daily with people I like and trust. Why should our managers — accomplished artists at what they do — see things differently?"

"In their relations with Berkshire, our managers often appear to be hewing to President Kennedy's charge, "Ask not what your country can do for you; ask what you can do for your country". Here's a remarkable story from last year: It's about R. C. Willey, Utah's dominant home furnishing business, which Berkshire purchased from Bill Child and his family in 1995. Bill and most of his managers are Mormons, and for this reason R. C. Willey's stores have never operated on Sunday. This is a difficult way to do business: Sunday

is the favourite shopping day for many customers. Bill, nonetheless, stuck to his principles -- and while doing so built his business from $250,000 of annual sales in 1954, when he took over, to $342 million in 1999.

"Bill felt that R. C. Willey could operate successfully in markets outside of Utah and in 1997 suggested that we open a store in Boise. I was highly sceptical about taking a no-Sunday policy into a new territory where we would be up against entrenched rivals open seven days a week. Nevertheless, this was Bill's business to run. So, despite my reservations, I told him to follow both his business judgment and his religious convictions.

"Bill then insisted on a truly extraordinary proposition: He would personally buy the land and build the store — for about $9 million as it turned out — and would sell it to us at his cost if it proved to be successful. On the other hand, if sales fell short of his expectations, we could exit the business without paying Bill a cent. This outcome, of course, would leave him with a huge investment in an empty building. I told him that I appreciated his offer but felt that if Berkshire was going to get the upside it should also take the downside. Bill said nothing doing: If there was to be failure because of his religious beliefs, he wanted to take the blow personally."

"The store opened last August and immediately became a huge success. Bill thereupon turned the property over to us — including some extra land that had appreciated significantly — and we wrote him a check for his cost. And get this: Bill refused to take a dime of interest on the capital he had tied up over the two years."

"If a manager has behaved similarly at some other public corporation, I haven't heard about it. You can understand why the opportunity to partner with people like Bill Child causes me to tap dance to work every morning".

Yes, Warren Buffett lost no time in realising that every leader must learn the skill of 'delegation of authority' to run a business and ensure its sustained growth. Beware! It is a natural inclination of a leader to control every minor and major incident connected to his work, venture and business and the people involved. However, any attempt to micro-manage so many jobs, ventures and businesses at the same time is like throwing many balls in air and attempting to prevent them from falling on ground, just like a circus juggling artist giving his performance. In such a case, even a slight loss of attention by the leader may have the risk of everything falling apart. Not only that, when a leader at the top tries to control every activity, his more important tasks in fact get neglected. But, if that leader delegates authority to able managers focusing on specific tasks and oversees and guides the entire business, all the jobs get executed smoothly and he does not lose his focus on more critical jobs.

This was the reason that Warren had picked highly efficient managers / chief executive officers for each of his companies and had also delegated to them all necessary executive authority to allow them to carry out their operational responsibilities related to concerned businesses. Just as Warren has given the example of Utah's home furnishing business, he delegates complete control of his business to every chief executive officer. When Berkshire acquired an American manufacturer of recreational vehicles, cargo trailers, utility trailers, pontoon boats and buses in June 2005, Warren made it clear to its founder and chief executive officer Peter Liegl not to expect to hear from him more than once a year. Not only that, Berkshire in May 2003 acquired American supply chain services company McLane Company from Walmart for USD 1.45 billion. When William Grady Rosier, who had been the president and chief executive officer of McLane since 1995, contacted Warren Buffett over phone for approval of purchase of some company jets, Warren told him, "This is your decision. It is your company to run".

Warren's this quote is quite popular, "We delegate authority almost to the point of abdication". Yes, Warren felt it would be sheer folly on his part to think he could competently manage each and every one of his businesses himself. He has hence delegated complete responsibility to all his managers and chief executive officers with regard to management of their related businesses and also authority to take all decisions for their operations. Yes, this is boldness almost to the point of abdication. However, Warren has also formulated some rules for delegation of authority: they are as follows:

Every business culture is unique: Warren Buffett was well aware that every business - small or large - has its own unique work culture. Workers and managers connected to every business have their own highly specialised skills that allow them to accomplish their tasks efficiently. Warren had quickly learnt that he could not perform jobs like those highly skilled managers and hence, he allowed those specialised workers only to perform their tasks without any interference. Warren also realised that the only responsibility he had as a management leader was to inspire his employees to attain their greatness. Warren has always held himself in the role of a cheerleader and never allowed himself to become a slave driver. He believes that his employees are the experts and they should be allowed to perform jobs in which they have expertise. This only would ensure utilisation of full potential of the workers in the interest of the company. And then only, it would be possible to protect the personal interest of the employees.

Competent managers like to do their business as their own: Warren Buffetthad quickly discovered the mystery of management psychology that most of the business-owners fail to understand. Warren felt that managers who were really competent liked to be left alone to run their business and they were unable to tolerate any interference in their work. They liked to manage their business the way they deem proper. And if they were allowed to consider their business as their own, they did wonders. Warren did the same thing. After completing the process of selection, he has been maintaining 100 per cent confidence in his managers and encouraging them to manage their 'own' business in their 'own' way. He has been taking pride in standing behind them in all instances of their minor and major mistakes. As a result, the managers/ chief executive officers of associate companies of Berkshire work hard like owners and ensure the best performance for their 'own' businesses. For them, it is a matter of pride.

Competence, hard work and passion must come with integrity: Before delegating full authority to his managers, Warren Buffett has been making sure that besides being competent, hardworking and passionate, they also have a great deal of integrity. Warren has sensed that a manager who is hardworking, passionate and expert in his business-related jobs but lacks integrity may use all his expertise to rob the company blind. Hence, Warren pays maximum attention to integrity in his managers - though rest all the qualities are of course required to run the business efficiently.

It is worth noting that, during the acquisition of Nebraska Furniture Mart, he had given maximum importance to 'Mrs. B' and allowed her only to run the business for her entire life. Mrs. B's motto was 'sell cheap and tell the truth'. And, Warren was just crazy about that line.

Initial Success of Investor Buffett

In 1956, Warren Buffett's guru Benjamin Graham had handed over the reins of his company 'Graham-Newman Corporation' to his partner Jerry Newman and like a celebrity, started living a luxurious retired life in Beverly Hills (a city in California, surrounded by Los Angeles and West Hollywood)while also teaching at California University, Los Angeles. During 21 years (1936 to 1956) of his teaching at Columbia University, Graham had firmly established his partnership investment concern 'Graham-Newman Corporation' in the world's largest capital market 'Wall Street' (New York) and earned an average income of 17 per cent that was more than 14 per cent growth of 'Standard & Poor's 500' index. This did not include the earnings on shares of Government Employees Insurance Company (GEICO), the best investment of Graham-Newman Corporation, though the same was available for distribution to its shareholders. The shareholders, who had held on to the shares of GEICO, were earning almost double in comparison to the S&P 500 index.

However, after completing his studies at Columbia University in 1950, Warren Buffett was regularly making investments at his own level silently and while working with 'Graham-Newman Corporation', had seen his personal investment capital jump from USD 9800 to USD 140,000 in 1956. With enough capital of his own, he was getting impatient to move back to his hometown Omaha. Another major reason was Benjamin Graham's relocation to Beverley Hills, as after that, Buffett was not enjoying working under Jerry Newman's uninspiring leadership.

Hence, during the spring of 1956, Warren Buffett and his wife Susan had rented a house a little away from his grandfather's grocery store 'Buffett Grocery' in Omaha. This time, Buffett had no plans to work for his father's brokerage firm or for anybody else. On the very day when he arrived Omaha from New York on 1 May, he arranged an informal meeting for his family members and friends. In the meeting, seven limited partners - Buffett's sister Doris and her husband, aunt Elis, Doc Thomson, his old hostel roommate Chuck Peterson and his mother and his attorney Dan Monen - together pooled USD 1,05,000. Warren Buffett himself contributed only USD 100 as a general partner. This was a very nominal amount but this time, Buffett was going to use this investment not for his father or guru Benjamin Graham but for his own proposed partnership firm Buffett Associates Ltd.

This was the time when medical practitioner Homer Dose, an old investor of Graham-Newman Corporation, had asked Benjamin Graham, "Who is now going to carry forward your 'intellectual legacy?" Graham had responded, "Warren Buffett". And when Homer Dose was on his trip to the West in his car for his summer vacation, he had made a stop-over at Omaha for sometime. After only a short conversation with Warren Buffett, Dose had announced his decision to invest USD 1,20,000 in Buffett's partnership firm and had continued with his journey.

Thus, Buffett started managing three small partnership firms from his bedroom and he could also visualise great potentials for the future of his family partnership. A few months later, Buffett returned to New York to participate in the last meeting of the shareholders of Graham-Newman Corporation. There, he mentioned to Benjamin Graham's another follower Ed Anderson that he was contemplating launching a partnership firm like 'Graham-Newman' with a minimum investment of USD 50000. After the shareholders of Graham-Newman Corporation had cast their formal votes at the end of their activities, the chief of Manhattan located brokerage firm commented that Graham had made a big mistake by failing in developing talents. He further elaborated that Graham-Newman could have carried on with its operations further only because he had an extraordinary lad named Warren Buffett. Who would like to drive with him now?

In the beginning of 1957, Warren Buffett was managing an investment fund of USD 300,000 of some of his relatives and friends. Now, Buffett needed large capital to do something different from other anonymous stock pickers in Omaha. But what else did Buffett have, other than demonstrating self-confidence in his abilities, to win the trust of large investors? Buffett did not have any track record of working as an independent investment operator. He had nothing, on paper, to indicate that he was worthy of people's trust. Still, Warren did not want mere discretion over people's money; he wanted absolute control over it. He did not want anybody to raise any question on his stock investment related decisions; he was not ready to have any boss as at 'Graham-Newman'.

However, by now, Buffett was quite familiar with all kinds of information related to almost every share of stock and debt security/ bond. He was regularly reading 'Wall Street Journal' and other financial newspapers and magazines besides Moody's Manual and its other books and financial reports, and in the process, was building the entire mental portrait of the Wall Street day by day. He had started to understand every movement in the stock market and the most important point was that he believed in his own analysis only and did not consider the analysis of any of the financial analysts of Wall Street trustworthy. In the situation, what more than Buffett's self-confidence and clear frame of mind could have won people's confidence? And, did Buffett really need anything else but these very features defining his character?

In the summer of 1957, he got a call from Edwin Davis, a prominent Omaha urologist. As Buffett had never met him earlier, he was a bit surprised also. But Davis had very soon made it clear that his investment consultant in New York had suggested Buffett's name. In fact, that consultant had come in contact with Buffett when the latter was working for Graham-Newman. Somebody had informed that consultant that Buffett was working in Omaha and he was looking for some big investment. That is how he had referred Buffett to Davis. Though Davis was not feeling comfortable to trust a novice like Buffett, he had made up his mind to talk to Buffett directly.

When Buffett reached Davis's home on the appointed Sunday, he found that Davis had gathered his entire family there. That was a great moment of Buffett's professional life, not only because he could raise large capital from Dr Davis but also because it could open door for him to other big investors. However, Davis family was surprised that Buffett had not told them anything that could make them happy. On the contrary, Buffett had made it clear that he would not reveal to them where their money was going to be invested. Not only that, Buffett had told that he would come back to them with results of their investments only at the end of year, on 31 December, when they would be free to add more investments or withdraw their capital. Otherwise, the invested capital would be under his complete control. Buffett, in his presentation, was just repeating the business principles of his guru Benjamin Graham. He was putting forward his points quite patiently but his intention was quite clear. He was badly in need of Davis family's capital but he wanted the same at his own terms.

Buffett had placed the terms of business in front of Davis family. Davis family would get a percentage of total profit in the capacity of a limited partner and out of the rest, 75 per cent would go to Davis family and 25 per cent to Buffett. And if the results were average or worse, Buffett would get nothing - no salary, no fee, no expenses. Thus, Buffett had convinced Davis family that he was not asking them to gamble alone; Buffett himself also was taking risk. Buffett had left after his presentation. Davis family deliberated on the matter after that. Though Buffett's terms were crystal clear, majority of the family members were not finding any solid reason to leave their capital in the hands of Buffett and silently wait for the year to end. However, Dr Davis's wife Dorothy unilaterally declared that she had liked everything about young Buffett, and finally, Dr Edwin Davis decided to put up USD 100,000.

Thus, by the end of 1957, Warren Buffett was running five small partnerships, totalling in the range of USD 500,000. His investment portfolio had gained 10 per cent during the first year whereas Dow Jones Industrial Average (DJIA) had got stuck at 8 per cent.

This was the time when Susan was to give birth to their third child. Buffett was quite optimistic about his future based on his first year's income, and as a long-term investment, bought a five-bedroom house on Farnam Street in anupper-middle class suburban neigh bourhood in Omaha for USD 31,500. The master bedroom had now been converted into Buffett's office and he would operate all his companies from there only.

In 1958, Buffett's investment portfolio had gained 41 per cent against 39 per cent return of DJIA. Thus, the original partnership capital had doubled by the end of third year. Simultaneously, Buffett was bringing new investors into his fold and he had also increased the minimum investment limit to join the partnership to USD 50,000.

Buffett had made a lot of effort to buy 10 per cent shares of stock of National American Fire Insurance, an obscure insurance company in Omaha, during its buy-back offer; this had given him the opportunity to make his first grand income of USD 100,000.

Buffett's next target was Sanborn Map Company, developer and publisher of maps for American towns and cities, whose once-lucrative business had been ruined by depression. Sanborn Maps had made lot of investments during its good times and its book value was around USD 65. But the same had come down to USD 45 on account of map business not doing well. As per the investment lesson learnt from Graham, this was a golden opportunity as today or tomorrow, the book value was in any case going to be reflected in its market price. Hence, Buffett had continued buying Sanborn shares during 1958 and 1959. As the original directors of Sanborn were holding just 400 shares and the falling price of 105,000 shares issued in the market did not impact them anyway, they were not showing any interest in lifting their price. Not only that, sitting on a huge investment portfolio, the company directors had paid dividends on only five occasions during the last eight years, though they had not affected any reduction in their own fees. In the circumstances, Graham had managed, on the strength of his shareholding, to take a position among the board of directors and had started putting pressure on the management for disclosure of the real value of the investment portfolio. Eventually in 1960, Sanborn management had agreed to utilise its huge investment portfolio and bring out a buy-back offer; and thus, Buffett had got the opportunity for 50% return on his investment. In fact, Buffett had invested 35% of all the assets of his investors in shares of Sanborn Maps only. Obviously, Buffett had got a chance to reap the returns on the risk he had taken.

Buffett understood the importance of the 'right manager'

Though Buffett had just been successful in winning the trust of a group of ten practitioners and attracting a total investment capital of USD 1,00,000 (USD 10000 per practitioner), he was yet to emerge as a large investment operator. Perhaps that was the reason that, after two very successful ventures, he decided next year to take the biggest risk till date and staked USD 1 million on Dempster Mill Manufacturing Company (Beatrice, Nebraska).

Located in Beatrice, Nebraska, 90-miles south of Omaha, Dempster Mill Manufacturing Company was an 80-year-old manufacturer of windmills and farm equipment. Though Dempster was sick due to static sales and negligible profitability of windmills, Buffett found the market price of its shares quite attractive. In 1961, he used 20% of the capital of his investors to acquire a controlling holding of 70% in Dempster and appoint himself as chairman of the company. Generally, investors try to keep themselves away from the hassle of management, but Buffett was marching ahead on an unknown path of future like a prophet.

Buffett convinced his trusted attorney and investor friend Dan Monen also to join the board of directors. Every month, Buffett, along with Monen, would make a 90-miles trip in his car to dusty town of Beatrice but he was still unable to have a grip on Dempster. The company required radical changes but they were beyond Buffett's expertise. He would instruct his managers every month to bring down overhead expenses and reduce inventory. They would even nod their heads in agreement. Buffett would return to Omaha and next time, Buffett would still find the problems existing as before. All this made Buffett to put the company on sale.

On the other side, Buffett had already invested partnership capital in, besides Dempster, 40 other shares of stocks. Though Dempster's issue was yet to be resolved, other investments brought in unprecedented returns for Buffett. In the first five years of his business, he was able to consistently beat Dow Jones Industrial Index (DJIA). (See table)

Buffett Versus Dow Jones

Year	Annual gain (%) for Buffett's Partners	Annual Return rate (%) of Dow Jones Industrial Average Index
1957	+10.4	-8.4

1958	+40.9	+38.5
1959	+25.9	+19.9
1960	+22.8	-6.3
1961	+45.9	+22.2
5-years' cumulative gain	**251.0**	**74.3**

Source: Buffett: The Making of An American Capitalist (Roger Lowenstein/ Random House/1985)

The above table 'Buffett versus Dow Jones' clearly indicates that while Dow Jones (DJIA) was up only three quarters during five years from 1957 to 1961, Buffett's portfolios two and half times. Word of Buffett's amazing success spread like wildfire among the investors in his hometown Omaha. People would descend on him and ask for tips whenever he visited his favourite Ross's steak House or Omaha Country Club. But Buffett wanted to use his skills only for himself. Hence, he would somehow manage, keeping his natural decency intact, to avoid them with his witting answers. He was possessive about stocks, like an artist with an unfinished canvas. He enjoyed narrating stories of his coups to others, but only when they were wrapped up.

Buffett's passion outside his work was the game of bridge. He had a regular game, the members of which included the nobility of the town like ad executive, Buick (car) dealer, judge, life insurance agent, mortgage service provider and railway attorney. Buffett would show up with six packs of Pepsi-Cola and entertain the guys with a stream of jokes and stories. But, he would not talk about the money he was making, as he did not want to. He played quite intensely as if taking decisions on stocks and bonds. He hated to lose and he would play for high stakes only when he thought his team had an edge. Buffett was also unique as he would just stare at the cards and calculate the odds like a machine.

And, Buffett was using this very talent to win over large investors in New York and collect six-figure cheques. For this, he was feeding off Benjamin Graham's network. He met Marshal Weinberg, a broker and fellow Graham alumnus, at 'New School', a private research university located in New York. He and Weinberg soon became friends and Weinberg and his brothers invested USD 100,000 in Buffett's partnership. Similarly, another broker friend Henry Brandt also invested and steered his clients to Buffett. Laurence Tisch, tipped off by Howard Newman, his former colleague at Graham-Newman, had invested USD 100,000.

Around that very time in New York, Buffett met David Strassler whose family was in the business of fixing distressed companies. Strassler had later flown to Omaha to look into acquiring Dempster. Being educated at Harvard Business School and Massachusetts Institute of Technology (MIT), Strassler was very proud of his merit. Buffett had come to the airport to pick him up. When Buffett, after driving a bit, started asking him questions about a company in which his family had a majority stake, he felt quite surprised. In fact, Buffett was asking him about Billings & Spencer that made metal forging products and only about 2% of it was public. But Buffett knew everything about the company. And Strassler was totally cold when Buffett started asking him questions about the balance sheet of the company. He was so impressed by Buffett that he had immediately decided to invest in his partnership.

By 1962, Buffett's partnership companies had a total capital of around USD 7.2 million that was bigger than that of Graham-Newman Corporation. Of that total, USD 1 million belonged to Buffett. Though Buffett's partnership was still quite small compared to large investment firms of Wall Street, it was not unproven. As such, Buffett was still unknown to the common people but he was no longer obscure among investors. Starting with just seven core investors, Buffett had, within just six year, grown the figure to 90 that included groups from California to Vermont. Hence, Buffett merged all his partnerships to form a new company 'Buffett Partnership Limited' and enhanced the limit of minimum investment to USD 100,000. His business had now outgrown his bedroom and hence, he moved his office to Kiewit Plaza, a fourteen-storey tower on Farnam Street near his house.

In the meantime, Buffett developed friendship with Charlie Munger, six years his senior. Having grown up in Omaha, Munger was the son of a lawyer and grandson of a judge. After completing his graduation at Harvard Law School, he had started practising in Los Angeles. In 1959, when Munger returned to Omaha to close out his father's practice, Edwin Davis's son, one of Buffett's investors, was struck by his likeness to Munger and invited the two of them to lunch at Omaha Club with the aim of introducing them to each other. And they soon became close friends. This friendship evolved further when Buffett went to California the same year on vacation with his wife and children. Munger was unimpressive physically but Buffett was quite impressed by his intellect and self-confidence. Buffett advised Munger to focus on his practice but Buffett was quite surprised when Munger had termed his practice as 'waste of his talent and time'.

In fact, like Buffett, Munger also had a considerable passion to get rich - not because he wanted Ferraris - he desperately wanted to be financially independent. This was the reason that even though he had started a new law firm 'Munger, Tolles & Hills'after returning from Harvard, he barely practised there. In 1962, when Buffett moved his office to Kiewit Plaza, Munger was running his own investment partnership. In the meantime, Buffett had started to consider Munger more a consultant than his friend. The same year in spring, Buffett went to Los Angeles to meet Munger only to discuss Dempster issue. Munger was no Benjamin Graham disciple. Munger advised Buffett to sell Dempster even at a loss, as he felt it was quite difficult to put things right for a troubled company.

But Munger knew a fellow named Harry Bottle who could be a suitable manager for Dempster. Buffett interviewed Bottle in Los Angeles and Bottle was on the job in Beatrice (Nebraska) six days later. Strictly following Buffett's directions, Bottle cut overheads, closed many loss-making plants and brought the inventory to the lowest level. That year-end, Buffett, in the letter to his partners, had referred to Bottle as the man of the year. One year later, when Dempster was quite trimmer and more profitable and its USD 2 million worth of securities were making its financial condition strong, Buffett sold it on a profit of USD 2.3 million. Thus, Buffett was able to triple his investment within three years.

Buffett could achieve this feat because he had bought Dempster at a very low price compared to its book value. Instead of selling the same in panic, he patiently held on to it and picked the 'right manager' like Harry Bottle for its turnaround.

This incident had made Buffett understand the importance of picking the 'right manager' for a company to succeed. Buffett later also felt that the 'right manager' should be retained as long as possible, as like changes in marital relationships, changes in management also are troublesome, time-taking and unpredictable.

Skill of Picking the 'Leader' in a Crowd

This quote from Warren Buffett is quite interesting:

"Would you rather be the world's greatest lover, but have everyone think you're the world's worst lover? Or would you rather be the world's worst lover but have everyone think you're the world's greatest lover?"

Buffett has thus developed his own principle - everybody has either inner scorecard or outer scorecard; he is either true to himself or becomes the one that he feels the world wants him to be. A true leader follows his own drumbeats while bureaucracy submits to others' perceived desires.

Yes, it is quite difficult to stand alone when popular public opinion is against you. However, this very talent of Warren Buffett made him so rich. He buys shares of stocks when everybody else is fearful. He always lives his life against herd behaviour. He has always been free from misconceptions and beliefs and has remained an independent thinker and that is the reason he never faced defeat and was always a winner. In fact, independent thinkers like Buffett never fall prey to misconceptions and beliefs. They are masters of their own destiny. The world-famous quote of Swami Vivekananda that 'You are the maker of your own destiny' also refers to the same.

What is the difference between a loser and a winner mentality? Psychologists believe the two differ in 'locus of control' only. If your locus of control is internal, you blame yourself for anything going wrong. You believe that you are in charge of your fate and can control your results. And in such a mental state, you blame your actions only for your failures. On the contrary, when the 'locus of control' is external, you blame others only, not yourself, for anything going wrong.

In fact, Warren Buffett thinking was highly impacted by his father Howard Homan Buffett. It was on 13 August 1931, just two weeks shy of Warren's first birthday, when his father returned from work with news that his bank had closed. It was the defining, faith-shattering scene of the Great Depression. His job as a securities salesman in Union State Bank was gone. Very soon, his savings also were exhausted. Though Howard's father Ernest had his own grocery store, he gave his son little time to pay for his grocery bills – a bitter pill, as he had inherited the Buffett's disdain for borrowing – "Save your credit, for that is better than money". He sensed bleak prospects, but soon he had announced opening of 'Buffett, Sklenicka & Co.' with an office in Union State Bank building on Farnam Street. This was the same street in Omaha where Warren Buffett was to later stay and work.

It is worth mentioning here that Warren Buffett's grandfather Ernest had married a girl of his own choice against the wishes of his elder brother and that had resulted in acrimony on both sides and they were not on talking terms. As a result, Ernest had to leave his family grocery store located at Omaha city centre. But Ernest wanted to take his family expertise forward and hence in 1915, he established a grocery store in the name of 'Buffett & Sons' in the west side of the town. This was Ernest's clever step as Omaha was expanding in the west. Sensing the opportunity in the suburbs, Ernest started the business with credit facilities and home delivery. Very soon, chefs of rich families started placing orders with Buffett & Sons over phone. Business picked up rapidly. Ernest would extract work from his workers for 11-hours shift quite brutally.

However, Howard Buffett did not have any interest in becoming the third-generation grocery store operator. He also had independent thinking like his father but had a comparatively soft nature – not used to scolding or threatening anybody. Howard worked for sometime for a company engaged in laying gas pipelines, but he was in fact interested in doing something intellectual. He had been editor of 'Daily Nebraskan' in Nebraska University (Lincoln) and longed to have a professional life in journalism. This was the time when Leila Stahl also had joined the university. Raised in West Point (Nebraska) 82-miles west of Omaha, Leila had to work for her father's weekly newspaper for three years after she finished her high school at the age of 16, to arrange funds for her fee for admission into a university. She had contacted Howard asking for a job in 'Daily Nebraskan'. Leila was beautiful. Howard hired her and also immediately asked her for a date. The attraction was there on both sides. When his graduation neared, Howard asked for her hand. Her father John Stahl gave his blessings hoping that Leila would finish her college. A day after Christmas in 1925, when West Point was freezing with temperature 10 degrees below zero, marriage of Leila and Howard was solemnised. They travelled to Omaha on bus instead of going on honeymoon.

Like a dream come true, Howard had already been offered a newspaper job, but his father's friend had also kept a $25-a-week job for him in an insurance company. Howard abandoned his dream of journalism and deferred to his father who had paid his university expenses. This was the need of the time. The couple started their life in a two-bedroom wooden bungalow with a coal furnace, on Baker Avenue, Omaha. For Leila who was raised by an invalid mother, this was a tough beginning. She was not ready to be a homemaker. Howard used his car while Leila would use public transport for her part-time secretarial or printing jobs and many a times, would make more in a week than Howard did. Leila had to attend to a load of housework after returning from work. Around that time, Leila had to go through an eye operation and she was getting regular headaches. When Leila delivered her first child Doris in 1928, she was having 105 degrees fever. And two years later, Leila delivered her second child Warren Edward Buffett on 30 August 1930 in humid summer, with cloudbursts breaking in the 89-degree heat.

By the time Warren began school, his father's fortunes were rapidly improving. When Warren turned six, Buffett family moved to a brick-house on suburban 53-North Street. The bad times in Buffett home were not discussed anymore; they were banished forever. The same year, when Howard took his family on summer vacation to Okoboji (a town located on east side of West Okoboji lake of North-West Iowa), six-year old Warren had tested his first endeavour. He bought a six-pack of Cokes for 25 cents and sold the same to tourists around the lake for 5 cents each, thus making a profit of 5 cents. Back in Omaha, Warren would buy soda pop from his grandfather's store and sell the same door-to-door on summer nights while other children played in the street. Yes, Warren developed his passion for moneymaking then itself. He was not thinking about getting pocket money but about advancing towards his great aspiration.

When Warren was seven, he was hospitalised with a mysterious fever. Doctors removed his appendix, but he still remained so ill that the doctors feared he would die. Even when his father offered him his favourite noodle soup, Warren refused to eat. But left alone, he picked a pencil and filled a page with numbers. These, he told his nurse, represented his future capital. Warren said cheerfully, “I do not have much money now, but someday I will and I will have my picture in newspapers”. Purportedly, even in his death throes, Warren was seeking succour not in soup but in dreams of money. It is said that after this incident, Howard Buffett got determined not to let Warren experience the hardships he had gone through. He also resolved that he would not follow his father Ernest and demean his son. After that, Howard unfailingly expressed confidence in Warren and supported him in whatever he did. As Warren could never develop close relations with his irritable mother, his universe revolved around his father.

Six-feet tall Howard Buffett with his imposing personality towered over the family, physically and in other respects. He worked hard for supporting his family, owning not only his brokerage firm but also the South Omaha Feed Co. But he was quite excited about money. His passions were religion and politics. He was a self-consciously moral man and had the courage to express his beliefs. Overall, Howard Buffett was extremely conservative. He would remind his children of their duty not only to God but also to community. He was true to his words. He did not ever drink or smoke. When a close investor’s securities performed badly, he felt bad enough to repurchase them for his own account. He was elected four times to the US House of Representatives as Republican candidate, but he always indulged in ethical politics. He would even tell Warren always that he himself, not the world, was in control of his life; hence he only would decide how he wanted to lead his life.

But it is not simple to keep ‘locus of control’ always internal. In that situation, if you succeed, it is only your success and when you fail, it is your failure only. You cannot make somebody else a scapegoat or blame others for your failure; and this situation is like cursing oneself. But a true leader takes responsibility for his success and failures both. This is the reason that when Warren Buffett's investments in two Ireland banks had failed and when he had bought shares of stock of multinational power corporation Conoco Phillips Company at high prices, it was his failure only. And Warren had even publicly owned the mistakes. This is the reason that Warren Buffett always picks managers/chief executive officers who are ready to own both their success and failures.

A Manager Needs to Have Many More Traits

Warren Buffett looks for many traits while picking the right managers'.

Do they love their job? Buffett makes sure that the person whom he is entrusting his business is doing what he loves to do. There is a very interesting Buffett's quote, *"There comes a time when you ought to start doing what you want. Take a job that you love. You will jump out of bed in the morning. I think you are out of your mind if you keep taking jobs that you don't like because you think it will look good on your resume. Isn't that a little like saving up sex for your old age?"*

In fact, many times we keep doing things that we do not like, just looking for money. But the irony is that we keep doing the same job day-after-day, year-after-year, until we reach end of our time. In the meantime, we keep ourselves under the misconception that we would eventually attain our dream job. This pain, in the name of earning, starts right in the initial years of one's life and is fore casted based on needs. If we look at the psychology behind the same, it would be clear that nothing but greed is behind this kind of pain. Warren believes not doing what we love in the name of greed is poor management of our lives. This state of our mind makes our job a hard labour, pushes us down and destroys our soul. We may be earning a lot, but 9-10 hours that we spend doing that are quite painful.

In the world of business, the people who are most successful are those who are doing what they love. The interesting fact is that the thing that always motivates them is not money. It is that same thing that motivates a singer to sing and a player to play - love for one's job. Irrespective of what you are - a carpenter, barber, butcher, salesman, security man, computer programmer, doctor, chartered accountant, lawyer or anyone else - you can attain any level of success if you really love what you do. Such people only earn the most money and fame in their profession. Obviously, loving what you do and attaining success and money - they both go together.

That is why Warren Buffett makes sure while choosing managers/ chief executive officers that they are assigned the job they love. Such people only feel happiness and pride in their jobs, motivate their colleagues to bring out their potentials and become driving force for the entire business. And their collective strength has only made Warren Buffett a great brilliant leader of this time.

Does he believe in his product? Warren Buffett, in the initial years of his professional life, had learnt that only salesmen who believe in their products are the best. People who are passionate about their products enjoy selling them and their sale levels are always high. Such people are equally interested in related matters like raw materials, production process, best utilisation etc. And salesmen who are familiar with all details relating to their products are able to easily impress their consumers. In his companies, Buffett has assembled such people only who believe in their products and businesses. This is the reason that majority of the chief executive officers in associate companies of Berkshire Hathaway have spent most of their professional life in managing a single company. The interesting fact is also that most of them have huge personal wealth.

In this context, the name of Buffalo News publisher Stanford Lipsey who was born and brought up in Omaha comes first; he worked with Warren Buffett for more than four decades. In 1969, Buffett had acquired 'Sun Newspapers', the group of local weekly newspapers founded and managed by Lipsey. In 1980, Buffett had appointed him as the publisher of Buffalo News where he continued at the same job for next 32 years and retired in 2012. He died four years later in 2016. Similarly, Irvin Blumkin had started working in 1967 at the age of eight in Nebraska Furniture Mart founded by his grandmother Rose Blumkin (Mrs B); his father Louie Blumkin was looking after operations there. Irvin assumed charge as CEO during 1980s and he along with his brother Ron Blumkin has been managing the business since then. These people were so rich individually that they could have taken retirement any time. But Irvin, just like Lipsey, was also passionate about his work. Irvin's grandmother was active till the age of 103 and his father Louie Blumkin is still the chairman emeritus. It is worth reminding that Buffett had in 1983 acquired 80 per cent ownership stake from Blumkin family but he has continued to retain business control of Nebraska Furniture Mart with the family members as before and they all love what they do. They believe in their products.

Is he passionate about his work? In Warren's view, "He is a great manager who thinks of business when he gets out of bed in the morning and dreams about the business when he sleeps in the night". He believes, "Obsession is the price of perfection". Warren expects obsession not only from his managers but he himself has also been obsessive his entire life. It was his obsession only that Warren was able to memorise Moody's Manual and even today, he is always ready with all the figures related to all his businesses. Warren had bought Nebraska Furniture Mart as the same was being managed by an obsessive lady like Mrs B who had made even her children obsessive.

Now, if we have a look at the professional life of Olza M. Tony Nicely, Chairman & CEO of motor vehicle insurance company Government Employees Insurance Company (GEICO), we find that he started working there as a clerk in 1961, at the age of just 18. Going up the ladder, he reached the current position in 1993. Thus, Tony had spent 56 years working for the same company. He is now going to cross 74 and his personal net worth is estimated to be USD 15 million (January 2017). Still, he himself never knew when he would retire, as obsessive people like Tony keep working till their mind and body are functional. And Buffett likes such managers only.

Somewhat similar story is that of Albert Lee 'Al' Ueltschi, founder of the world's foremost aviation training organisation 'FlightSafety International'. After listening to the radio broadcast of Charles Lindbergh's solo transatlantic flight in 1927, Albert Ueltschi got obsessed with flying. Then, he opened a hamburger stand named 'Little Hawk'to pay for flying lessons. He had started making solo flights at the age of 16. Very soon, he dropped out of his classes at the University of Kentucky to move around the country to provide flight training to student pilots, and finally began his career as a pilot with Pan American World Airways (Pan Am). After flying for

10 years there, Ueltschi felt that corporate pilots did not receive the same rigorous training that airline pilots received and at the age of 50, he founded Flight Safety International in 1951. By the time the company went public 17 years later in 1968, Ueltschi was considered the 'father of modern flight training'. In 1996, Ueltschi sold majority stake in his company to Warren Buffett in exchange for 16000 shares of Berkshire Hathaway at USD 1.50 each; however, Buffett ensured that Ueltschi remained connected to the company for his entire life.

At the time Al Ueltschi died in 2012 at the age of 95, Flight Safety International was operating more than 4000 individual courses for 135 kinds of planes through 1800 trainers and was using more than 320 flight simulators to offer services to its customers in 167 countries. Warren Buffett had later commented about Ueltschi, "Al understood what I was doing. I knew the mission of Flight Safety and I could say he loved his profession. The first question that I ask about the position of an individual is - does he love money or his profession? But, for Al money was entirely insignificant. He loved his profession and he was the kind of person I need; had he loved money he would have left the company very next day it was sold".

Yes, the first thing that Warren Buffett always tries to find out about his prospective manager is whether he has been loving his profession ever since his childhood. Buffett believes that if a manager has taken more interest in some petty profession than his studies during his childhood, he may be able to achieve better success as compared to many educated managers, as his childhood love for a profession makes him passionate to succeed. Thus, the first thing Buffett looks for in his manager is how much he loves his job and how passionate he is about the same; and if he is educated and has other skills also, that comes as the icing on a cake.

How loyal and honest he is? Buffett believes if a worker or manager is loyal and honest towards others, there are greater chances of him correcting himself by learning from others. On the contrary, if a worker or manager overlooks his mistakes or tries to blame others for his mistakes, it is quite probable that he would lie to himself in other important matters also and there would be no possibility of him getting corrected. Buffett believes "Managers that always promise to 'make the numbers' will at some point be tempted to make up the numbers". This was the reason that he would shy away from picking managers who discussed more about their employment contracts than work. He maintained that it was not possible to do business with people who get excited by their contracts. In the business world, a manager honest as the brightness of the day is like balance lying in your bank account. And Buffett would always look for such managers only.

Can he do cost-management? Profit is the life blood of business. Just as end of blood circulation brings end to life, end of flow of profit stops the business, and the only way to maintain profit flow is to keep production cost lower than the sale price as much as possible. The difference between sale price and production cost is what is known as profit margin. There cannot be any other way or formula for making profit. If you are unable to maintain your profit margin, you are definitely not going to last in business for long. And if you are able to make great profits, you may not only earn your livelihood but also become affluent.

As the manager of a business, a person has mainly two goals - sell products at maximum prices by motivating sales team to improve sales and keep production costs at the lowest level by motivating teams procuring products and raw materials. It is most important to keep production costs to the lowest level as they only determine sale prices. It may be easy to sell a product with low production cost in good quantities and thus maintain better profit margin. In such a case, if a business manager is not 'watchful about costs', it would not be possible for him to maintain costs at the lowest level. Buffett maintains that a manager not disciplined for little things would be undisciplined in more significant matters also.

In this context, Warren Buffett narrates stories of Tom Murphy, CEO of Capital Cities Communications; he was so conscious of costs that he had not allowed painting of the rear wall of his office building, as the same was not visible to anybody. Not only that, Murphy never created public relations and legal departments in his office, as he believed these services could be obtained from freelance professionals whenever required at very low costs. And when Murphy merged Capital Cities into ABC, he had even closed personal dining rooms along with other cost cuttings.

Does he have a long-term perspective? Warren Buffett says, "In fact, managing and investing have lot of overlapping. Managing has made me a better investor and investing a better manager".

Yes, Warren Buffett has always been a long-term investor. He has always tried to maintain his majority stake in favourite companies providing durable competitive advantage, as their inherent economics work in their favour. Warren's this very long-term perspective has made him such a great and successful investor. However, most of the managers in corporate world work with short-term perspective, as their performances are measured by their quarterly and annual results. If they surpass their estimated quarterly or annual performance, they are rewarded with fat bonuses and promotions, and if they fail to reach those quarterly or annual targets, their jobs are in danger.

In Buffett's view, such short-term perspective of management kills long-term potentials of the business. He calls this management perspective as 'reactive management' and tries to keep himself away from the same. Buffett believes that management should be proactive, not reactive. He has attained great success as an investor by adopting long-term perspective only, and hence he has implemented this very perspective in his acquired businesses also. The most important point in his prefatory instructions that Buffett conveys to his managers after appointment is that they should stop worrying about short-term ups and downs of the business and concentrate on making the business strong and profitable in the long-term.

At the time Warren Buffett acquired Berkshire Hathaway, it was an average grade company that was making capital investments more than its income in a desperate bid to compete with foreign textile manufacturers. He soon realised that textile manufacturing required continuous capital investments though its chances of making profit was quite low. Hence, he stopped spending on working capital of Berkshire's textile production and used that capital to acquire an insurance company that had much better potentials in long-term perspective.

How? This was a result of Buffett's intensive study of inherent economics of various businesses. We have already seen this in the first chapter. Buffett was well aware that the textile industry required constant capital infusion to stay in business and that it was eating away income and preventing the company to become profitable. Hence, Buffett knew that any extent of capital investment in Berkshire would not have made any significant impact on its profitability. On the other side, constant cash flow is maintained in insurance business through premiums whereas the claim payments are comparatively quite less. Building an insurance network requires one-time capital investment that is negligible in comparison to manufacturing businesses. Thus, an insurance company always has a good amount of cash for investment in other profitable avenues. This was the reason that Buffett had eventually stopped all textile manufacturing activities of Berkshire and started to gradually transform it into a financial powerhouse. And this is the reason Buffett directs his managers to manage businesses with a long-term perspective.

Provision of Performance-Based Emoluments- Buffett says, "If you have a great manager, you want to pay him well". But how much? Buffett has a simple formula to decide compensation for his managers. He compares the performance of his manager against average performance of the related industry. Obviously, only if Buffett's manager delivers a performance better than industry average, he considers the manager worthy of bonus. If for some reasons, the company fails to achieve industry average, Buffett finds out how much the manager has contributed towards making the company strong and profitable with long-term perspective and determines manager's annual bonus based on the same. He considers his manager an expert coach in different sports. Just as inherent economics of different sports are not the same and coaches of all sports are not paid the same salary, Buffet determines compensation for his managers of various businesses based on financial potentials of related businesses.

❑

4

Motivation of Workforce

Warren Buffett had realised, right at the start of his professional life, that once he had chosen the right businesses and entrusted full authority for their operation to right managers, the only job he was left with as the owner and leader of the businesses was - to constantly motivate the managers for their outstanding performance. Yes, Buffett's management motivational skills have played a major role in transforming Berkshire Hathaway into a financial powerhouse. In this chapter, we are going to discuss in detail these very Buffett's skills - what all he learnt from the father of 'self-improvement' Dale Harbison Carnegie and others and how he adopted them in his winning management style. Be it the skill of impressing others in very first meeting or magic of using appreciation or risk of using criticism or precise use of counselling - Warren Buffett is placed at the top of the most skilled leaders of this age in terms of encouraging, motivating and influencing his managers.

Impact of Friendly Gesture in First Meeting

Warren Buffett says, "You should open talk in a friendly manner when you meet somebody the first time". Though Buffet has just repeated the age-old saying about practical skills "First impression is the last impression", he has used the same successfully to leave a magical influence on his managers.

Beryl B Raff, Chairperson and CEO of Helzberg Diamond Shops, a subsidiary of Berkshire Hathaway, has recounted her first meeting with Warren Buffet in an interesting way in her interview (1 May 2014) published in Kansas City Business Journal. It was sometime in 2009 when she was working as Executive Vice President in Fine Jewellery Division of American departmental store chain J C Penny. Starting her professional career in 1975, Beryl Raff was one of the most experienced workers in retail jewellery business. An acquaintance had asked Beryl Raff about her interest in the interview for the position of chief executive officer of Helzberg Diamond. It is worth noting that Helzberg Diamond, founded in 1915 by Morris Helzberg, operated 270 diamond jewellery retail stores across the United States of America and Warren Buffet had acquired the company in 1995.

Beryl Raff was fully aware of the distinguished history of Helzberg Diamond and she was also a long-time admirer of Warren Buffet; she was also aware of Buffett's well-known working style and excellent quality of the professionals working with him for long. She could not ignore this great opportunity to work for a world-famous leader like Buffett. For her, just having the opportunity to talk to Buffett for some time was itself not less than the greatest achievement of her life. And when she landed at Omaha airport for interview, she had never imagined that Warren Buffett himself would be waiting there in his golden Cadillac to receive her.

Naturally, Beryl was quite nonplussed, but Buffett soon allowed her to calm down with his simple behaviour. She found Buffett a jovial and attractive person and she quickly got rid of her fear. At Berkshire headquarters, Buffett asked her many questions relating to jewellery business. After spending few hours there, he took Beryl to his favourite Omaha Club for lunch. After that, he took her around his hometown and finally also offered her the position of Chairperson and CEO of Helzberg Diamond Shops. All this was just like a dream for Beryl. She however composed herself and asked Buffett, "Would I be reporting to you?" He responded, "No, you wouldn't report directly to me. You do not report to anybody. It is your company. You run it, and if you ever want to talk about anything, just call me".

Warren Buffett had chosen Beryl Raff as his manager, but Buffett's simplicity had made Beryl so stunned that she just could not say anything at that moment. Buffett's words were still echoing in her ears when she took return flight for Dallas. She was finding herself unable to believe her luck. Beryl took 2-3 days to come to senses and she conveyed Buffett her acceptance of his offer. In his press note released on 6 April 2009 from Berkshire Hathaway headquarters, Warren Buffett announced appointment of Beryl Raff, "Beryl is widely recognised in the retail industry as an outstanding merchant and a strong multi-store retail executive. In her new position, she would bring with her finely balanced blend of merchandising instinct and analytical sharpness".

And within just a few months after taking charge at Helzberg Diamond, Beryl Raff realised that she had already been accepted as a member of Warren Buffet's extended family. Yes, this was the result of Buffett's management motivational skills that impressed her in the very first meeting. Just imagine what would have been the impression on Beryl if Buffett had not gone himself to receive her or he had not shown warmth in his behaviour or had not personally taken her around the city or for lunch. Beryl might have still worked for Helzberg Diamond as she was getting a great professional opportunity and was going to be a part of a mega financial empire like Berkshire, but she would not have considered Warren Buffett anything more than the billionaires interested only in their business profits. Buffett has been understanding this psychology quite well - if you want to have your own way, you must start off your interaction with people in friendly manner only. And this management motivational skill has played a major role in helping Buffett assemble a group of the world's best professionals.

Magic of Appreciation in Human Resource Management

Warren Buffet says, "We all have a deep and genuine craving to be appreciated". Yes, Buffett always understood well the practical psychology of the magic of appreciation in human resource management. He recognises this psychological fact that we all have a natural basic need to feel important. To a great extent, this is also a biological need of every human being. There is a famous quote of William James, referred to as the 'Father of American psychology' and counted among the greats of psychological and pragmatic philosophical traditions of 20th century, that says, "The deepest principle of human nature is the craving to be appreciated".

However, Warren Buffett had learnt about the amazing power of appreciation in human resource management after studying the management skills of the legendary professional of American steel industry Charles Michael Schwab. He had started his professional career as a simple labour in Edgar Thomson Steel Works and Furnaces (Braddock, Pennsylvania) of American steel magnate Andrew Carnegie. Impressed by his diligence, hard work and leadership skills, Carnegie was constantly assigning him major responsibilities. However, Schwab had given the best demonstration of his abilities when Carnegie assigned him the responsibility of setting things right at Homestead Steel Works, a large steel plant suffering from labour troubles. He brought about amazing reforms in its financial condition as well as labour-management relations. In 1897, at only 35 years of age, he became president of the Carnegie Steel Company. Soon, Carnegie Steel grew to be the world's largest steel company. In 1901, he played a significant role in negotiating the historical deal of USD 480 million (equivalent to USD 14.1 billion in 2016) for sale of Carnegie Steel to a group of New Yorkbased financiers led by J. P. Morgan, and later also became the president of the United States Steel Corporation, the company formed out of Andrew Carnegie's former holdings. However, after several clashes with J. P. Morgan and his supporter fellow executive Elbert Gary, Schwab left USS in 1903 and took charge of the Bethlehem Shipbuilding and Steel Company (Bethlehem, Pennsylvania). Under his leadership, Bethlehem Steel soon became USS's biggest competitor and second largest steel company of the United States of America.

Yes, Charles Michael Schwab was the first highly successful manager and chief executive officer who was paid an annual remuneration of USD 1 million. By 1920s, Schwab's fortunes had reached the level of USD 200 million. Though Schwab's luxurious lifestyle, shoddy investments and the Great Depression had robbed his fortunes and he was almost broke at the time of his death in

1936, professionals around the world even today acknowledge his management skills. The interesting fact is that Schwab was not recognised as the most respected manager of his time just because he was the greatest specialist of steel industry but also because he had an extraordinary ability to motivate his workers and he did the same using appreciation and encouragement. Schwab had once said, "I consider my ability to arouse enthusiasm among my people the greatest asset I possess, and the way to develop the best that is in a person is by appreciation and encouragement. There is nothing else that so kills the ambitions of a person as criticism from superiors. I never criticise anyone. I believe in giving a person incentive to work. So I am anxious to praise but loath to find fault. If I like anything, I am hearty in my appreciation and lavish in my praise".

Charles Michael Schwab had learnt all this from his boss Andrew Carnegie. Carnegie never hesitated in appreciating his workers not only privately but also publicly. Warren Buffett follows this advice from Schwab as if appreciating workers and managers for small things and being too enthusiastic with them on major affairs are religious tenets. Yes, Buffett has been hearty in his appreciation of his workers and has been their greatest admirer. He never misses a chance to appreciate his managers privately or in Berkshire's annual public meetings and annual reports. Yes, this is what Buffet has learnt from Schwab - if you appreciate people even for petty things, they would present to you much bigger achievements in coming times to get your appreciation. Thus, in Buffett's view, appreciation and praise are priceless gifts that always give something much bigger in return. Obviously, if you expect to constantly receive something great from your employees, you must keep on showering them with your praise and appreciation on regular basis.

Importance of Living with Your Dignity

Warren Buffet had learnt from the world's greatest steel magnate Andrew Carnegie the importance of allowing his workers to live with dignity. In this context, he often narrates the story told by Carnegie and impresses upon his managers to ensure that they themselves as well as the people working with them are able to live with dignity.

Carnegie's story goes like this. A manager was working with a trustworthy old employee. Monotony of job had made the employee slack in his work. This had resulted in fall in his workmanship and productivity. The manager reviewed his performance. He could have shown the employee the door, but in that case he would have had to work in his place. The manager could have even threatened the employee to fire him but being an old worker, this would have made him upset. In the situation, the manager talked to the experienced employee directly in a friendly manner. The manager, during the conversation, mentioned him as the best employee and the one who inspired other workers. The manager also told him that even many customers appreciated his workmanship. In the end, the manager calmly conveyed to him that he was rapidly falling behind in his work for the last few days. The manager let the employee know that he was worried for him and was wondering if he could help him in any manner. The manager thus provided the employee an opportunity to realise his old dignity again. Obviously, this was going to have a positive impact. Everybody likes to live with dignity. After that meeting, the employee started showing sudden improvement in his work behaviour. He got rid of the boredom. He started to work with his old enthusiasm. He soon attained his earlier productivity levels and people started to appreciate his workmanship once again.

Sitting at the top of a huge business empire, when Warren Buffet appreciates his CEOs publicly, he actually encourages them to live with dignity. Buffett knows very well that when a manager tries to live with dignity, he would inspire his employees also to do the same, like the story above.

Buffett had even suggested Ireland's rock band U2's lead vocalist and primary lyricist Paul David Hewson, known by his stage name 'Bono', that if he wanted to secure encouraging assistance and financial support from Americans to fight poverty in Africa, he should have appealed to their 'greatness' rather than awakening their 'conscience'. In fact, Bono is counted among the world's most distinguished philanthropist actors and is known as the most politically effective celebrity of all time. Since 1999, Bono has been active in raising awareness of the plight of Africa and AIDS. In this regard, he met several influential politicians, including former US President George

W. Bush and former Canadian Prime Minister Paul Martin. In March 2002, after meeting with Bono, George W Bush had announced from the White House a financial assistance of USD 5 billion to Africa and had remarked, "This is a significant first step and a serious and effective level of commitment.... this should happen immediately as this is a crisis".In the same year, Bono had taken US Secretary of the Treasury Paul H. O'Neill on a tour to four African countries. In the same course, Bono had met Warren Buffett and had sought his advice on making Americans aware of his campaign. In an interview published in 'US Today' (15 September 2003), Bono had revealed Buffett's advice to him, "Do not appeal to the conscience of America, appeal to its greatness, you'll get the job done".

If you notice, you may find why Warren Buffett advised Bono to appeal to America's 'greatness' and not to its 'conscience'. In fact, when we try to awaken anybody's conscience, we indirectly try to awaken his or her sense of 'right' and 'wrong'. Thus, when Bono was appealing to the conscience of Americans, he was indirectly telling them, "What kind of humans are you if you are not ready to help the poor and hungry in Africa?" And hence, though unknowingly, Bono was playing with the sense of guilt of the Americans and rebuking them. Obviously, nobody would like a person who stirs up his sense of guilt and rebukes him. And that was the reason he was not getting expected response from the Americans in his campaign.

After that, Bono changed the tone of his appeal during his American music programmes, "You are the most intelligent nation on this earth. You won the World War II against all odds and created hole in the heaven to land man on the Moon. Faced with the serious issue of helping the Africans who were in poverty and pain and had lost their souls, I wondered whom I should turn to? I had then felt a manifestation of Lord Jesus. I should turn to the greatest nation of the world - the kind of people who can really solve tough problems, the nation that can attain the impossible". Obviously, Bono had appealed to the greatness of America and its distinguished reputation at the advice of Buffett. And, he really got his job done. After that, many individuals and social service organisations including 'Melinda Gates Foundation' had wholeheartedly donated for Bono's campaign.

Obviously, Warren employed the same psychology for expansion of his financial empire. He has tried to appeal to the greatness of his managers instead of awakening their sense of guilt, as he knows well that if you appeal to others' greatness, they would always work in your interest. Of course, Warren's managers and employees have done the same thing to him.

Grave Dangers of Criticising Your Own People

Warren Buffett says, "Use of criticism for motivation is useless, as it makes a person defensive, hurts his precious pride, impairs his sense of importance and arouses discontent". Buffett is aware of this psychological truth that uncalled-for criticism is something that we hate to hear. This generates discontent. This may force people even to leave their parents' house. This is the main reason behind failed marital relationships. Still, most of us keep showering others, especially the people at our workplaces, with uncalled-for criticism. Managers and leaders of work-groups often make this mistake of publicly criticising their own people with the aim of motivating them. However, Buffett had understood right at the beginning of his professional life that uncalled-for criticism could never motivate anybody. This could not bring about durable change in a person and this demolished all kinds of productive work-relationships.

This is the reason that when any of the managers at Berkshire makes a mistake, Warren Buffett first of all tries to understand what made the manager to make that mistake. He looks at his manager and his work situation and tries to visualise things by putting himself in his position. This helps him to make out the real purpose of that risky management decision. If the manager has taken a calculated risk with the aim of doing something good, Buffett has an amazing capacity to withstand even huge losses on account of such occasional mistakes committed by the managers.

In this context, the case of rise and fall of David L. Sokol, Chairman and CEO of Mid American Energy Company (Des Moines, Iowa), a subsidiary of Berkshire Hathaway, and regarded as the likely successor to Warren Buffett, is worth mentioning. Raised in Buffett's hometown Omaha and civil engineering graduate from Nebraska

University (Omaha), Sokol started his professional life from an architectural engineering firm. In 1982, Sokol was appointed in Citi Bank (New York City) where he advised customers about investment in large waste-energy projects. After that he moved to energy-to-waste business with USD 500,000 seed money of a real estate company named Ogden. In the next six years, this had become a corporation earning revenue of USD 1 billion with more than 1000 employees and two plants at Oklahoma and Oregon, and had gone public in 1989. Thus Sokol, at just 32 years of age, became the CEO of a company listed in New York Stock Exchange. However, he was shown the door in 1990 after an altercation with the son of Ogden director. Sokol then joined JWP, a contractor company in New York, as president. He resigned from there in 1992 after an argument with the board of directors on accounting related issues.

This was the time when David L. Sokol was contacted by Walter Scott, CEO of Omaha based national construction company Peter Kiewit Sons. Walter had earlier worked for Ogden. Walter requested him to return to Omaha and work along with him on something new. Thus, Scott-Sokol partnership launched a small geothermal business that later took the shape of the large and profitable Mid American Energy company. Buffett's childhood friend Walter Scott, who was also a member in the Board of Directors of Berkshire, then made David Sokol also a part of Buffett's expanded family. In 2000, Berkshire acquired 80% ownership of Mid American. After that, Sokol executed many successful acquisitions and besides two-third ownership of Mid American Iowa, expanded his services to parts of Illinois, South Dakota and Nebraska. During the next 10 years, Buffett had compensated Sokol with a total of USD 8.8 million as salary and USD 53.9 million as bonus for his hard work. During the same period, Sokol had also received dividends of USD 26.3 million on his shares of stock and had sold shares amounting to USD 145.5 million.

In the meantime, in 2010, Douglas County (Nebraska) Judge Gary Randall found Mid American guilty of acting in 'improper, wrongful and unscrupulous manner' in its dealing with the shareholders of an irrigation project in Philippines and held David Sokol responsible for the same. Overall, Mid American had to pay 7% of its net profit of 2010 (around USD 84 million) as compensation. However, in his statement on 30 March 2011, Warren Buffett had also congratulated David Sokol and his confidant Gregory E. Obel for the excellent performance of Berkshire's public utility companies. It is worth reminding that David Sokol had made a grave investment error between 2002 and 2004 and Warren Buffet had on 13 September 2004 announced writing off a loss of USD 340 million in Mid American's Zinc Recovery Project. Buffett had not awarded any punishment in both the cases, as he did not find in them any intentional mistake by Sokol.

Not only that, earlier on 26 February 2011, Buffett in his annual letter to the shareholders of Berkshire, had credited David Sokol for financially rescuing Berkshire's subsidiary company Net Jets during the previous two years. Net Jets (Columbus, Ohio) operates the world's largest fleet of 700 private commercial jets and sells their part ownerships to its clients. In 1995, Warren Buffet had bought 25% share in 'Hawker 1000'. He had soon determined that the concept of part ownership was the future of private aviation and in 1998, Berkshire had acquired the entire company. But, when total pre-tax loss of Net Jets rose to the level of USD 157 million in the next eleven years, Buffett had appointed David Sokol as its CEO to turn it around. Buffett had indicated in his above letter that Net Jets loss would have been several hundred million greater, but for the backing of valuable goodwill of Berkshire. But, Sokol had turned the company around within a year. Sokol had carried out large scale retrenchment, sale of assets and fundamental changes in management to bring Net Jets to a position of pre-tax profit of USD 207 million in 2010.

In fact, Sokol had made a lot of money for Buffett and that had developed a lot of self-confidence in his ability. Besides managing Berkshire companies, Sokol had also explored opportunities for their investments. After the deepening crisis of Wall Street in 2008, Sokol had spent most of his time as a representative of Buffett for evaluation of potential deals created out of economic chaos. As per the 2010 report of US Bankruptcy Court on Lehman, Lehman Brothers' Chief of Investment Banking Hugh E. McGee III had contacted David Sokol in September 2008 to enquire if he had any idea or advice for saving Lehman. On getting a 'No' from Sokol. Lehman had filed for bankruptcy.

However, after the fall of Lehman, Sokol had brought to Buffett's attention the rapidly falling prices of shares of Baltimore's utility company Constellation Energy Group(CEG) and after receiving Buffett's consent, Sokol as the chief of Mid American had almost pulled off the deal at heavily discounted price of USD 4.7 billion to acquire CEG and save the same from bankruptcy. However, before the process of acquisition could start, a French competitor had entered the fray with higher bid. But Sokol's hard work and foresight did not go waste. CEG had to compensate Berkshire with a payment of over USD 1 billion towards breakup fee and other terms of the deal. Thus, Sokol was successful in making a good amount of money for Buffet within a short span of few months.

Yes, this kind of 'profitable opportunism' has been a major part of the investment formula of Berkshire (Warren Buffett); this however gets very little appreciation. Buffett is reputed to be a 'generous owner' that lays emphasis on efficient management and puts the same in practice. As a result, many of the companies remain eager to get acquired by Berkshire. Not only this, Buffett's personal aura and the record of his previous achievements open for him the doors for such non-ownership investments that others can only dream of. Among the typical examples of such non-ownership investments are the deals in 2008 for Goldman Sachs (USD 5 billion) and General Electric (USD 3 billion) when both the companies had gone financially broke. Buffett had shown his goodwill towards the two companies at such a highly sensitive moment; but in return, Berkshire could earn, besides repayment of its principal (USD 8 billion), more than USD 4 billion towards redemption fee and warranty fee along with interest. Can other regular investors secure such profitable deals? And, David Sokol had played a significant role in all these deals.

But Warren Buffett surprised everybody on 30 March 2011 when he announced that David Sokol was going to tender his resignation from Berkshire. Later, 27 April, Berkshire's audit committee had released 18-page report wherein it had charged Sokol of violation of company standards by misleading Berkshire about his personal shares in chemicals manufacturer Lubrizol (LZ) that he had recommended to Buffett as an acquisition target. The committee had concluded that Sokol had committed the crime of 'Insider Trading' under Federal Law when he bought Lubrizol shares for USD 1 million in January and then recommended acquisition of the same company to Buffett. Of course, it would not have been easy for Warren Buffett to take the decision of

Sokol's removal. Sokol had made mistakes earlier also and Buffett had been condoning them, as nothing came out of his investigations that could prove that the mistakes were made intentionally. But this was the first instance where Sokol had made the mistake for his personal gain; this had dented Berkshire's historical reputation and Buffett had to take the decision to remove him.

Praise by Name, Criticise By Category

Buffett knows very well that 'praise' and 'criticism' are two most important tools for any manager. If he is able to use them properly, he can motivate his workers to work hard, be creative and attain great achievements. If the tools are used incorrectly, they may demolish enthusiasm, aspiration and creativity of employees at work and even ensure their failure. Buffett believes learning how to effectively use 'praise' and 'criticism' is the primary task of a manager. The manager who understands properly the sensitivity of these tools and the challenges of their use can get anything done by his colleagues and employees. Warren has been expert in utilising these tools. He has this simple rule - 'Praise by name, criticise by category".

We all like to be appreciated. We crave appreciation as a child from parents, as a student from teachers and later as employee from seniors. We need appreciation from all of them, as we want to know if we are on the right path and this also inspires us to move ahead and do still better. On the contrary, nobody wants to hear his criticism. Whether we do anything or not, there is nothing more frightening that our own criticism. This is generally enough to destroy our enthusiasm. We were not ready as children to listen to our own criticism and now even as adults, we are not able to tolerate the same, as criticism proves us wrong. Be it parent or teacher or senior, we are unable to have regard for the person that criticises us and then, we start ignoring their words. Obviously, there is nothing greater than 'praise' to win friends and nothing greater than 'criticism' to make enemies. Now it all depends on you whether you want to appreciate somebody and make friends with him or criticise him to turn him into your enemy.

Many of the managers are never able to learn how to use 'praise' and 'criticism' in their conversation. As a result, they quickly become unpopular among their colleagues and employees and managements soon show them the door. However, Warren Buffett is considered to be an expert in using 'praise' and 'criticism' quite precisely and he has been successful in motivating his managers through the same to give their best performances. As we have read earlier, Buffett never misses any small or big opportunity to appreciate his people. He is adept at memorising the names of his people and always praises them by their names. Pick any of the annual reports of Berkshire Hathaway and look at Buffett's detailed letter addressed to the shareholders, you will surely find, along with the review of performance of various businesses, mention of the names and works of the employees showing outstanding performance in those categories. Yes, Buffett boosts self-esteem of his people by publicly appreciating their achievements and inspires them to lead their life with their elevated goodwill. The language that Buffett uses to praise also indicates that he himself also enjoys doing that. However, he not only praises his managers but also offers them promotion and huge monetary benefits much more than their expectations. This way, he makes his people feel 'special' and encourages them to do still better. This is the reason that the managers at Berkshire always keep vying for their best performances, as if they are working not for money but for their 'self-esteem'.

Though Warren Buffett considers every personal criticism poisonous, he is a realist also. He agrees that criticism is essential in certain situations and the same cannot be cast aside. However, when a personal criticism is necessary, he follows Dale Carnegie who advises that a person should be praised before he is criticised; according to him, people are not able to bear their criticism without a word of appreciation, and hence they just would not accept the same. But, when the good works of a person are appreciated profusely during conversation and then his mistakes are raised before him, he listens to the same, accepts them and also tries not to repeat them. Thus, if you are looking for a positive result of criticising a person, you should always start conversation with his appreciation.

Better to Avoid Conflicts and Arguments

Warren Buffett had learnt from Dale Carnegie that instead of arguing, it was better to agree with someone in order to win his confidence and have him listen to your ideas. Warren adopted this philosophy from the very beginning and he has been famous for trying to avoid conflicts and arguments. He has been well aware that you do not have to be at a higher position to win an argument. When you, in your attempt to win an argument with someone, pick his mistakes to correct him, he may even feel insulted and in that situation, instead of agreeing to your ideas, he may even get displeased with you.

In fact, when Buffett agrees to others' views in order to avoid conflict or argument, his primary aim is to respect their opinions even if the same are contradictory to his own views. And when Buffett, instead of arguing, accepts others' contradictory opinions, they feel comfortable and naturally get anxious to listen to his ideas. And this is the adroitness of Buffett; he is well aware that putting across your ideas to others is the first step towards winning an argument. As a securities salesman at the start of his career, he used to readily agree to the points raised by his potential customers.

In fact, invaluable ideas of Benjamin Franklin, one of the founding fathers of the United States of America, had played a significant role in shaping the academic growth and personal and professional lives of Buffett and his friend and Berkshire's Vice Chairman Charlie Munger. Pick any of Berkshire's annual reports; you will certainly find some of Benjamin Franklin's quotes there. Franklin also was adept at avoiding arguments and respecting others' opinions. Possibly, that was what had influenced Buffett to adopt this strategy.

Talk About Others' Wants and Needs

Warren Buffett says, "When you want people to do something, think not what you want but think what they want". Yes, as a leader and business owner, the key to Buffett's management success lies in the fact that he has always been able to understand and discuss the needs and wants of his managers/chief executive officers. In this respect, Buffett was influenced by the great industrialist of 20th century and founder of Ford Motor Company Henry Ford. Ford has written in his autobiography, "If there is any one secret of success, it lies in the ability to get other person's point of view and see things from that person's angle as well as from your own".

Buffett had embraced this idea in his personal as well as professional life. When he wanted to discipline his children, he would talk about their needs instead of making comments on them. Like, when he wanted his children to mind their health and control their weight, he would propose a reward programme for the same. Buffett understood adolescent psychology quite well and he knew that the children would not listen to him until their cash requirements were met. Similarly, when Buffett tried to acquire a family-owned private company, he would first of all talk about the prestige of the owner in that business. In fact, Buffett understood this very well that besides selling his company at the maximum possible price, the owner also wanted to ensure that the company was going in the hands that was capable of carrying forward its reputation. This was the reason that even after acquiring companies, Buffett used to hand over the same to the same previous owners who took pride in managing them for life.

We have already seen this in the case of Nebraska Furniture; after acquiring 80% stake in the company, Buffett did not go for any change in its management team consisting of Mrs B and his sons and members of the same family are still managing the same. Similarly, after acquiring FlightSafety, Buffett offered its founder and chairman AL Ueltschi the opportunity to run the company for life. And Buffett more or less tried to do the same with other companies, as he wanted to maintain the owners' reputation for their businesses. Thus, Buffett fulfilled the needs and wants of those owners and in return for his investment and magnanimity, they produced amazing financial results.

Besides this, Warren Buffet also gives his managers the chance to set their own goals and standards. He does appoint people on jobs but does not tell them what they are expected to do. This way, he prompts his managers to come up with their own views. And when managers feel free to set their own goals and standards, they always try to set higher goals and standards to project a better image in the eyes of their boss. As such, managers do know that though Buffett does not tell them anything, his silence conveys a lot. While he permits his managers to have complete freedom and authority to work, his expectations from them are also equally high. He expects extraordinary performance from his managers. Buffett believes that when we ask somebody to do something, it indirectly amounts to an order only. And it is psychological truth that nobody likes to be ordered and an order restricts the potentiality of performance. This is the reason that, instead of passing orders to his managers, Buffett confronts them with a number of questions and managers pick up Buffett's expectations from these questions only. In fact, Buffett's questions are indirect 'orders' as he shies away from passing 'orders' directly.

And...Warren Buffett believes that everybody makes mistakes and hence, one should inculcate the habit of promptly accepting his mistakes so as to ensure its timely correction.

❑

5

Risks, Challenges and Opportunities

Warren Buffett maintains that roads of business are full of pitfalls and planning is required to avoid them; this is called 'plan of disaster'. Risks of too much debt, breach by employees, good thoughts going astray, unintentional mistakes, managing yes-men and missing opportunities - are all examples of those pitfalls and special management techniques are required to handle those risks and challenges. In Buffett's view, only when we manage all of them properly, we are able to see related business opportunities. Buffett had learnt all this the hard way. In this chapter, we are going to discuss Buffett's these very invaluable experiences that would help every leader to keep away from managerial risks and extricate himself from such situations.

Too Much Debt is Like a Gamble Only

In Buffett's view, the managers resorting to too much credit are actually gambling. The irony is that these managers mostly have the misconception that they would not encounter any financial pitfalls on the long roads of their businesses. But they do need special business plans to move ahead avoiding those financial pitfalls. However,

Buffett, based on his experience, cautions that if a business, though being managed exceptionally well, over-utilises its leverage to avail loans expecting profits exceeding outstanding payables, it cannot always cheat or avoid its financial problems.

Buffett maintains that over-utilisation of 'leverage' results in banking disaster in the world economy every twenty years. Banks are the masters of 'leverage'. Whatever credits they extend are all out of funds received from depositors on credit. However, while they go for short-term borrowing from depositors, they have to extend long-term credits. This goes on smoothly till the time banks are able to keep adding new depositors. But when most of the depositors demand payment of their short term credits at the same time and banks are not in a position to honour their demand, a situation of banking crisis comes up. In economic scenario, such situations of change also create many opportunities. But we may be able to take advantage of such situations only if we have enough cash in hand. And economic swings may even prove to be disastrous if we have already availed too much of loans. Buffett believes such economic changes have been taking place always and will be coming up in future also. The question is - are we capable of withstanding those changes?

Warren Buffett says that leverage is quite tempting and always takes us to crisis. The question is - why is leverage so tempting? Because it can dramatically boost the performance of managers of a business provided, of course, the managers know how to use leverage. Suppose you are running a business that normally generates a profit of ₹ 1 crore without depending on any credit. In the situation, you expect that an additional ₹ 10 crore of investment may lift profit by ₹ 2 crore. This is a very tempting situation. But the problem is that your business is not in a position to fund that transaction. But you may use the leverage of your business to easily secure ₹ 10 crore on credit from investment bankers sitting in capital markets, as they keep waiting for such opportunities only. They would happily offer you loan provided you agree to pay them annual interest of ₹ 1 crore. This means that after paying ₹ 1 crore out of gross profit of ₹ 2 crore in your new venture, you would be earning a net profit of ₹ 1 crore. Thus, you may be able to report a net profit of ₹ 2 crore (₹ 1 crore from existing operations and additional ₹ 1 crore from new business) in the balance sheet of your company. Your business would thus show a 100 per cent jump in performance over previous year and you would be in a position to claim sizeable bonus from your management.

However, you as manager would be able to continue with this game of boosting your performance by using the leverage of your business only up to the point conditions continue to be normal and you are able to generate profit as expected. But the moment economic conditions change and recession sets in, your game would start getting into a bad shape. You would not be able to generate your expected profit. It may be possible that you are not in a position to pay even the interest amount. In the situation, your performance bubble would burst and your business would get into a financial crisis, leading the company into a possible bankruptcy. How would your board of directors deal with you in such a situation? The plain answer to the same is that it would replace existing management and you would lose your job.

That is why Warren Buffett terms too much of credit a gamble and does not invest in companies that have heavy long-term debts. Yes, Buffett had never allowed Berkshire to get entangled into debts. He never uses borrowed funds to buy a business. He allows cash to get accumulated until he finds a definitely attractive deal. In this respect, Warren Buffett is a conservative businessman who never tries to increase his income by using borrowed capital.

Great Ideas Also May Prove to be Bad

In his professional life, Warren Buffett had found this saying of his guru Benjamin Graham - 'Good ideas may deliver worse results than bad ideas' - to be true. Graham believed that managers never knowingly worked on bad ideas, as bad ideas got killed in the very beginning. But good ideas are put into practice. If a good idea succeeds, it becomes tradition. And when an idea turns into tradition, nobody even thinks of the same resulting into a failure. In such a situation, good ideas start getting misused. And as no caution is exercised in this regard, misuse of good ideas keeps on growing until the entire system collapses.

For example, subprime mortgage loan was basically a good idea that allowed worthy individuals with marginal credit to buy houses.

As these schemes selling mortgage loans provided opportunity to earn sizeable commissions, they started selling 'subprime mortgage loans' even to undeserving individuals by claiming them to be worthy. As such, the number of undeserving borrowers started going up. They were buying more than one house and brokers were getting the chance to earn more. This had started creating an environment of boom in the real estate market. Racing to meet their ambitious targets, banks had started to blindly accept proposals from brokers. Thus, the annual rate of growth of subprime mortgage loans went up from 8 per cent in 2004 to 20 per cent in 2006.

Just to remind, constantly increasing extravagant habits had lifted the ratio of debt to disposable personal income of average American family, that was hovering at 77 per cent in 1990s, to exceptionally high level of 127 per cent by the end of 2007, especially due to subprime mortgage loans. In the situation, when real estate prices, after peaking around middle of 2006, started falling down rapidly, borrowers were finding it difficult to re-finance their houses. Hence, they had to go for refinancing at higher interest rates resulting in their EMI sizes going up and payment defaults becoming common. As real estate prices were going down rapidly, financial institutions stopped investing in securities backed by subprime mortgage loans, thus creating a situation of loan crisis in the American banking system.

On 15 September 2008, the Lehman Brothers declared themselves bankrupt. After Goldman Sachs, Morgan Stanley and Merrill Lynch, this was the fourth largest investment bank in the United States, with 25000 employees worldwide. Lehman Brothers had at that time USD 619 billion in assets and USD 619 billion in liabilities. Thus, Lehman Brothers became the largest victim of the financial crisis of 2008 and the biggest bankruptcy in history. As a result, within just one month in October 2008, stock markets around the world went through a historical loss of USD 10,000 billion in their market capitalisation.

In fact, Lehman Brothers traces its roots to a small grocery store opened by the German immigrant Henry Lehman in Montgomery (Alabama) in 1844. In 1850, Henry Lehman and his brothers Emanuel and Mayor founded Lehman Brothers. Though, in the following decades, unabated economic development of the United States of

America provided ample opportunity to Lehman Brothers to prosper, it had to face many challenges also during that period. Lehman Brothers survived the railroad bankruptcies in the beginning of 19th century, the Great Depression of 1930s, two world wars, a capital shortage when it was spun off by American Express in 1994 and the long-term capital management collapse and Russian debt default of 1998. However, its headlong rush into subprime mortgage market proved to be a disastrous step that brought it to its knees.

In 2003 and 2004, when the US housing bubble was well under way, Lehman acquired five mortgage lenders including BNC Mortgage and Aurora Loan Services, which specialised in the most-risky Alt-A category loans extended to borrowers without full documentation. These acquisitions and jump in real estate business enabled Lehman revenues in capital markets to surge to 56% from 2004 to 2006; this was much more compared to the growth of other investment bankers. Lehman securitised USD 146 billion of mortgages in 2006 - a 10% increase from 2005. Though Lehman reported net profits every year 2005 onwards, it announced in 2007 a record net income of USD 4.2 billion on a revenue of USD 19.3 billion. In February 2007, Lehman stock price reached a record USD 86.18 per share, taking its market capitalisation to the level of USD 60 billion. In the meantime, loan defaults had reached a seven-year high and the crisis of subprime mortgage had become apparent. On March 14, 2007, when stock markets had their biggest one-day drop in five years, Lehman had reported record results for its first fiscal quarter.

However, Lehman's stock fell sharply as the credit crisis erupted in August 2007 with the failure of two Bear Stearns (New York based investment bank, securities trading and brokerage firm) hedge funds; during the same month, the company eliminated 2500 mortgage-related jobs and shut down its BNC unit. It also closed offices of Aurora Loan Services in three states. Even as the correction in the U. S. housing market gained momentum, Lehman continued to be a major player in the mortgage market. In 2007, Lehman underwrote more mortgage-backed securities than any other firm, accumulating a USD 85 billion portfolio that was four times its shareholders' equity. Though, in the fourth quarter, Lehman's stock rebounded as global equity markets reached new highs, but the company did not go for trimming its massive mortgage portfolio and thus, it had lost even the last chance to save itself. By the end of 2007, Lehman's degree of leverage - ratio of total assets and shareholders' equity - was 31 and with the deteriorating market conditions, its large mortgage securities portfolio was rapidly weakening its financial condition.

Later in March 2008, when Bear Stearns' - second largest investment banking firm underwriting mortgage-backed securities - was close to collapse, it was being widely anticipated that the king of mortgage loans Lehman Brothers was the next to fail and its shares plummeted nearly 48%. Confidence in the firm returned somewhat after an issue in April of preferred shares of stock - which were convertible into Lehman shares at a 32% premium to its concurrent price - yielded USD 4 billion. However, the company's stock resumed its decline as hedge fund managers started to question the valuation of Lehman's mortgage portfolio.

On June 9, 2008, Lehman reported a historical second-quarter loss of USD 2.8 billion. This was its first loss since it was spun off by American Express in 1994. The company also reported that it had raised USD 6 billion from investors. The company also informed that it had boosted its liquidity pool to USD 45 billion, decreased gross assets to USD 147 billion, reduced its exposure to residential and commercial mortgages by 20% and cut down leverage from a factor of 32 to 25. But the markets found all these measures to be just too little, too late. During the next few months, Lehman's management made unsuccessful overtures to a number of potential partners. The stock plunged 77% in the first week of September 2008.

On 10 September, the company reported USD 3.9 billion loss for the third quarter, including a USD 5.6 billion devaluation of its assets. On the same day, Moody's Investor Services announced that it was reviewing Lehman's credit ratings and opined that the only way for Lehman to avoid a rating downgrade would be to sell its majority stake to a strategic partner. All these developments led to a 42% plunge in Lehman's market price on September 11. Over the weekend, when Lehman was left with just USD 1 billion of cash, it even made a last-ditch effort with Barclays and Bank of America for a deal; and Lehman Brothers was left with no option other than declaring its bankruptcy on 15 September.

There is Ample Money Within the Scope of Law

Warren Buffet keeps on clearly telling his managers that a lot of money can be made while remaining within the scope of law. Of course, it requires being aggressive to make money, but you can do so while remaining within the limits of law. Experience has taught Buffett that when a manager breaks law in a bid to make too much money too soon, his single step exposes entire business to risk. In this context, it is worth mentioning the example of the US Treasury Bond scandal of 1991 when the very existence of the Wall Street's famous investment banking firm Salomon Brothers was in danger as two of its bond traders were found to have broken law. In the situation, Warren Buffett as the largest investor and director of the firm, had to step in and he somehow managed to save the company after paying a heavy fine of USD 290 million.

In fact, American investor Ronald Owen Perelman, notorious as 'takeover specialist', had started his bid in August 1987 to takeover Salomon Brothers by acquiring 12% stake of Minerals & Resources Corporation Limited (a subsidiary of mega South African group Anglo American) in the company. Ronald Owen Perelman, founder of MacAndrews & Forbes Incorporated, was listed among the world's richest persons in 2016 at 80th position with total personal assets of USD 12.2 billion. The Salomon Brothers' Chairman and CEO John Gutfreund had then contacted Warren Buffett. On 27 September 1987, Buffett had acquired 12% stake in Salomon Brothers for USD 700 million through Berkshire Hathaway. This was Buffett's largest investment in a single company till date. However, Salomon Brothers had to pay USD 809 million to buy back 12% shares to save itself from Perelman's takeover plot, i.e., Buffett had made this shareholding investment to help Salomon Brothers at a heavy discount of USD 109 million and that also in the form of Convertible Preferred Shares that could be converted to common shares of stock any time. And, Buffett had made this investment because John Gutfreund had helped him in many deals during the last few years. For the first time, Warren Buffett had joined the so-called 'greedy community' of the Wall Street that he had always been avoiding.

In less than a month after this deal, on 19 October 1987 (Black Monday), Hong Kong and European stock markets experienced sharp declines followed by crash of stock markets in the United States; the Dow Jones Industrial Average (DJIA) fell 508 points (22.6%). Market price of a share of Berkshire Hathaway, that was USD 4230 a week back, came down to USD 3170 on Monday; and the company lost USD 5 billion in its market capitalisation within a day. Warren Buffett's personal net worth went down by USD 342 million. However, it is interesting to note that Warren Buffett had sensed the unexpected bounce in the market and sold most of the shares in his portfolio at highest prices to accumulate a lot of cash that could be used for investments at extremely low prices.

Warren Buffet's rescue proved to be momentary for Salomon Brothers and it was going to face a lot of financial issues in coming days. But the biggest crisis came in 1991 when U. S. Treasury Deputy Assistant Secretary Mike Basham learned that Salomon trader Paul Mozer had been submitting false bids in an attempt to purchase more treasury bonds than permitted by one buyer during the period between December 1990 and May 1991. The case forced the Chairman and CEO John Gutfreund to lose his job in August 1991. Later, U. S. Securities and Exchange Commission (SEC) imposed a fine of USD 100,000 on John Gutfreund and barred him from serving as a chief executive of an investment banking or brokerage firm. Meanwhile, in the absence of John Gutfreund, Warren Buffett being the largest investor took charge of Salomon Brothers and provided all assistance in SEC investigation. Though SEC did not ban Salomon Brothers from buying Treasury securities, considering Buffett's previous reputation and his honest assistance in the entire episode, but levied a fine of USD 290 million to cover damages; this was a historical penalty at that time. After running Salomon for nine months, Buffett handed over charge to competent managers in the company. Eventually, Travelers Group acquired Salomon in 1997 for USD 9 billion and Warren Buffett sitting in Omaha headquarters felt a sigh of relief, as his investment of USD 700 million had more than doubled to USD 1.70 billion. However, for Warren Buffett, this was a bitter experience involving investment in a Wall Street firm and by 2001, he was fully out of Salomon. Travelers merged with Citi Group in 2007.

This experience, however, came in handy for Warren Buffett to caution his managers. He has been using this example to explain to his managers that breaking law for immediate profits can prove to be highly detrimental to personal professional life as well as to very existence of the business.

Successes More Important than Mistakes

Warren Buffett also did not drop out of heaven! He has also built his fortune by learning from mistakes. He says, "I make plenty of mistakes and I'll make plenty more mistakes, too. That's part of the game. You've just got to make sure that the right things overcome the wrong ones". You may not always escape mistakes, but yes, you may surely attain greater success by learning from them. Hence, wisdom lies in ensuring that your successes overcome your mistakes. But, if the equation turns opposite, you are sure to get caught in troubles. We may learn from Buffett's experience to take following precautions:

Do not take decisions in hurry: In his letter to the shareholders of Berkshire Hathaway in its 2011 annual report, Warren Buffett had referred to his mistake in making heavy investment in bonds of Energy Future Holdings. He had written, "A few years back, I spent about $2 billion buying several bond issues of Energy Future Holdings, an electric utility operation serving portions of Texas. That was a mistake – a big mistake. In large measure, the company's prospects were tied to the price of natural gas, which tanked shortly after our purchase and remains depressed. Though we have annually received interest payments of about $102 million since our purchase, the company's ability to pay will soon be exhausted unless gas prices rise substantially. We wrote down our investment by $1 billion in 2010 and by an additional $390 million last year. At yearend, we carried the bonds at their market value of $878 million. If gas prices remain at present levels, we will likely face a further loss, perhaps in an amount that will virtually wipe out our current carrying value. Conversely, a substantial increase in gas prices might allow us to recoup some, or even all, of our write-down. However things turn out, I totally miscalculated the gain/loss probabilities when I purchased the bonds. In tennis parlance, this was a major unforced error by your chairman".

Two years later, in the annual report for 2013, Warren Buffett had written to the shareholders of Berkshire Hathaway, "Most of you have never heard of Energy Future Holdings. Consider yourselves lucky; I certainly wish I hadn't. The company was formed in 2007 to affect a giant leveraged buyout of electric utility assets in Texas. The equity owners put up $8 billion and borrowed a massive amount in addition. About $2 billion of the debt was purchased by Berkshire, pursuant to a decision I made without consulting with Charlie. That was a big mistake. Unless natural gas prices soar, Energy Future Holdings (EFH) will almost certainly file for bankruptcy in 2014. Last year, we sold our holdings for $259 million. While owning the bonds, we received $837 million in cash interest. Overall, therefore, we suffered a pre-tax loss of $873 million. Next time I'll call Charlie".

Yes, Buffett's presumption was correct and EFH, acquired by private equity firms KKR, TPG Capital and Goldman Sachs Capital Partners in 2007, could not withstand the burden of debt amounting to more than USD 40 billion. This deal executed in anticipation of rise in gas prices proved to be too costly when, on 29 April 2014, EFH filed for bankruptcy. But, more than losing money, Buffett was regretting his mistake of not consulting his old friend and vice chairman of Berkshire before making his decision. There are very few people as fortunate as Buffett to have a friend like Charlie Munger for sharing ideas. However, we may certainly strive to avoid doing what Buffett did - he took a decision in a hurry. It is always better to take some time before finalising an investment decision, even if the same involves much less than Buffett's mistake of USD 2 billion. It may be noted that the mistake of USD 2 billion was quite insignificant compared to Buffett's achievements, and he could comfortably bear the same.

Make thorough analysis of company and industry: In 2015, Buffett had written to the shareholders of Berkshire about performance of manufacturing, services and retail operation of the company till date. Most of them, not all, had given good results. In most of the cases where companies were not doing well, he had accepted his mistake in evaluation of the company and related industry. Possibly, the most notable example of Buffett's error in evaluation of an industry was the main company Berkshire Hathaway. Berkshire was then a textile manufacturer and Buffett had a great opportunity to sell his shares and make good money. Instead, Buffett had continued with his investment in that textile company that he later accepted to be a dying business. Yes, Buffett had acquired Berkshire in 1965; but when textile operations were completely shut down in 1985, it was already 20 years since then. Thus, even an intelligent investor like Buffett may end up wasting time as well as money. This only proves that nobody can be always right. But this also does not mean that we keep ignoring facts and avoid taking hard steps. Hence, a thorough analysis of the company and related industry is imperative before making investments.

Check out competitions also thoroughly: In his 2015 annual letter to the shareholders of Berkshire, Buffett had mentioned that not checking out competitions before buying Dexter Shoes was one of his 'most gruesome mistakes' till date. Everything looked good when he bought the company in 1993. Buffett could not see foreign competition coming and the value of his initial investment of USD 44.3 billion in Dexter Shoes going to zero. The incident teaches us that, irrespective of the company you are buying the shares of or the industry that the same belongs to or the size of the investment, the first thing you need to check out is the competition existing in the related market segment. Keep in mind that every market segment is thronged by companies that were once strong but could not compete with the rivals having better quality, better speed and better prices.

Do not use well-invested fund to make fresh investments - More than his mistake of not checking out competitions before finalising deal for Dexter Shoe, Buffett regretted using shares of Berkshire Hathaway for the transaction. By the time Buffett informed the shareholders in 2014, the shares that he used to buy Dexter were worth USD 5.70 billion that was later going to rise further by 40%. This incident teaches an important lesson that a well-invested fund should not be used for investment elsewhere.

Here, the words of great ancient Indian economist Acharya Chankya look to be so apt, "योध्रुवाणिपरित्यज्यअध्रुवंपरिषेवते। ध्रुवाणितस्यनश्यन्तिअध्रु मनष्टमेवच।", i.e., whosoever leaves behind a task that can certainly be completed, and runs after another task completion of which is uncertain, not only the previous task gets spoiled but even the uncertain task would get spoiled. Yes, even prudent investors sometimes make grave mistakes of selling stocks earning them assured profits and investing the money in options with uncertain prospects. Hence, if a share of stock is giving good income and the related business has strong fundamentals, it is better to continue with the same.

Do not doubt yourself much: Berkshire Hathaway had acquired General Reinsurance Corporation (Gen Re) in 1998. Immediately after that, Warren Buffet started having doubts on his own decision. There were issues that prompted external observers feel that billionaire investor Buffett had made a grave mistake this time; but Buffett had not made any mistake in buying 'Gen Re'. Of course, the biggest mistake he was making was to 'doubt' his own decision because of the questions being raised by external observers. However, Buffett did not allow that 'doubt' to overwhelm his decision, as a re-evaluation had given him confidence that his decision was perfect as per basic investment principles and he did not have to heed external opinions. Fortunately, Buffett maintained confidence in his decision and in his own words, 'Gen Re' proved to be a 'gem' later. The incident provides the lesson that it is not proper for anybody to doubt himself too much. If you have bought any share based on sound investment principles, you may definitely review your decision based on external observations but should not doubt your decision over and over again. Keep in mind, you have taken the decision as per your perspective that needn't match those of others.

Avoid greed when it is time to sell: It is common perception that once Warren Buffett buys a stock, he holds the same 'forever'. But this is not entirely true. Leaving some exceptions, he keeps churning rest of the investment portfolio. In 2013, British multinational groceries and general merchandise retailer Tesco was included in the list of companies with maximum holdings in Berkshire's portfolio; but it completely disappeared from the list next year. Though Buffett had come to know of the management problems in Tesco in 2013 itself and he had even made profits by selling a part of his holding in the company, he had taken a lot of time, in the hope of things turning around, to sell rest of his holding. Thus, when it was time to sell, Buffett was gripped by greed of better returns in future. And as a result, Berkshire had to provide for a net loss of USD 444 million at the end of 2014 towards that deal.

In his letter to the shareholders in Berkshire Hathaway's annual report of 2014, Buffett had described the sequence of events like this, "Attentive readers will notice that Tesco, which last year appeared in the list of our largest common stock investments, is now absent. An attentive investor, I'm embarrassed to report, would have sold Tesco shares earlier. I made a big mistake with this investment by dawdling. At the end of 2012 we owned 415 million shares of Tesco, then and now the leading food retailer in the U.K. and an important grocer in other countries as well. Our cost for this investment was USD 2.3 billion, and the market value was a similar amount."

"In 2013, I soured somewhat on the company's then-management and sold 114 million shares, realising a profit of USD 43 million. My leisurely pace in making sales would prove expensive. Charlie calls this sort of behaviour 'thumb-sucking.' (Considering what my delay cost us, he is being kind.)"

"During 2014, Tesco's problems worsened by the month. The company's market share fell, its margins contracted and accounting problems surfaced. In the world of business, bad news often surfaces serially: You see a cockroach in your kitchen; as the days go by, you meet his relatives. We sold Tesco shares throughout the year and are now out of the position. (The company, we should mention, has hired new management, and we wish them well.) Our after-tax loss from this investment was USD 444 million, about 1/5 of 1% of Berkshire's net worth. In the past 50 years, we have only once realised an investment loss that at the time of sale cost us 2% of our net worth. Twice, we experienced 1% losses. All three of these losses occurred in the 1974-1975 period, when we sold stocks that were very cheap in order to buy others we believed to be even cheaper".

Thus, the incident teaches us that when it is time to sell our stocks i.e., when we know that the investment is not safe, we should not delay or feel afraid of selling the same in the hope of making better profits in future.

Do not vacillate over buying: But Warren Buffett's biggest mistake was a different kind of vacillation. In 2014, he had told the shareholders that almost all his huge errors were in 'not making a purchase' when he should have. In this context, he had mentioned about his serious hesitation in buying Walmart stock. The interesting fact is that Buffett in his annual letter to the shareholders in 1990, had written how low operating costs of Walmart allowed it to sell at prices that its competitors could not touch and it could constantly increase its market share. But Warren Buffett took fifteen years to take a final decision to buy; he had not bought any shares of Walmart before 2005. In the middle of 2016, Buffett was left with Walmart shares worth USD 3 billion, but he started selling the same after that and in February 2017, he had shares worth USD 100 million only. In fact, Buffett had indicated to his shareholders in the very beginning of 2016 that the days of mega retail companies like Walmart were over and future belonged to e-commerce companies like Amazon.

Thus, this serious mistake of Warren Buffett teaches us that we should not vacillate over buying stocks when it is time. Buffett had accepted that had he not hesitated in making investment in Walmart and had he seized the opportunity in 1990 itself and bought Walmart shares then, Berkshire Hathaway's net worth would have gone up by at least USD 50 billion (till 2014). This means that when we know that the future prospects of shares of a particular company is great and we still delay buying the same, it is just like the mistake of not picking a bag of gold lying on a table. Hence, whenever we get a buying opportunity, we should grab the same.

And...finally, Warren Buffett also advises his managers to keep away from sycophants.

❑